RIGBY SHLEI ᴵ ᴵᴵᴱᴿᴸ

A Memoir of Terence Rigby

(1937–2008)

Juliet Ace

COUNTRY SETTING

RIGBY SHLEPT HERE

A Memoir of Terence Rigby (1937–2008)

by Juliet Ace

Text copyright © Juliet Ace, 2015

Cover design by Anna Trussler

Available from Amazon.com,
CreateSpace.com, and other retail outlets

British Library Cataloguing-in-Publication Data
A catalogue record for this book is available
from the British Library.

ISBN PB 978-0-9559998-6-4

Produced by Country Setting,
Kingsdown, Kent, CT14 8ES, UK

www.countrysetting.co.uk/

Printed in the UK

'A fascinating and unusual memoir of a fascinating and unusual actor. Terence Rigby was an extraordinary actor, adored by his colleagues. His highly original mind is displayed in the extracts from letters and diaries, which suggest he might have been a great writer as well. There is unknown and detailed documentation of his work with Pinter, Peter Hall and Ian McKellen, among others, some of it quite shocking, as Rigby sought the unvarnished truth in his work and his life. This book should be read by anyone who likes the theatre, but should be a compulsory text for young actors and drama students, who will learn what it is to be a true artist in the theatre. Oh . . . and they will have a lot of laughs too.'

PETER EYRE

'Terence Rigby would be astonished by the sight of himself, I think . . . His shade, and his memory, have been fortunate in their chronicler. [Rigby's] almost threatening contradictions speak throughout the whole narrative – no wonder he got on so well with Pinter – but always in a strange harmony with his lovable qualities. As an account of the complexities that can beset an acting life, it's unparalleled, I think. And the way that the bones of the book are allowed to show through, in the progress of its compilation, seems absolutely right. Surely it is destined to be a 'real' book, rather than a virtual book. The sheer solidity of Rigby requires hard covers.''

RUSSELL DAVIES, *critic and broadcaster*

Dedication

For George, Masha and Stanley

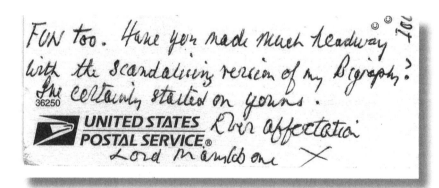

i. Section of the postcard to Juliet Ace from Terence Rigby asking,
'Have you made much headway to the scandalizing version of my biography?'

Foreword

On a postcard to Juliet Ace, Terence Rigby wrote: 'Have you made much headway with the scandalizing version of my biography? I've certainly started on yours. – Ever affection, Lord Marylebone X.' Although he would not live to see it, Juliet Ace has written much more than a 'scandalizing' life of the wonderfully memorable and professionally esteemed actor that was Terence Rigby.

Famed as one of the finest performers of Harold Pinter's work, he was equally lauded for his creation of Albert, the lugubrious horse, in Alan Bennett's dramatization of *Wind in the Willows*, and for numerous classical performances from Ibsen to Racine. While the theatre was his natural habitat, his commanding presence, and stillness, is recorded in numerous films and television appearances – memorably as the burly spy Roy Bland in the television classic *Tinker, Tailor, Soldier, Spy*, and as 'Big Al' in Alan Plater's *The Beiderbecke Affair*.

For those lucky enough to have seen him in Pinter's *No Man's Land,* with Ralph Richardson, John Gielgud and Michael Feast, his delivery of the famous speech about the impossibility of navigating to Fitzrovia's Bolsover Street is an unsurpassed theatrical vignette, a moment to match what was arguably Gielgud's finest performance in a modern play. Rigby's work was full of such moments.

Rigby – just plain 'Rigby', as he was known by most of those who knew and loved him – kept the company of great actors, and was admired by them. In the last ten years of his life, dividing his time between the United States and England, he became a keeper of the Pinter flame, reporting back on the successes and deviations of American productions. Those dispatches were sometimes the only clues to what was happening in his intensely private life, and the success of Juliet Ace's account of his life is in unpeeling more than a few layers of the onion to grant insights into the man and his work.

Marylebone (of which he appropriated the honorific title 'Lord') was his restlessly foot-patrolled patch of London, even occasionally agitating the council to maintain the area's cultural heritage (and park benches). But from the time he first trod the stage in the Scouts, and at his grammar school in Birmingham, his passion and rightful place was in performance, and he continued until his death to learn and explore his craft

Juliet Ace was one of what she calls Rigby's 'Cup-of-Tea Ladies', a select group of women friends, rigorously separated in space and time, who catered to his mixed intellectual, theatrical, culinary, and social needs. Writing from the dinner table where Rigby had placed a small brass plaque staking claim to his place – 'RIGBY SHLEPT HERE' – she has succeeded, where he had run out of time, in regaling the reader with at least some of what *The Times* obituary called 'the treasury of stories that he held'.

As a dramatist, Ace has written wonderfully *for* actors, from *EastEnders* to film and radio, but here she does not shirk from that notoriously difficult task of writing *about* acting. She achieves, through shrewd and astute interviews with his peers, through the family collections of clippings, and through her own diaries, in evoking the man at work.

In his memorial tribute, the critic Michael Billington defined Rigby's 'vital quality' as an actor as 'physical and emotional weight'; a decade earlier, Bernard Levin had endorsed Rigby's application for an American Green Card by describing his 'amazing flexibility'. While he never went on to write Juliet Ace's biography, he made three starts on his own before his death in 2008, turning to Ace for editorial inspiration. It fell to her to gather his family papers, speak to his friends and illustrious theatrical colleagues, and call on her more-than-forty years of memories of Rigby to tell his story. It is perhaps not the 'scandalizing version' that he predicted – from the hard-drinking days of his younger self: he gave up alcohol for the last decades of his life – but her portrait of this 'mournful Brummagem nag in battered felt hat' (as Billington described his performance as the horse in *Wind in the Willows*) is by turns intimate, reflective, unsparing, and warm, evoking his large presence on every page.

The riddle of Terence Rigby remains – there are so many private places, and private doors that are never opened, mysteries even to the agent who represented him for most of his career – but there are insights aplenty into the life and work of a generous and richly talented man.

What lifts this story from a deserved tribute to a creative artist to something that rewards the reader with something greater is Juliet Ace's decision to build the story around that plaque-marked table where they shared long nights and pots of tea, reminiscences and rehearsals. The table provides the gravity that brings us, as readers, into Rigby's orbit, to share and learn from a life well loved.

Ned Chaillet

List of Illustrations

Contents

Key to Symbols

❑   *memories from Juliet's table*

☞   *other written material*

✉   *correspondence*

☰   *published clippings*

☎   *phone conversations*

✎   *diary*

⊗   *filmscript*

RIGBY SHLEPT HERE

ii. The plaque on Juliet's table:

❏ Juliet's Table

'Oh, Mrs Probert, I feel such passion for you!'

And with that he flings me down on to the sofa, roaring, as loudly Welsh as Dylan himself.

'Bugger off,' I tell him. 'We don't want your sort round 'ere.'

I open the sitting-room shutters, reassemble the sofa-bed while he uses the bathroom, then go downstairs to see what's left in the fridge for breakfast.

I hear the front door close. He's cleared off without a goodbye, without a wave, even. Not a word of thanks for all the food he chomped his way through last night; no apology for keeping me up until dawn reminiscing, hearing lines . . . *And* I took him a cup of tea in bed this morning. By the time I've compiled a list of misdemeanours as long as your arm, he's ringing the doorbell.

He's carrying bacon, eggs, bread and – for some inexplicable reason – pig's trotters. Obviously he intends hanging round until lunch, at the very least. But one never knows with Rigby. Chances are he'll be here until midnight and suddenly remember that he should be at so-and-so's.

I am one of a handful of 'Cup-of-Tea Ladies' in his life. We're not romantically attached to him, but each of us enjoys a special friendship. One woman satisfies his intellectual needs, another his worry over religion, a third, theatrical gossip. I regard myself as his vulgar, common friend.

But no, that's too easy. Within each categorized friendship, we satisfy other Rigby needs. So the physical roistering of the Mrs Probert element, in my case, is just a small part of the whole. He feels he can come to my house bearing greasy kebabs for him and two tasteless fishcakes for me. The former are accompanied by several large mugs of tea. I keep a yellow Slim-Fast mug of giant proportions (presumably for powdered soups, I can't remember) exclusively for him. I prefer a small glass of Merlot, which I try to make last for as long as possible, and invariably fail. The kebab is followed by gargantuan chunks of Cheddar cheese, which must always be in the fridge in case he shows up. If there's a slice of apple pie going begging, then we're in for the perfect gastronomic evening. If not, there's possibly a bar of Fruit & Nut which he slaps on the table.

The table is significant. It's actually a battered old partners' desk that I bought from a stripped-pine shop in Camden Road when I first moved into my house in Camden Town (the rough end) in the Spring of 1988. It has a wonky leg and is slightly warped, but it seats ten people comfortably. Rigby loves this table and he always sits in the same position on any one of eight non-matching chairs. One day, when a new man has come into my life, he arrives with a brass plaque inscribed with the words 'Rigby Shlept Here'. He insists that it is screwed into the table top. In King Lear tones he asserts that 'This is my place and no other bugger is going to sit in it'.

*

Origins

Terence Christopher Rigby was born on 2 January 1937 in Birmingham. He died in London on 10 August 2008, aged 71 years.

A few days after he died, I was invited to dinner at Strada in Marylebone High Street – just around the corner from Devonshire Street, where Rigby had a mansion flat. Father Michael McGreevy, an old family friend from the Birmingham suburb of Erdington, had also been invited – as I was – by Rigby's brother and sister, Joseph and Catherine. I'd brought some of my collection of funny photographs to show them, taken in my kitchen over a period of twenty years; Father Michael had brought mementoes from schooldays. Joseph asked me whether I would consider writing a memoir of Rigby. Without hesitation I said I would. Silly, perhaps. But Rigby had himself asked for my help in writing his memoirs, the Christmas before he left for America for the last time.

Over the following months, Rigby's nephew John (Joseph's son), who was the main executor, brought round several large boxes, and piles of yellowing newspaper reviews, as high as Snowdon. This was Terence Christopher Rigby's life: a giant muddle of material that, nevertheless, had many pieces missing. I took several deep breaths, then suffered mild panic attacks and sleepless nights, before I eventually took the plunge.

After four years I had assembled a first draft. Reading it through, I found it slightly boring; my son found it over-long; a close friend who scanned its pages thought that it was probably a 'compendium'. Depression set in, and then I decided I must find a new starting point. And this is it.

I am hoping to take the reader with me on my discovery of a man I thought I would never fathom. After all, Rigby's life *is* a compendium of . . . what? Games? Truths and lies? Public success and personal failures? Alcoholism and sobriety? Crescendos and crashes? The journey is beginning to sound like a mystery tour, so I need to find its magical elements. That's easy, because Rigby was – and still is, in the surviving footage of his performances, and in the memories of his many friends and colleagues – a quite magical man.

Quite early on in the process, I sent an email to one of Rigby's old girlfriends in the Antipodes. I began by mentioning something that Rigby's one-time flatmate had declared ('David Sinclair told me that Rigby is a eunuch'), before asking more questions about his relationships and his work. I got the immediate response back from New Zealand that Rigby was certainly *not* a eunuch: they had been lovers for years. Then a week later I got another email berating me for asking such questions – what right did I have to write a memoir of him in the first place? Oh, dear. I was mortified. I wrote an apology straight away.

After that unfortunate start, I realized that I had a lot to learn about interviewing people. It also became clear that, as well as meeting people face to face, there would also have to be both telephone and email interviews. I have a horror of telephoning strangers, so I bought a clever recording device that fitted on to the telephone and into my digital recorder – another of my new toys. I'd also acquired something called Dragon Speak, which would take my dictation and transfer it on to computer – with hilarious, often unintelligible results.

To play it safe, I decided that my first face-to-face interview should be with someone I knew well, who would forgive my incompetence, and with whom I felt comfortable. The actor Stephen Thorne was my first choice.

Stephen first met Terence Rigby in the Buckstone Club, just off Haymarket, in the early Seventies. He'd gone there with David Sinclair, a fellow member of the BBC Radio Drama Rep, Rigby's flatmate. By this time, Rigby was established in the role of PC Snow in the popular television series *Softly, Softly* and was becoming more famous by the minute.

'This is my friend Stephen Thorne,' Sinclair had said.

Rigby, who was standing at the foot of the stairs, was expressionless.

'Hello, Stephen Thorne. What do you do?'

Stephen replied that he was an actor.

'Are you?' he said. 'I suppose you want to know about my dog.'

This was a reference to the police dog, Radar, his constant appendage in Softly.

Stephen responded sharply by telling Rigby that he had a dog of his own, which took up all of his time. Rigby grunted, and that was that. The rest of the conversation was a monologue from Stephen, interjected by grunts and monosyllables from Rigby, who eventually ambled off. They met up several times after that, until Stephen was eventually invited to the holy of holies – one of Rigby's Sunday lunches: 'the onion sauce on the lamb and all that stuff'.

Stephen thought Rigby was an amazing character, and would just sit and watch him, 'as one would watch a character that you'd been asked to play':

I marvelled at him, and developed a theory about him, which was that all the drinking and grunting, and whatever, was a basic insecurity of the social situation. You could tell that he was a very good actor because you could see his work. That was not in question. But as a human being, I used to think that the drinking and the persona he employed was a sort of skin he put on to keep the world at bay and to soften the feelings of social inadequacy.

This was probably quite true in relation to his flatmate Sinclair in particular, who was supremely confident. 'I suppose you're a Public School chap, Thorne,' Rigby said, inventing a character for Stephen as a news reporter that would last the rest of his life. Whenever Stephen embarked on another of his stories, Rigby would say something like, 'Ah, yes . . . Stephen Thorne, *News at Ten*, Marrakesh,' as he sat on his bar stool, sipping a vodka.

I asked Stephen whether Rigby ever lost his temper with him. He never did, although he and Sinclair would often have public disagreements. To Stephen, Rigby appeared to be almost a hermit-like figure, living like a monk in a cell. Sinclair once invited Stephen to see Rigby's 'wardrobe'. Imagining a fine piece of furniture, all that he was shown was a single hook behind the bedroom door. There was a bed with a table next to it, and a small table and chair on the other side of the room. And that was it. It wasn't a room to spend time in; it was merely a room for sleeping – and that's all Rigby used it for.

But there were wonderful drunken nights in the flat when renditions of the duet from *The Pearl Fishers* (which was one of Rigby's favourites) would be played. Sometimes the music would reduce him to silent tears; other times he would sing along, the tears pouring down his cheeks.

❏ JULIET'S TABLE

He's sitting at the far end of the table, devouring a cheese sandwich. It's a few days after our reunion. We'd 'walked out together' (his term) in the mid-Sixties, and here we are, twenty-five years later, rediscovering our friendship. I'm wary.

The actor-couple Rio Fanning and Karen Ford had brought him along to my pre-New Year Party as a surprise for both of us. He'd looked at me blankly and walked off to flirt with my daughter's girlfriends. Obviously I was disappointed that he hadn't recognized me, so I enjoyed everyone else's company instead. But after midnight, when all my friends had gone, Rigby took my arm and led me upstairs to the sitting room. We sat on the sofa and he asked me to jog his memory. He hadn't had a drink all evening.

7

Back at the table, he says, 'It's jolly nice to see you again. It took me some time to find the house.' He presses more cheese and beetroot on to a slice of bread. 'Tell me again, in great detail, how we met. I think it's coming back to me.'

'Oh no it isn't,' I insist. But I tell him anyway. 'We met in the Buckstone Club in the Autumn of 1964. You were in the chorus of *Pickwick*—'

'And understudying several parts,' he butts in. 'You didn't know I could sing, did you?'

'I was an usherette at the Piccadilly Theatre where Jennie Paul was understudying Joan Sims in *Instant Marriage*. I shared a flat with Jennie and four other girls in West Hampstead. I'd just gone back into teaching, but had to take an evening job for a few months until I'd been paid.'

He remembers the flat and Jennie. They were both in the tour of *Fings Ain't Wot They Used T'Be*, the Joan Littlewood hit show.

'You said you were glad I wasn't an actress. You told me you didn't like actresses.'

He laughs at that. He's developed a 'tee-hee' ironic sort of titter – he rarely laughed in those Sixties days.

'On Boxing Day you turned up and invited me to RADA to see the premiere of Ken Campbell's *Events of an Average Bath Night* with Warren Mitchell.'

'Was that our first date? I definitely remember that. I love Ken. He met a pal of his the other day who said they were holding auditions in some West End Theatre, so he thought he'd have a go. It was a Shakespeare . . . He was carrying two plastic shopping bags. Just walks on to the stage and says, "Good morning." Then he groans, grabs his chest and staggers on to the floor. After a very long pause he gets up and tells them that's the dying scene. He fishes out a bag of sausages, splays them across one hand and says, "Pick a sausage. Any sausage."'

Maybe he's had enough reminiscence for one day. I don't know how this man ticks any more. I refill the teapot.

'It's coming back to me. All this.'

I decide to leave out what happened after the show. That can wait until I get to know him a bit better.

'We met up in the Buckstone one night,' I say, 'and you told me you'd auditioned for Pinter's latest play – *The Homecoming*. I think you'd been called back about three times. Anyway, they offered you the part of Joey. God, I was impressed. I hadn't realized how good you were. I'd never seen you perform.'

He looks interested. Stops eating for a moment. He wants me to go on.

8

'I congratulated you and said you must be over the moon. But you weren't. You said the contract was only for six weeks and you would also be playing a small part in *Henry V*. I mean, it wasn't just Pinter. It was Peter Hall directing, and it was for the RSC. You pulled a face and said, "But I'm getting eighteen pounds a week in *Pickwick*. I've got a long contract. It's steady work."'

'It was twenty pounds.'

'I told you you'd be mad not to take it. No doubt other people would have told you that. But I was horrified.'

At long last he's eaten enough and I've filled the teapot several times. He suggests a walk to Camden Lock. I tell him we can go there along the canal towpath. He's nicer than he was in the Sixties.

*

The Homecoming (1964–65)

It took several weeks to set up a telephone interview with Sir Peter Hall. It involved a host of emails to his PA where we agreed on a specific time when he would be available to talk to me. I bought the device that linked the telephone to my recorder and tried it out on long-suffering friends until I got the volume right; then I worried about the questions I should ask. I knew that Rigby had a sometimes ambivalent relationship with the great man, and I was petrified of saying the wrong thing. Sir Peter had recently been one of Andrew Marr's guests on BBC Radio 4's *Start the Week*, but hadn't joined in that much in group discussions and sounded rather reticent, tired even. So it was with pounding heart that, later that week, I dialled the number and began my interview.

It took less than ten minutes, but I did it.

Sir Peter told me that he had first met Rigby when he came to the Aldwych Theatre for an audition he was holding:

☎ [*Peter Hall*]

It was a sunny afternoon and we were all auditioning in the auditorium. There was Harold Pinter, Stage Management and myself . . . Rigby ambled in, looking like no actor that ever was, and I mean . . . *was* Joey. I really thought of him as Joey. He was one of those people who need to act in order to survive. That sounds melodramatic. I think the life he had as an actor set off his ordinary life, which was private and secret somehow. He had such a sense of identity. I have actors who pretend to be working class and put on accents and patronize the reality. And from Day One, Terry never did that. I believed him as an actor.

I asked Sir Peter how he elicited such a brilliant performance from Rigby as Joey – as there's no doubt that he was supremely confident in the role:

☎ [*Peter Hall*]

Just by seeing what the dramatist had asked him to do and helping him find it. Some actors are extrovert and some are introvert. Terry was an introverted actor. Whatever was going on inside his head was private, was his world. He was a 'limited' actor in the sense that versatility wasn't his strongest point. But what he could do, he did with immaculate precision.

Rigby had wanted me to see *Pickwick* before he came out of it, and arranged a comp for me at the box office for the Saturday evening performance. Sadly, one of my flatmates had been dumped that day by her boyfriend. She was so depressed, I felt I couldn't leave her. On the following Monday, Rigby rang to find out what had happened, and why I hadn't come.
I explained and apologized profusely. – Silence.
I apologized again. – Silence.
After the third apology and a very long silence, I put the phone down.
'You put the phone down on me,' Rigby said to me the next time we met, at the Buckstone Club.

'I was an awkward bugger in those days,' he confessed, when I reminded him of this episode, over twenty years later. We had already begun to drift apart – and I had met my future husband. But I still kept up with his news, and was relieved to read that he'd accepted the part of Joey in *The Homecoming*.

☞ [*Terence Rigby*]

And that led to very advanced things [*Rigby later wrote*], like working with the actors Paul Rogers, Ian Holm and Vivien Merchant, Michael Bryant and John Normington – all well-established, big names. We rehearsed in Stratford-upon-Avon, and finally opened: we went straight to the provinces – which is the interesting thing: rather than opening in London, we opened in Cardiff, the New Theatre. Lots of people walked out in Cardiff, there were plenty of empty seats due to the nature of the play. Then we opened in Cambridge, Brighton, and then we played Sunderland. And then the play was 'put to sleep', as we say, set aside whilst other works by the RSC commenced, such as *Henry V*. But although the reviews of *The Homecoming* were not particularly good – a lot of reviewers did not understand the piece, but that was par for the course, anyway as far as Pinter was concerned – it was judged to be a success.[1]

We went to see *The Homecoming* when it came to the West End, and I thought it was an extraordinary play, and felt immensely proud of Rigby's performance. He played Joey with great authority, something he never lost in all his years in the theatre. The character of Joey is nearly always described along the lines of 'a thick-witted, would-be boxer', but beyond the dumb facade, Rigby managed to show Joey's brooding temperament – someone who sits on the periphery, watching the proceedings and looking

---

[1] Written in four weeks, Harold Hobson considered *The Homecoming* Pinter's cleverest play, while John Lahr regarded it as the last and best play of Pinter's fecund early period (1957–65).

for an opportunity to make his mark. When, almost out of the blue, he makes an unexpected move on Ruth (played by Vivien Merchant), Rigby tackled the kiss and the rolling about on the floor with great confidence. He made the scene believable. It was the first time I'd seen Vivien Merchant, and was mesmerized by her stillness, her magnetism. And in the last scene where Rigby kneels at her feet, his head in her lap, the relationship was clearly established with mere nuance. It was also the first time I saw how expressive Rigby's hands could be – he had very fine hands, which he used with enormous delicacy.

We went backstage and took Rigby to the pub. As we crossed the road there was a sudden commotion a few yards off. Rigby excused himself and then, after a few minutes, joined us again. He'd split up a fight between Harold and Vivien – and behaved as if he was very used to this scenario. In my 1965 diary, the date recorded for that outing was 16 June. On the 23rd, we went again to the Aldwych to see him in *Henry V*. And that was the last time I saw Rigby for nearly twenty years. I moved to Devon with my new husband and I watched his progress from afar.

❏ JULIET'S TABLE

'Have you ever been to Dieppe?' he asks.

'I've been to Calais, Boulogne and Le Touquet . . . oh, and Cherbourg. Did you ever see *The Umbrellas of Cherbourg*?

He hasn't. But he thinks we should go to Dieppe for a few days. I lighten up considerably. He's been coming round for weeks now and we've never been anywhere except for the Tandoori round the corner and another one in King's Cross owned by Mr Mustapha. Perhaps I look too eager, because he changes the subject. The trouble is, I need distractions. The man I have loved for a long time has been told that he is terminally ill. It's affecting my wellbeing and my work. The main problem is that I can't see him because he is married to someone else. On *EastEnders* (where I have been one of the writers for some time), my script editor John Maynard is worried about me. He decides we need a week in the sun and books a holiday in Santorini. I haven't been abroad in ages, and Rigby invites me round to his place before the flight, which is at the crack of dawn. He'll make sure I get a cab to Victoria from there. He prepares a delicious supper of home-cured ham and Montgomery cheese. There's even a bottle of chilled white wine in the fridge. He checks my case and isn't satisfied with the contents. He packs a beach towel, a red Aertex shirt and some white tennis shorts. (I don't realize at the time what a privilege it is to be given the shorts.) Then he gives me an envelope of dollars, because they always come in handy no matter where you are.

I come back home fighting fit. But my dear friend is slipping away fast. I am about to experience one of the greatest kindnesses ever shown to me. We're having supper with my son Daniel, who is home from university. It's a good round-the-table sort of evening, and Rigby is on sparkling form, talking about Pinter's obsession with cricket and how on one occasion, Vivien had forgotten to pack his whites, prompting an almighty tantrum. Then I get a phone call to say that my friend has died. No one wants to eat any more. When I've recovered somewhat, Rigby says we should go for a walk. He hails a cab and asks to be driven to the Duchess Theatre. Despite my grief, I'm bemused. But what a clever decision. The auditorium has been transformed into a theatre bar-cum-cabaret. The show is down, but some of the actors and their mates are still there drinking. So I am surrounded by delightful people who know nothing of my circumstance – and Rigby doesn't tell them.

Very late, we walk to Devonshire Street and eventually get a cab home to Camden Town. It's four in the morning and we're sitting back at the table. Rigby reads the Shakespeare sonnet 'Let me not to the marriage of true minds admit impediments', and I know he won't leave until he's sure I'm tired enough to sleep.

We've found out when the funeral is going to happen – in some other town. Rigby invites me to lunch. He's organized the day, he says. He's baked some cod, boiled some potatoes and opened a tin of peas. Before we eat he drifts off into the sitting room and puts on Elgar's 'Nimrod' – 'I thought we'd have some solemn music.' That makes me smile. Just before 3 p.m. we make our way to Marylebone Church, where my daughter Catherine is waiting for us. We sit separately in the nave and contemplate a life lost – a beautiful and talented friend. I thank God for Rigby.

In the pub afterwards Catherine and I drink champagne, Rigby drinks tea and there are several toasts. And then we walk in Regent's Park and eventually find the secret garden, passing rose bushes labelled BERYL BACH and REMEMBER ME. It's just Rigby and me now, and I feel an overwhelming sense of loss. We don't speak for a while. He understands exactly what must be done. It's a gift he has – when to talk, when to be silent in complete ease.

And again, he won't leave me until he's certain I'll sleep. As dawn rises, he leaves.

Agents, actors, mentors

After my rather unsatisfactory telephone interview with Sir Peter Hall, I decided that, if possible, I would try to talk to people in person, so I made an appointment to meet Peter Charlesworth, who had been Rigby's agent off and on for most of his career.

Peter, and his long-time assistant Cherie, were extremely welcoming, and eager to provide as much information as possible, though I was first asked to provide some kind of background to my relationship with Rigby. By the time I'd outlined where I was coming from, Peter reckoned I knew more about him than he did. It was a good introduction, because we both felt we could be open and properly critical about a man we both loved and admired. He told me that I was sitting in the same chair that Rigby always sat in – sometimes for hours on end, chain-smoking and with the inevitable cups of tea. If he arrived with cream-cakes, he said, Peter knew that Rigby had a pressing problem.

My first encounter with Terry was after the second Pinter play, *No Man's Land*. I did the deal for that. He was still in *Softly, Softly* when I took him on. He said he needed guidance. So I did the deal for the second *Softly* series, and then he did the Pinter. From then on he was with me, off and on for sixteen years. Then he suddenly left me. I didn't find it very humorous at the time, but I do now. Laurence Olivier's dresser told him that if he went to London Management, they would get him into Hollywood films. So he disappeared for about six months, then he suddenly turned up again and said he wasn't getting any work.

He was with me for another period – for a number of years. All in all, he left me three times before he died. I've got a collection of his firing letters somewhere, which were always written very acutely and sensibly. When he came back for the third time, he was suffering from a form of angina. He sat there very nervous, not knowing what to do. He said his consultant was Australian and didn't say much (which is very unusual for an Australian). So I rang the man, and he was able to reassure Terry.

But one never really knew an awful lot about Terence Rigby: you knew as much at the beginning as you did at the end. For instance, he would disappear to Paris – he would just go, and not tell me. Do you know what he did in Paris? You must tell me. It used to confound and anger me terribly because I'd have some very nice jobs lined up for him and I couldn't find him.

I tried to persuade him to buy an answering machine. He flatly refused. I told him we couldn't go on if he didn't have one, and he said in his charm-riddled tone, 'Well, I don't know where to get one and I don't know what to do.'

So I told him I'd get one and take it round to his apartment and fix it up for him. He said, 'I don't know if I want that.'

'Yes you do, because you're going to lose money if you don't.'

Anyway, that's exactly what I did, and he never stopped moaning about it. To begin with, he refused to use it, but eventually he put a recorded message on it. And I realized after a while: he just left it on to pick up messages! He was having a wonderful time – it suited him beyond belief because he could hide behind it and he never had to speak.

My other big moment with Terry was when he was doing a big American series in Yugoslavia . . . You probably know all about that. He'd been drinking very heavily – doing a bottle of vodka during the day *and* in the evening. He stopped just as he was setting off, and this caused pink elephants to come out of the walls. When he arrived at the hotel in Zagreb he saw his mother being eaten by a wolf. I quashed the newspaper story by getting a PR man of mine to say he'd been taken very ill on the set, and that's what went out. His brother Joe brought him home. Terry was eternally grateful to me for a few more years . . . until he fired me again. The funny part of that story was that the actor who replaced him was Robert Stephens, who was always drunk.

I absolutely adored him. I loved him to bits, and I think he was one of the best character actors we've ever bred.

I'm very glad you've enlightened me about Paris. I had no idea there was a girl in his life. He mentioned a few girls but as if they were more distant cousins than girlfriends. I never met any of them. We went out sometimes, to parties, but not many. There was one woman he *did* like. He liked Britt Ekland very much, *very* much. And she liked him – not romantically, I have to add very quickly, because she has always gone for very young men. But she thought he was great. She made that film *Get Carter* with him. I didn't know Terry had a girlfriend to this day. My impression was that he was asexual. I never thought he was gay, because there was never the least sign of it. But several people thought he *was*. I just thought he was like Kenneth Williams – but of course he was asexual in a different way. Kenneth always had a good-looking young man with him – not to touch or be touched, he hated being touched.

But I'd love to know who those girls were. Have you got any interviews with them? There was one he told me about that he lived with for about ten minutes, and he said, 'I couldn't stand her around any more.' I assumed it was a friend by the way he talked about her, but this was some years back. Britt once said to me, 'He's a bit strange, isn't he?' And I said, 'No, he's not strange, he's just a bit unusual.' And she said, 'Yes, well, I was expecting him to jump at me and I didn't want him to because he's such a big man. I don't think I could have handled him.' And I said, 'Were you disappointed?'!

I don't think you could ever properly analyse Mr Rigby. He was a true eccentric, but I was very fond of him. We got on extremely well . . . but he could turn on a penny – and you didn't know why. But he stayed with me to the end. He actually rang me when he was diagnosed with lung cancer – I was amazed. He said, 'What shall I do?' They were doing *A Woman of No Importance*, and I said, 'Terry, go back on the stage. That's where you belong'.

I was made aware, over the time Peter Charlesworth and I spent together, that Rigby was a mentor to so many actors. He would nurture them, give them advice, watch their performances, and, if he felt they were good enough, he would introduce them to Charlesworth. That's a supremely generous act: to share your agent with other actors. And Peter took at least three of them on: James Stephens, an English actor who had lived in New York for many years; Maria Miles, who appeared with Rigby in *The Wild Duck*; and Angie Bull, who met him when she was a young schoolgirl in Birmingham. With their permission, Peter was able to give me their contact details so that in due course I could talk to them. There were many more who spoke highly of his generosity – of both time and experience.

Peter said he used to take Rigby out to lunch, and it wasn't until the third of these lunches that he said, 'I hate this.'

'What?' asked Peter. 'What?'

'Lunch,' said Rigby. 'I'm not a lunching person.'

'All right,' said Peter. 'Well . . . don't come again.'

❑ JULIET'S TABLE

I keep telling him that stair carpet is very low on my list of priorities. The house is now leak-proof and most of the walls have been covered with lining-paper to hold the crumbling plaster in place. But it offends him, he really feels uneasy about it.

They've just put in a new lift in his mansion block, and the Residents' Committee decided to lay new carpet. The old Axminster, pure wool and barely worn, is in the boiler room all neatly rolled. For a donation of ten pounds to charity, I can have it. He won't take no for an answer.

Tonight he's delivered another two rolls by taxi from Devonshire Street to join the other six he's already brought. He looks up, imagining the umpteen stairs in my house and reckons we've nearly got enough.

'Don't forget the passage and the landings,' I remind him. He tells me not to be so greedy. He wants a bit for his place.

All this effort deserves a proper home-cooked beef stew before the Cheddar.

He's in the middle of rehearsals for *The Wild Duck*, directed in 1990 by Peter Hall and starring David Threlfall, Nichola McAuliffe, Alex Jennings, and himself. He seems dissatisfied with his progress, doesn't like the messing-about in rehearsal, and feels he has to protect younger actors from incipient bullying. I listen to his lines. He has to be word-perfect. I established the ground-rules when he was doing Pirandello's *Man, Beast and Virtue* – when I should prompt, how pernickety I should be about accuracy, whether I should emote or just give a bland reading . . . Today we're concentrating on the scene where Dr Relling discusses his philosophy on 'Life Lies'.

Rigby puts the script down. 'Life Lies' is the topic for the night.

We debate every interpretation until we are utterly exhausted. I suggest he talks to his director. As it's way gone midnight and it's a Friday, he stays the night.

When he surfaces on Saturday morning he says we ought to lay the carpet roughly to see how much more, if any, we're going to need. We lug a couple of rolls to the top landing and others on subsequent landings. It looks very good. The traditional Victorian decorated-lozenge pattern is exactly right for the house. By the time we get to the passage, it's clear we'll need one more roll.

'Come on,' he says. 'Let's roll it up again'.

We climb to the top landing, somewhat breathless. He sits on the top stair and tells me to sit close behind him. Then with a whoosh, we helter-skelter down the stairs to the very bottom, landing on top of the mountain of carpet piled up by the kitchen door.

I tell him he's bloody daft, but it's the kind of thing we do. I laugh out loud more with Rigby than with anyone else in my life.

At rehearsal on Monday Rigby asks Sir Peter about 'Life Lies' and whether there's anything in the subtext that could help his understanding. Sir Peter says he wishes Rigby hadn't asked at this point – that the translator would be coming in later in the week and would clarify the whole scene.

*

The Wild Duck was highly acclaimed by the critics. When it came to town it was well grounded and the performances were strong. It was a brooding production that also managed to be comic. For a change, Rigby was quite pleased with his performance and particularly with the way he looked. I believe that the publicity photographs were among his favourites and one, in particular, where his face is wreathed in cigarette smoke, would be used quite often.

17

iii. 'Life Lies': Rigby as Dr Relling in The Wild Duck

≡ 'Terence Rigby is on top form as the doctor who introduces a welcome note of common sense, but who has somehow managed to make a hopeless mess of his own affairs.'– John Gross, *Sunday Telegraph.*

≡ 'Terence Rigby . . . a particularly impressive Dr Relling, whose heartfelt outbursts against idiots with absolute moral creeds ends the play so tellingly.' — Charles Osborne, *Daily Telegraph.*

≡ 'Terence Rigby's sceptical doctor deals with the best of the new translation (by Sir Peter Hall and Inga-Stina Ewbank) – natural, immediate, direct – so as to set an example to his colleagues.' – Milton Shulman, *Evening Standard*

Family and childhood

O f course, I had to talk to the Rigby family. I met them all at the funeral, and at various homes and restaurants. It was good to put them all in context. I felt I knew some of them already because Rigby talked about them quite often.

After the Requiem Mass at St James's, Spanish Place, in Marylebone, there was a second Mass at the Abbey in suburban Erdington, a few miles north of Birmingham. Jane Morgan and Peter Acre (very close friends of Rigby) made the journey by train with me. Father Michael McGreevy officiated, and both he and Rigby's sister Catherine spoke very movingly about him.

I met many of his schoolfriends at the celebration after the service. There were old sweethearts, football pals, classmates from the Abbey schools and St Philip's, his Catholic grammar school, and others, all of whom had fond memories. Group photographs of football teams and amateur productions show that the young Rigby was something of a teenage heart-throb. Looking round, I realized that Erdington was crucial in those formative years. There were the abbey church, the primary school, the social club where Rigby's father Charles worked – amidst a religious community of Catholic Redemptorist brethren. Catherine Rigby, Cousin Peter, and Father Michael all gave me insights into those early years.

Charles Rigby was born in 1903 in the Birmingham suburb of Nechells, the son of Joseph Franklyn Rigby, who owned a hydraulic-packaging business. It was a successful enterprise, and when he died, Charles and his brother took it over. Charles met and married Trixie (Teresa) in 1933. He was able to buy a semi-detached house on a brand-new housing estate in Erdington.

After the Mass and celebration, Catherine showed me round the house (now occupied by Rigby's brother Patrick). There were two rooms and a very small kitchen downstairs, and a neat garden. Upstairs, Catherine showed me how the three boys – Patrick, Terence, and Joseph – had shared a room, two of them sleeping top to tail, the other in a single bed. Next door, his two sisters, Catherine and Caroline, shared a bed, and their mother Trixie slept in a single bed squashed against one wall. Charles had contracted TB, and had to sleep alone in a small box room. There was a shelf for his statuettes of the Virgin and the Pope and other religious figures, Catherine told me. Every night, when he came in, he would stand on the landing and bless each room with the sign of the cross.

While Charles was in hospital, the business failed, and life was extremely difficult for Trixie. She had been used to a fairly comfortable existence and could afford help around the house. Now she had to take on jobs herself and sell her fur coat and jewellery to make ends meet.

The church elders gave Charles a job as steward of the social club. The boys belonged to the church youth club and the Scouts, and Rigby helped form an amateur drama society. In his teens he had already developed an interest in both acting and tennis. The children were lucky in that Trixie always gave their friends a warm welcome. Sometimes a whole football team would arrive, wet and muddy, and somehow she would feed them all. Cousin Peter Rigby has fond memories of Trixie, and of being part of the 'Bretby Grove clan':

> During the Second World War the family were evacuated to Upton-on Severn. We never went there then, so my first meeting with him would have been sometime in 1946 when we joined them for our first ever holiday together. The cottage in Upton was a two-up, two-down with no running water. The five children topped and tailed in one bed. We were given chewing gum by American soldiers and Terry fell in the river. He had to be rescued by a young local girl.
>
> Terry and I attended the Abbey Primary School and later the Abbey Secondary Modern School. We were in the same class until Terry passed the entrance exam for St Philip's Grammar School. That would have been around 1948. Away from school, we made frequent visits to each other's houses. Trixie was a fun-loving person, daft as a brush and lovely with it. The house was always full of children. My mother and Trixie were good pals and would go to church together. Trixie only knew the words of one hymn – 'Hail, Glorious St Patrick' (being Irish) – and would sing these words to every other hymn.

Father Michael said the Rigbys, the McGreevys and the Mackeys were at the very heart of life in Erdington. The kids were a wild bunch: 'At the back of the Primary School were great sand pits – a huge cliff of sand, and rampageous, wild games. Thank God no one was injured. Later on we developed a football team called The Abbey Wanderers. I thought we were very good, but the scores don't bear that out. Terry's mum, Trix, was a wonder. She could produce a bit of nosh without any bother, in what were difficult times.'

He explained that the Abbey Church was run by Redemptorists (The

Congregation of The Most Holy Redeemer), a 250-year-old order whose communities he has always served. He now lives in the Church House of St Mary's on Clapham Common, where Rigby would occasionally drop in, if he was in the area, for the rest of his life. 'But to go back to those sheltered years in the Forties and Fifties: you felt a kind of attachment.'

Rigby made several attempts to write about these early years but was never satisfied. I've tried to assemble these fragments into some kind of coherent order:

☞ [*Terence Rigby*]

Perhaps it might be said that it all started in Upton-on Severn, a large village between Worcester and Tewkesbury to which Hitler's Luftwaffe had caused Father to steer myself, my two brothers and mother when too many stray bombs meant for Coventry began falling on the Birmingham suburbs – though, no doubt, the man Goering was also aware that the Fisher and Ludlow factory near our house, made, and wheeled across the road in the dead of night, sparkling new Spitfires, which operated from RAF Castle Bromwich – literally across the road. For what seemed like many years after the war had gone away, a lone Spitfire stood in all weathers at the entrance to the decommissioned airfield. I certainly recall some degree of sadness when it one day disappeared, as did the whole remaining outfit, to make way for a housing estate.

By the time I was fifteen and had been attending the RC Grammar School, St Philip's, on Hagley Road, Edgbaston, since sitting the eleven-plus – I had amassed a considerable amount of amateur acting experiences, including *The Pied Piper of Hamelin* at the Abbey School, a couple of Gang Shows with the Church Scouts, and the St Philip's annual school play: my Shakespearian 'début' as Dogberry in *Much Ado About Nothing*. This was directed by our English master, Mr Gilchrist, who had spotted me during our rehearsed reading of [Norman McKinnel's 1901 play] *The Bishop's Candlesticks*. I have a memory of making every part I played funny and comedic – no doubt to amuse my schoolmates – but with the *Candlesticks* piece I gave it, for the first time, its full dramatic weight. I distinctly remember the boys being very confused at this departure, as it wasn't nearly as much fun. However, it led to Dogberry – a great honour – subsequently well received in the school magazine: 'Apart from a certain monotony of body movement, Rigby's Dogberry was one of the successes of the production.' Later, when Mr Larkin, the headmaster, called up the entire cast to take a bow at morning assembly, I was, as usual, late and missed the applause.

I left school at sixteen after a poor showing at School Certificate exams, achieving only French and History (and RI, which I didn't count). Indeed, most school reports were dull, with praise only for my footballing and running skills. I somehow knew that the sixth form and university was not my bent, and indeed the family, being large, needed the input of what small offering of ready cash any job would provide. So I was soon working the telephones in a local factory, R.M. Douglas, eventually upgrading to a trainee Quantity Surveyor – which made it possible for me to add £1 a week to the family economy.

Meanwhile, some good local good lady had presented me with a real pudding of a tennis racquet. Amateur acting and amateur tennis now vied endlessly for my total attention. I joined two tennis clubs and belonged to the local amateur dramatic society, and as well as playing in the Warwickshire Open, I became a founding leading light in The Yentonians, a company started by Anne Thomas, a local Erdington girl, supported by a life-long friend, Audrey Waterson.

Father was Steward at the local Church Men's Club and I got drafted into their amateur society as well, making my 'major' début in *Uncle Henry*, and more memorably, in *Arsenic and Old Lace* as Dr Einstein. I was particularly suited to this role, and although one night I drank from the poisoned bottle by mistake – confusing the audience somewhat – I was feted for my young performance. The director was a local enthusiast, Mr Ray Moran.

The young Rigby was obviously a big fish in a small pool, in demand from all quarters, and living life with undoubted enthusiasm. But in common with all young fit men of his generation, Rigby was called up for National Service:

☞ [*Terence Rigby*]

When I grew up, I went into the RAF, though my romantic vision of flying Meteors and NF-11s was skippered [*sic*] by impaired eyesight and the fact I had not passed English Language in School Certificate. I spent the greater part of two years in darkened rooms staring into TV sets, plotting the courses of aircraft going off somewhere, or practising a dogfight somewhere over Peterborough. Once in a blue moon a signal on the screen would indicate something at seventy or so feet, travelling at twice the speed of any known plane. A buzz would go round, only to be played down by the officer in charge of the watch, declaring 'freak weather interference'. However, we knew that he (or she) knew that we all knew that all the weather was perfectly normal, and that what we had tracked was some hush-hush enterprise from Boscombe Down or some such . . . Boscombe Down being, as far as I recall, something Naval, something very secret.

In 2007, probably in London, Rigby wrote – somewhat optimistically – as follows:

☞ [*Terence Rigby*]

What follows here is an account of forty-six years of work, by an actor, born just before the outbreak of World War Two and written at the ripe old age of seventy, perhaps as his tolerance is on the wane – despite being still actively involved in working at his trade.

To kick off abruptly, I have recently made a film with the Hollywood icon Faye Dunaway and, only last week, somehow raced through six tricky scenes in a BBC soap [*Doctors*] up in Birmingham, where I was born, and where I first put foot on a professional stage, having to black up – well, brown up, in fact – for Derek Salberg, the gentle boss of the Alexandra Theatre, playing a Nubian steward. I was a student at the Royal Academy of Dramatic Art, on holiday, having just had my appendix out. Tony Steedman, Brian Kent and Derek Royle were the leading players in the company. After this short baptism, it was back to RADA.

After three goes, I think Rigby has covered most of his early years with almost no mention of his family and how he related to them all. It's another part of the mystery of the man.

When he returned home from National Service, Catherine, then about ten years old, watched as this handsome figure in his RAF greatcoat, carrying a kitbag, walked up Bretby Grove. It would be some considerable time before the age difference between the siblings would cease to matter, but at this point he was a virtual stranger, and she was in awe of him.

❏ JULIET'S TABLE

As soon as I say it, I regret it.

'You're not going to take me to Dieppe, are you?'

'We'll go tomorrow.' But there's no enthusiasm. Maybe because we've just eaten a good supper, he feels obliged in some way to take me. This doesn't bode well. He goes home before midnight. So I don't sleep and it serves me right. After tossing and turning for several hours I realize the wind's got up and there's torrential rain.

At 9 a.m. Rigby rings to tell me that all crossings have been cancelled because of gale force winds. The demon inside me is still on duty.

'I still want to go somewhere – even if it's just across the Thames.'

I hear him laugh. So that's how we find ourselves on a Thames Pleasure Boat crossing the river to Greenwich. Rigby is in an excellent mood. We're the only passengers, and it's clear the foul weather has set in for the day. We go below to the saloon which has a wooden floor and pillars that support the upper deck. There's nothing to see through the steamed-up windows so we dance instead. Fred Astaire and Ginger Rogers, in macs and heavy boots, grabbing pillars and swirling round, lifting a leg and sweeping round and round with gay abandon. The bugger's made me laugh again and my bad mood lifts.

Greenwich is just as grey as Charing Cross, but we wander round the obvious sights and eat in a cheap cafe. By four o'clock we're ready to make the return journey. As we approach the Strand, he says, 'Let's go to Leicester Square.'

I'm not best pleased because there's still that drizzle that creeps into one's boots so that they squelch uncomfortably. The square is bursting with crowds and umbrellas. The red carpet is down and people press themselves against the barriers. Rigby pushes through to the front. I would never have put him down as a stargazer. And here they come – John Hurt, Joanne Whalley, and some tanned faces that mean nothing to me. Then I look up at the billboard. It's the premiere of *Scandal*, the 1989 film about the Profumo Affair, and there in the cast list is . . . Terence Rigby. So he's spent the day with a cranky old witch instead of preparing for the stars' get-together. Not a bit of it. He hates this sort of theatrical shindig and I was just an excuse to stay away.

We sit in the French church for a little while, and then in an anonymous little pub where we're too tired to talk much. He tells me he's off home now and that I should do the same and get out of my wet clothes. On the bus back to Camden Town I'm not sure if I've had a good day or not. What I do know is that Rigby is not best pleased with me. Oh dear.

He'll stay away now, I say to myself the next day. The phone doesn't ring and there's no one at the door. Finally a letter arrives from him to say he thinks we've spent too much time together and that we should give it a rest for a while.

OK. Let's do that.

*

RADA

In a newspaper interview – so faded I had to use a magnifying glass – I read that Rigby had borrowed money from a work-mate for his train-fare to go to the RADA auditions. When he went home for Christmas after the first term, he put on his practice clothes – a leotard, tights, and ballet shoes – and posed for the family. His father wondered what Rigby wanted to go to drama school for, and why he didn't have a proper job, while Trixie hoped he wouldn't become one of those 'pooves'.

I could understand why Rigby had mixed feelings about the place. He had told me often enough that Peter Barkworth, and one or two others, had said he'd never lose his Brummie accent and he wasn't much good anyway. It's no wonder he became moody with the family and all his friends. And that's how I knew him – Birmingham's answer to Marlon Brando and James Dean. There's a photograph of Rigby from that time, brooding, fag in mouth; on the back he's written: 'What have they got that I ain't got?'

'They' included such distinguished contemporaries at RADA as John Thaw ('Inspector Morse'), who, Rigby recalled, won a student prize to work in Liverpool; and Tom Courtenay, who was swiftly cast in a Chekhov play at the Old Vic. Rigby, it would appear, went largely unnoticed. An American student, Barbara Caruso, who was reunited with Rigby in the 1990s, was also at RADA with him for a while. She had graduated in Drama at university in the States and had done a lot of sketch work, comedy and radio before coming to London. Unlike Rigby, she got on with Peter Barkworth, who then taught Technique and Improvisation. She thought he was a brilliant teacher and feels that Mike Leigh, who was also at RADA at the same time, was inspired by his working methods. Barbara, who was used to improvisation, liked the precision of the work – but says Barkworth could never see anything in Rigby and frankly told him to give up the business.

Perhaps this explains Rigby's lifelong aversion to improvisation and acting exercises. Barbara thought it was because he was totally intuitive as an actor, but Rigby never forgot Barkworth's complete dismissal and the deep hurt it inflicted. He felt he was on the outside of it all, Barbara said,

iv. 'What's he got that I ain't got?' Rigby at RADA

but that he was also on the outside of life. He still admired many of his fellow students, she said, and they certainly regarded themselves as 'tough guys': British versions of Dean and Brando, following in the footsteps of Albert Finney at a time when the 'working-class thing' was burgeoning.

However, one visiting tutor, Robert Peake, a professional producer who directed student productions at RADA, championed Rigby and encouraged him to persevere. They remained good friends, and Rigby always spoke of him with respect and affection, always regarding him as one of his favourite directors. His end-of-course report, from Clifford Turner, Ellen Pollock and Michael Gover, was excellent, and John Fernald, the Principal of RADA at the time wrote: 'Very good work: it has got steadily better and better and I feel I can predict a good future for you with every confidence. Good luck!'

❏ JULIET'S TABLE

It's several days since I gave the most nerve-racking dinner so far. For some reason, at their 'Farewell to *EastEnders*' party at the Roof Garden in Kensington, the show's creators, Julia Smith and Tony Holland, tell me that they want to come to my house for a meal. Since I no longer work for them, I feel I can oblige – but can't for the life of me understand why they want to come to the rough end of Camden Town to be entertained. My daughter Catherine tells me to make shepherds's pie so as not to over-complicate the evening. 'Don't be pretentious, Mum,' she says. So I fill the table with friends rather than colleagues, and she comes too. It turns out fine, and here I am, about to finish off the last of the leftovers that have been hanging around the fridge for days.

The doorbell rings, and I'm amazed to see Rigby. It's probably a month since I last saw him, so it's quite a shock. He tells me to put my coat on because we're going to Mr Mustapha's place in King's Cross. I barely speak as we make our way down to the towpath. I love this walk past St Pancras basin, where a proprietary heron stands one-legged as passenger trains crawl along the viaduct into King's Cross, and the wrought-iron gas holders stand majestic. This evening, I'm not singing their praises as I usually do – I'm waiting for His Lordship to speak.

He doesn't tell me what he's been doing; he asks endless questions instead. I tell him I've been working hard, seen a film, been to the theatre – oh, and I've had a big dinner, with guests including Julia and Tony.

'Why didn't you ask me?'

'Because you wrote a letter telling me we've been seeing too much of one another.'

He grunts and grumbles for a minute or two, by which time I've decided to take the bull by the horns. I stop and face him full on.

'Do you fancy me at all?'

'No.'

'Good,' I say. 'Because I wouldn't go to bed with you if you were the last man on earth.'

'Why's that then?'

'You call love-making "thrashing about in bed". I don't hold with that. That's not making love.'

I get the tee-hee laugh. So that's sorted that out.

We carry on walking towards King's Cross, climbing up to York Way before we reach the tunnel. He tells me if I don't behave, he'll take the carpet back.

I'm really glad he's in my life again but I've been warned. Any show of amorous intention is unquestionably out of order. No matter how solicitous he is, no matter how scornful and dismissive he is of anyone else interested in me, I am just his very good friend. I can live with that.

As ever, he orders six 'pompadoms'.

*

In his own words . . .

In sorting out all the archive material, I'm heartened to find more of Rigby's writing. It's all in his beautiful – but nevertheless sometimes difficult to read – penmanship.

☞ *[Terence Rigby]*

Having seen out my extra term at the hallowed Royal Academy, I returned home to Birmingham for Christmas and wrote letters to various repertory companies declaring my availability and no doubt outlining some of the work I'd done in the Vanbrugh Theatre, which was the RADA showcase on Malet Street. One piece of which I was very pleased was Shaw's *The Apple Cart*, directed by the special and wonderful Ellen Pollock. We had even played this – as students – at the Belgrade Theatre, Coventry and also toured in Switzerland. I played Boanerges.

My brother Joseph, intent on a BBC career, was at the time working as a cub reporter for the *Catholic Herald* and had by chance recently interviewed Bernard Hepton, the artistic director/actor at the old Birmingham Rep theatre in Station Street. Naturally I had written to him for a job and was able to mention this when I was granted an interview. Clearly the connection proved beneficial, as he gave me a part in the upcoming *Antony and Cleopatra*, so I had clinched my début despite some vague nepotism – or because of it – at the great salary of £12 a week, which, considering that accommodation cost around 30 shillings a week, was indeed a princely sum. It was also an improvement on my civilian wage of £8.10s that I earned at the Witton factory of Salisbury Transmissions as a material control clerk. Although Mother was fairly loath to take any cash from me, I used to give her £1 towards my upkeep; I didn't of course have a place in London at that time to keep up.

In January 1961 I duly started out on my acting career at Station Street. The fact that a few months earlier, during term breaks at RADA, I had blacked up for the first and last time as a Nubian steward in [Agatha Christie's] *Murder on the Nile* didn't strictly count, as I was still then a student. The theatre's reputation stretched back far more distantly than I was aware of, and included great shows starring Laurence Olivier, Paul Scofield, Ralph Richardson and Miles Malleson. My start was in the (no doubt) great tradition of 'News, my good lord, from Rome' and just two or three tricky lines like 'Labienus, this is stiff news . . .' etc. I also managed to convince myself that I was understudying the part of Antony, but realized later that if anything should happen to Tony Steedman, Brian Blessed would, in fact, step into the role. I did struggle to learn the role, although I don't think I had it securely, so if both actors had fallen ill, it would have been risqué [*sic*]. My star chance was lost. One can imagine the *Birmingham Mail* headline: 'IGNOMINY OF FAILED UNDERSTUDY' – such dreams and imaginings are the lot of actors.

There weren't any understudy rehearsals but I would endlessly watch the lead actors doing their roles through a crack in the proscenium stage-left arch. It was always illuminating to watch Bernard Kilby playing Caesar and Robert Marsden as Enobarbus. As it happens, Derek Jacobi was also in the play, having recently made his début, and there was Elizabeth Spriggs and Paul Anil – the list for this play is quite long. But Bernard Kilby was everything REAL. Many years later he sustained a rotten and tragic death – caused by a stage fall at the Belgrade, Coventry. I seem to remember several obituaries describing him as a 'leading Midlands actor' – and perhaps only so because he lacked theatrical representation and the wider opportunities he merited. He most kindly gave me, from time to time, the benefit of his wider wisdom, and so his loss was doubly personal for me.

An event of great note while I was at the Rep was actually meeting, if but briefly, the great man himself – Sir Barry Jackson – who as well as being kingpin of the Rep also had a long association with George Bernard Shaw, and had established the Malvern Festival where so many GBS plays were premiered. Sadly, Sir Barry died while *Antony* was playing – I remember meeting Felix Aylmer at his wake. Another actor in the company, Robert Marsden, joined me on the train home. It took me a long time to realize that his sight was impaired. Years later, when he and I were in *Henry V*, and he was alternating the Chorus with Eric Porter, the steps he took on stage were carefully measured, counted – as by that time he was technically sightless. The wonderful Esmond Knight had the same problem – these gentlemen must have lived in a continuous purgatory.

. . . And in other words

Rigby stayed on at Birmingham until 1962. A friend tipped him off that there might be a job in Hull, so he followed it up and stayed there for a season, playing the usual rep fodder.

As his reputation as a serious actor grew, it was time to spend more time in London: agents rarely ventured far from the metropolis in search of new talent. There he shared shabby rooms with other actors and signed up with agents who specialized in television 'walk-on' parts. The money was good, and if one dropped in the odd line or two, the rate was increased. Most of the time, though, they were 'noddies' – the only response they were allowed being a nod – because that cost less. Nevertheless, television was a relatively new medium, so working in a studio or on location with experienced actors and directors was to stand Rigby in good stead for the future.

Phyllis MacMahon, then an aspiring actor who became a lifelong friend, met Rigby in the street. There was a crowd of them who frequented Lyons Tea Shops, the Kismet Club, and various pubs including the Round Table, and they would tip each other off about any bits and pieces of work that might be going.

My very first meeting with Terry was in the Sixties, after RADA. I lived in Burleigh Mansions [on the Charing Cross Road] . . . He saw me twice in the space of half an hour wearing different clothes and he said, 'D'you live around here?' There was an agent next door to the Arts Theatre club. In those days you could just walk into an agent's and see if there was any work going. Walk-on parts, etc. I was a young actress from Ireland. And I worked in a restaurant called Le Bon Gourmet. And he would come in and have a cup of tea. He wouldn't say much. But we were a group, and we drank together . . . we'd all tell each other what was going on, who to ring . . . At the Buckstone, for some reason, I would pay the bill – It was quite funny – and one night *he* paid, so the next night I asked him if he had, and he just said, 'Fuck off.'

And if things got a bit hot in Chiltern Street, with him and David Sinclair, he would telephone me from a telephone box opposite my mansions, and he'd stay the night, and the next morning, there'd be a note: 'Thanks, doll.' He hardly talked at all, but one night he talked on and on. I can't remember what about, but it went on. When, much later, my husband

Bruno died, [Rigby] was rehearsing at the Mermaid, and he would come up, and we renewed our friendship then – that would have been around 1984–5 . . . He was very good at keeping in touch with people. If he met somebody, he would take their name and address and send them cards. He liked that, but if they got too friendly, he would run a mile.

In those days one could approach an agent directly and ask for work. Phyllis remembers that Rigby was monosyllabic, but at least he acknowledged her presence. (In due course it was sometimes difficult to stop him talking.) It was through Phyllis that he met Maria José, who came from a wealthy Spanish family, but was then working in London as a cleaner. When she was sacked because she had no idea how to clean, Phyllis took her under her wing and introduced her to Rigby in the Buckstone Club. He liked her very much – but the relationship was volatile. She gave as good as she got and was very demanding. Phyllis thinks they should have married, because even though it probably wouldn't have lasted, it would have given Rigby a taste for marriage. When she moved back to Spain, Rigby would hook up with her on his annual trips to Lew Hoad's Tennis School in Mijas.

Rigby supplemented his meagre wages with work at the Royal Opera House in Covent Garden, clearing tables. It was a job-share with his room-mate, a fellow actor. At the end of each evening they were allowed to take home the leftover sandwiches, which provided a free supper. But the biggest perk was that occasionally he would be given free tickets to see an opera or ballet. This is where his lifetime love of opera began, at the same time as entertaining a fantasy that he might retrain as a dancer, or even a singer – he had a lovely voice and was always light on his toes, despite his size-12 feet. (I remember once telling him I had to dash, and running across the road, then for some reason turning back – to witness Rigby mirroring my run, like Polly in *The Boy Friend*, his hands and feet flapping.)

They liked him so much at the Opera House that he was promoted to manager of one of the bars. This meant he was on nodding terms with some of the stars and chorus, thirsty after a strenuous scene on stage. But much as he enjoyed the work, he kept his eye on the future and took any theatre job that came his way. This included a travelling theatre based in Keswick. He also worked in Sunderland and Dublin, where he played Sir Toby Belch in an open-air production of *Twelfth Night*. It ran into financial difficulties, largely due to wet weather; cheques bounced, and Rigby was unable to get back to England. Luckily he was offered work by Jack and Vincent Dowling, who were putting on a new play by Donagh McDonagh, called *Let Freedom Ring*. It was a celebration of the founding of the trades unions in Ireland. Rigby played the Liverpudlian leader.

☰ 'The first half of the evening was saved only by one cynical touch – the use of "Moriarty" as a footnote to the baton-charge and by the quite magnificent performance of Terence Rigby as Larkin.' — *Irish Times* (1963).

The Dowling brothers never forgot the impact he had made on them in Ireland, and were influential in his success in the USA later in life.

By now Rigby had found himself touring in Joan Littlewood's *Fings Ain't Wot They Used T'Be* with Jennie Paul (through whom I eventually met him), and knew his way around London – where to sign on, which Lyons Corner House to frequent, which agents to pester. He would drop into the *Spotlight* office to find out about auditions and interviews. Rumour had it that auditions were being held at the Saville Theatre in Shaftesbury Avenue for a new musical: *Pickwick*, starring Harry Secombe. Rigby called in at the stage door and was seen by the director. He was cast in three different roles, and understudied many more. It meant he was being paid more than ever before and he was appearing in the West End.

The Buckstone Club

By around this time in the early Sixties, Rigby had also met and fallen in love with a nurse. He was very serious about her, but discovered her in bed with his flatmate. He was broken by the experience and sometimes said that he never quite recovered from it. He began drinking more as a result, and looked for places where he could drink out of hours. He'd already discovered the Buckstone . . .

☞ *[Terence Rigby]*

Of the few contemporary actors lives I have read, there has been almost no reference to a veritable haven for actors called the Buckstone. It was located in Suffolk Street, almost opposite the Stage Door of the Theatre Royal, Haymarket. Originally known as 'The Under Thirties Club', in so far as my knowledge stretches, it had as its nominees the actors Oscar Quitak and Gerald (Gerry) Campion, plus others. I became acquainted with it in 1962 or so, and by then it was simply known as the Buckstone. I was taken there after one of my first TV jobs, a piece written by Henry Livings, starring Lee Montague, John Sharp, Anne Cunningham and Roy Kinnear, and directed by Gilchrist Calder.

It was down some steps off the street, and inside resembled not much more than an air-raid shelter which was rather easily filled up. Out of the bar area it led out into only one floor, to a modest restaurant area of mostly four-person booths – with a cooking area and toilets – with one ominous feature of a fruit machine which (it turned out) would almost always be commandeered by a gentleman actor by the name of Gerald Cross. You could dine with good wholesome food – whitebait being a favourite starter – prepared by Peter the chef, and served mostly by Lillian (Lil) and Nancy. There was also Patrick – Nancy's lodger, it seemed – who did things around the place. It was also possible to take an early afternoon tea there – no doubt developed for the matinee actors at the Haymarket. I recall feeling very special the first night I was taken there – to be in a real professional actors' club where talk was all around, about shows in the surrounding West End theatres, with many of the working actors from those shows relaxing and drinking there.

Although it was a club and required membership arrangements, it soon became clear that if you were taken down there by a member – and if you were there frequently enough – you would be assumed to be a member, etc., etc (though I believe I did eventually become a member through official channels). Actors gathered there from all standpoints – many were working in the West End, others were returning from the regional theatres until the next show came up, some were down on their immediate luck, and others (like me) were working in London TV shows: an immense crowded gathering of actors of all standings and various degrees of success at that time.

It was, frankly, a home from home *for* actors, which was essentially run *by* actors – via a committee, some of whom were then working in shows, or 'resting', or had given up the Business.

From time to time there was a full professional manager and one I recall was John Anderson – a real gent, who gave the place a real feeling of class and respectability. Not that the club was ever less than respectable, but with so many actors around, one could say quite fairly that it was all a bit crazy. The amount of drinking that went on was legion – and there always seemed to be pals there who would endeavour to sub you a few beers if it was the wrong end of the week – or you had not yet managed to sign on at the Chadwick Street job centre in Victoria. There was a warmth and a camaraderie about the place that was just not present in any other establishment in London – and you simply never quite knew who would turn up – and believe me, someone always did: those who were at the top of their profession – those in the middle – and brand-new beginners. Agents and casting agents weren't allowed to be members but *were* allowed as guests: this was because actors often got smashed and could get dangerously out of hand and be saying the wrong things to such people – and could do themselves harm. There were, naturally, some unavoidable scenes from time to time, but over the years it mostly worked out all right. Among the many customers was Michael Gambon, who on odd nights would do a very amusing double act with a dog belonging to an RSC stagehand.[2] And one night, as a guest of Pauline Stroud – a beautiful actress – Mr Neale Fraser, the Australian tennis player, appeared, which sent shivers down my back as tennis was a love of mine. I made the most unforgivable error by saying I was so sorry that he had never managed to win Wimbledon . . . which of course he *had*. He corrected me in an easy, unfazed manner. I was staggered.

The Buckstone, as well as being a social drinking haven, was also where actors could pick up information about what was about to be produced – and it was there, through a bunch of RSC actors, that I first learned about Harold Pinter's play *The Homecoming*, since it was at the nearby Aldwych that it was going to be produced by Peter Hall, the Royal Shakespeare Company chief. The information I gathered led me to phone Gillian Diamond, the RSC Head of Casting, and a rather curious audition. Could I come along and do a piece of Pinter for her? I had the cheek to say that although I didn't know a Pinter piece, I had recently done an Osborne play, and would be prepared to recite it as if Harold Pinter had written it. She laughed and agreed to it.

---

2   Gambon has no memory of this, but still reckons it probably happened . . .

I was at the time at the Saville Theatre with Harry Secombe in *Pickwick* – a musical, in which I was playing three roles, and understudying another nine or ten, for £18 a week – and was keen to get into straight drama. *Pickwick* was my first West End show, and I remember ringing home very excitedly and letting them know I'd had an offer, and Mother saying, 'Oh well, it's better than nothing, isn't it, love?' Mother, as it happens, was a fine mimic – of Father and the entire family.

It's important to say that apart from the Buckstone, the Salisbury pub on St Martin's Lane was also an important place to pick up information about work, and it was there that I heard about *Pickwick*.

But back to Gillian Diamond and the new Pinter play . . . Having got away with my Pinter/Osborne rendering, I was next sent on to audition for the author (Harold Pinter) and the director (Peter Hall), and they asked me to read for Joey, since there were some quite long speeches. I noticed there were a couple of other actors present. Following my reading there were the usual conversations carried on in the blackness of the auditorium, and I had no idea who was who, as I'd never come across either of these people in the flesh.

I was asked back for the third time – but this time I had to enact a scene where Joey takes Ruth in his arms, kisses her and then rolls around the floor, lying on top of her. To my amazement, Gillian had volunteered to stand in for the actress. Somehow we effected the kissing and the rolling around, being careful not to tumble into the pit or the stage furniture, which was in fact the set for *Marat/Sade*. I must say, Gillian was pleasing and helpful during this most unusual situation.

Feeling that I'd done fairly well, I pitched my voice into the darkness and asked if they would mind if I said a few words. A voice came back to go ahead. I went on to say that I had enjoyed my third trip and much appreciated their time – but that I didn't think I wanted to come back again as I thought I had shown them all that I could offer – and also that I'd noticed that there were even more actors now waiting in line to be seen than there had been before, and that somehow, as far as I was personally concerned, the situation was becoming counterproductive. It was indeed a bold move but it was what I felt. Out of the darkness and down to the footlights came a figure dressed in black, who of course turned out to be Harold Pinter. He told me my comments were appreciated, that I had done very well, that Peter was going back to Stratford for the weekend to examine the play once more, and that word would be sent to me by the following Tuesday – so off I went.

By Tuesday I knew I had the job. To be honest, I had no idea how important it was, how important Pinter was as a writer, or how important it was for my career to be involved in a production of this stature. My agent at the time was Hilda Physick, who had a shadowy room up several flights of wooden stairs in Long Acre (part of the original Covent Garden), and the pay was to be a lofty £28 per week – to do, not only this one play by Pinter, but also several roles in *Henry V*, directed by John Barton. A brilliant scholar, John Barton also became very famous for falling off the top of his chair with a cigarette in his mouth – a feat he performed more than once during the subsequent rehearsals.

I effectively joined the RSC, and had to resign my position in Harry Secombe's musical – which they weren't very happy about. But I was on a particular contract, so I was able to give my notice in, and there was nothing much they could do.

❏ JULIET'S TABLE

I've come to realize that Rigby sometimes arrives at my house with a 'topic' that he wants to be thrashed out within an inch of its being. During *The Wild Duck* it was 'Life Lies'. Tonight he says:

'Tell me about iambic pentameter.'

This from the actor who went on for Albert Finney in *Macbeth* and to my knowledge has never had a problem. He finds my Collected Shakespeare and opens it up at *Henry V*.

'Hold on,' I say. 'Are you testing me or something?'

He spots the tape recorder which I recently bought in a jumble sale and demands that I load it with a cassette.

'You go first,' he says, so I begin the prologue.

'O for a muse of fire, that would ascend / The brightest heaven of invention . . .' I stop, embarrassed. He insists that I continue, but I play for time by saying I'd prefer to do the prologue from *Romeo and Juliet*. I recall that when I was a student at Rose Bruford, it had been one of my voice exercises, and some of the tricks were still lingering in my tired brain.

'Not bad,' he says when I've finished. 'Not bad at all. I like the way you emphasize "Do" in "Do with their death bury their parents' strife".'

Then I record his reading of it, and several sonnets. I feel privileged but I can't understand why we're doing this. He's performing it all brilliantly. But he's adamant: 'Tell me what it is.'

With the help of a dictionary and my inexact knowledge, I suggest that iambic pentameter is defined by its rhythm of pairing ten syllables for each line into five pairs. He looks perplexed. I try again. 'Each pair is known as an iambus – a common metre in poetry consisting of an unrhymed line with five feet or accents.' Then I remember in the sonnets the lines are rhymed ABAB/CDCD/EFEF until the end, which is always a couplet – GG.

I distract him with a light supper and fill the teapot again. I reach for the wine bottle and hope and pray we're done with it. But he's determined to pursue the subject despite the fact that I've given my all. I tell him I'm no expert – it all sounds good to me.

'D'you mind if I ring Stephen Thorne?'

The same questions are asked of Stephen and I feel relieved that he's talking to an expert. If anyone can help, it's got to be Stephen. When he's finished his call, he says, 'Stephen says I should sing "The Banana Boat Song". So that's what we do. Over and over. Later he tells me he's been cast as the vizier Acomat in Racine's *Bajazet*. Alan Hollinghurst, who has translated it into English, has abandoned the original form (alexandrines) and has opted for iambic pentameter. And Stephen has promised to photocopy Peter Hall's paper on speaking in iambic pentameter. He's hung on to it since the Sixties when he was a young actor with the RSC in Stratford. When I'm alone, I am conscious of the fact that Rigby trusts Stephen and me enough to expose his frailty – not an easy thing to do when you've built up a reputation for being solid and grounded in your art.

*

Bajazet (1990–91)

Performing in this Racine play was one of the most important experiences in Rigby's life. I was close to him during the whole process and observed that he was completely focused, and felt comfortable with the director and other actors, so I knew I'd be able to ask more relevant questions of its director, the actor Peter Eyre. It took weeks to track him down because he'd changed both his address and agent, but finally my letter reached him and he agreed to a telephone interview. After my feeble efforts with Sir Peter Hall, I girded my loins and prepared questions that were as open as possible. I needn't have worried – he was so communicative, ready to answer everything I wanted to know and much more.

☎ [*Peter Eyre*]

I may have met Rigby briefly around the time he was in *No Man's Land*, but I really met him when I directed *Bajazet* and I was looking for someone who had real authority to play the part. I'd just seen him as Dr Relling in *The Wild Duck*. He won a prize [a Clarence Derwent award] for that performance. I hadn't seen much of him on television, but I thought he had incredible attack – he was wonderful. I got in touch with his agent, met him and explained that I wasn't a seasoned director, but we got on. I rang the casting director of Peter Hall's company and she said, 'You know, he's very slow in rehearsal.' But I told her that every actor has his own different rhythm on how they arrive at something. But he didn't ask a lot of questions on motivation in rehearsal. But because Racine is rather unknown to actors – he was rather slow to get going, but on the other hand he was terribly open.

The translator/adapter, Alan Hollinghurst, and I both knew what was wanted. There was some problem with Rigby's contract because he was due to play in *The Wind in the Willows* at the National,[3] but I thought: I won't tell him, but I'll be his understudy. When the play opened, I told him and he was very sweet about it. And he was excellent.

We were in *Hamlet* together after that, which went to Broadway. He played the Ghost, the Player King and the Gravedigger. He was loved by the cast and he was a dedicated actor. He told me he was very, very frustrated because he hadn't done much Shakespeare and he hadn't been

---

3   This was the second, remounted production of Alan Bennett's adaptation.

thought of as a classical actor, maybe because he'd done all that TV stuff being a policeman and that. So he was doing this play by Racine which was so stringently classical – and he liked being in it. He told me later that being in *Bajazet* and in *Waiting for Godot* had been the two things he'd enjoyed the most.

I told Peter that I'd found a diary entry where Rigby had told me that after the first night, he felt he had given the performance of his life, which pleased Peter very much.

☏ [*Peter Eyre*]

I'm not sure I remember the first reading of *Bajazet* very well. The play, in translation, was in iambic pentameter. It was unknown territory for the actors, but they were very enthusiastic about doing it. I don't know whether you remember it, but I didn't allow people to wander about on stage. I imposed a physical restriction on the play. I choreographed it like a ballet. Rigby was open to it – very, very open. Some actors can be subversive about the way they act, but he wasn't. It's not the way one usually directs, but I had been in a few Racine plays before, when I was in France, and I felt to do the play in English, I had to replace the French formality. This was something I slightly copied from a director I worked with in the Lyric Hammersmith, in a Racine play – because it worked.

One day I was talking about the vocal requirements of Racine. In Racine, more than in Shakespeare, people talk in very long speeches. It's very rare to find a speech that is four or six lines long. Rigby had a very, very long speech at the beginning of the play when he is recording the history of the situation. I played a recording of Sarah Bernhardt and some of the actors laughed. I told them that the recording was over a hundred years old and that she was acting in a different epoch and in a different tradition, and they should listen to her breath control and the sound she makes. They laughed, but Rigby wasn't one of them.

When I did *Hamlet* with him, he was brilliant as the Gravedigger, but he never got on top of the Ghost – probably because of the way he was directed. He had terrible trouble with the speech and how to find his way in. He was always working on it. The way I did it in another production, I made it very personal and intimate. He was in armour and in a special light. It was a bit oratorical, I think.

I reminded him that Rigby was elevated on to a platform way above the set.

☏ [*Peter Eyre*]

He just didn't feel happy. He asked me one night what I thought of it, I told him I didn't know what the hell he was talking about. He swore. We always had a very humorous relationship but I didn't see as much of him as I would have liked. After that he stayed in America a lot. But when I moved quite close to where he lived in Marylebone, we used to have tea or something. One day I took him to the private gardens in Regent's Park and he told me he used to play tennis there.

I told him that Rigby had invited me to the dress rehearsal of *Bajazet*. The only other person in the balcony was Alan Hollinghurst. (Alan was very fond of Rigby, I later learned, and was sad when he died. He reckoned he was a true artist.) During the interval we introduced ourselves. He said that Rigby's research into Racine, into palace life, customs, and harems in the Middle East, was astonishing – he knew more than Alan knew! This did not come as news to Peter:

☎ [*Peter Eyre*]

He'd just done the Ibsen, and I'm sure when he did anything, he went into it very thoroughly. There aren't many people like that now, frankly.

I had an adviser, Rana Kabbani, who is a historian. She'd written a book about the Orient and had talked to people who lived in closed communities and in isolation – particularly women. And we had that wonderful designer Chloé Obolensky, who worked for Peter Brook in a Greek play. So Rigby felt as if he were in a different world – a Middle Eastern play by a French writer. It was prime to him and to everyone. He was incredibly dedicated.

Actors have intense friendships while they're rehearsing a play, but I wouldn't say I was an intimate friend. I remember not long after *Bajazet* he said he wanted to see me and we arranged to meet at Fortnum and Mason. He was completely silent. He didn't say a word. I tried to engage him in conversation, but after an hour, I said, 'Terence I've got to go now.' And he said, 'But we haven't really started yet.' I'd given him all the prompts, but he hadn't picked them up. He had a very good sense of humour about himself. I think he was shy, in a way. Most actors who are good are shy, I think. He didn't drink any more and people who drink a lot and are the life and soul of the party use it very often as a cover for shyness or great insecurity.

It was typical of Rigby's shyness – and his kindness – that, some weeks before the opening, Rigby asked if I would invite one of the younger members of the cast to Sunday lunch. He was concerned that she was overdoing things. In fact she was pregnant, and simply needed some TLC, which it was my delighted pleasure to supply.

When I told Peter about Rigby's 'problem' with iambic pentameter, he recalled Rigby once telling him he'd been to Stratford to see a friend: he'd stood on the stage and tried out various scenes from Shakespeare, just for himself. Peter thought that was an incredibly sweet thing to do: he wanted to spread his wings. 'He did a lot of Shakespeare after that,' he said, 'and I don't know whether *Bajazet* gave him a taste for it.'

I told him that Rigby had already understudied Macbeth and had given a memorable performance when Albert Finney was off. 'Iambic pentameter is poetry,' he replied.

☎ [*Peter Eyre*]

I don't think Rigby had a natural feeling for it. He didn't have the facility for it – it wasn't his thing. But he completely mastered it; in the end he knew completely what was required. I'm not pedantic about things like that. Most people now have to learn how to speak Shakespeare. I know that when Peggy Ashcroft was at the RSC and Peter Hall was expounding his theories on feminine endings, line endings, and stops, etc., she said, 'You don't have to tell me that stuff. You don't have to explain how to speak Shakespeare because it's in my ear. It's my generation.' That generation heard Shakespeare very young. Their parents read it. It was a transference thing.

In a way, having doubts about yourself makes you an artist. Rigby did have doubts, but he had very good reviews for *Bajazet*. Everyone said he was good – and he was.

Peter Eyre later told me that on one of their walks in Regent's Park, Rigby recited the whole of his part, Canon Chasuble, from *The Importance of Being Earnest*. This was not unusual. He would quite often recite the 'Bolsover Street' speech from *No Man's Land*. After I moved to Hanson Street, we were once on our way to a restaurant when he stopped under a street sign. I looked up and saw 'Bolsver Street'. The sign writer had left out a letter and Rigby, of course, had noticed. I often regret that I didn't run home for my camera. That photograph would have been priceless. Sadly, the mistake was rectified within days, so the opportunity never presented itself again.

Alan Hollinghurst wasn't the only person to be impressed by Rigby's erudition. The actor Douglas McFerran recalled another reaction, this time from the casting director Gillian Diamond. 'You know, I remember Terence in the Sixties in *The Homecoming*,' she told him, 'the guy who could hardly string a sentence together . . . and to see him now, reeling off those great reams of Racine, is quite extraordinary.'

The critics agreed:

▬ 'Terence Rigby's magisterial Acomat stands almost motionless, his steady gaze seeing past and future, his voice unhurried, measured, deep, unflurried by the questions from Oliver Parker's attentive acolyte . . . When Rigby is on stage the drama is gripping . . . the look of the production is marvellous – velvety costumes, excellently still postures – but without the matter-of-fact reality of Rigby these scrupulous Ottomans would be much too refined.' — Jeremy Kingston, *The Times* (November 1990).

As Peter Eyre mentioned, during rehearsals for *Bajazet*, Rigby was also at the National Theatre performing Albert the horse in Alan Bennett's adaptation of Kenneth Grahame's *The Wind in the Willows*. He sent me this postcard:

✉ [*Terence Rigby*]

Thanks for your card, your handwriting is terrible – nevertheless, Racine drones forward – we had a bookless run yesterday, Friday, and I imagine it's steadily moving forward – a great deal of skill is required. Monday (today) is Day 1 at my old stamping ground – well, the pay cheque will help. I don't think Albert the horse is likely to put me in for a Sony award, but as we are meant to run for a while – perhaps a guest appearance at Regent's Park May Day parade might achieve a 2nd, or a 3rd.

❑ JULIET'S TABLE

He wipes his plate with bread and tells me that a breakfast like this would cost £40 in the Connaught. This is meant to be a compliment, but I can't help thinking I wouldn't mind making the comparison for myself. We're not going to Dieppe because he thinks we'd end up in bed and that would complicate things. I've already come to the same conclusion; what we've got is a very comfortable friendship – one that acknowledges all flaws, frailties, and fantasies. I like it when he gets up from the table and goes into the back room, rummages around until he's found a broom, secateurs, and a black plastic bin bag. He'll sort out the back garden, and that's his way of saying thank you.

When we break for tea, I listen to his lines. He's rehearsing Alan Bennett's *Wind in the Willows*, directed by Nicholas Hytner at the National Theatre. He's playing Albert the horse with a Brummie accent. It's going to be an extravagantly staged Christmas show with a starry cast including Michael Bryant (one of my favourite actors) and Richard Briers. It's the only time I ask Rigby to get tickets for me – not comps, I hasten to add. The visit will be a Christmas present to my young niece and nephew. He tells me he's been down to Brick Lane to a brewery that still uses Shire horses and drays to deliver beer. I'm interested that he takes himself off to study animal behaviour in such a detailed way.

'You should see Frank Windsor's goldfish impersonation,' he tells me.

Then he proceeds to open and close his mouth in the goldfish 'O' mode, and then with a darting movement to the side, repeats the process. He doesn't stop for at least two minutes until I'm helpless with laughter.

He's got into the habit of telling me about his ladies. The ones he thinks he could have a chance with. I never want to know their names; to me, they are New Zealand, the Black Widow, the German Woman, Mrs G., the Vicar's Daughter, the Police Woman, and many others who come and go. We keep an imaginary list and even in letters he might write, 'Here's another one for the list.' His answering machine is a godsend: he just listens late at night and makes a note of their names, some of them having rung several times in a day. I make a mental note to ring him as little as possible – I never want to be on that list – and thank the Lord that I'm not fond of telephones.

Inevitably he wants to know what my ideal man would be like.

'The exact opposite of you.'

When I ask about his ideal lady, she is, predictably, young and blonde – 'Don't fancy my chances there. What, what?'

There's a kind of innocence about him, I think . . . or is he just playing games? One can never tell. At a memorial service he encounters a charming woman he meets on the way out. He invites her to join him at the wake, but when he asks her about her relationship with the deceased, she says she never met him, she just turned up at the church for something to do. He says he was highly amused by this admission and let her down gently over a respectable period of time. I realize that he chats up young waitresses and usherettes. A pretty face – almost anywhere – initiates a reaction from him. It's not particularly complimentary if you happen to be his companion at the time. 'Here we go again,' I mutter to myself, but no amount of sighing or groaning puts him off in his pursuit of 'skirt'. Heigh-ho.

In retrospect, I remember the New Year's party and how at the end of the evening his attention was all mine.

*

45

The Wind in the Willows (1990–91)

Jack, a friend of mine, recently alerted me to a theatre exhibition at the Victoria and Albert Museum. He thought I'd be interested in a *Wind in the Willows* workshop caught on film. It shows the company working on animal movements and how they can be translated into human-like behaviour. The actors are taking the whole thing very seriously. Then I spot Rigby in his red braces, wearing the usual bespoke, eight-hole policeman boots. He's involved, but not quite as eagerly as the rest of them. Improvisation and acting exercises had to be tolerated – he much preferred his own working methods that were largely based on instinct. Stephen Thorne told me that the cast had all been given videos of the animals they were playing. They had the weekend to study them. On Monday morning, Michael Bryant was asked if his badger video had been helpful. His arch response was that the badger moved remarkably like Michael Bryant. Clearly, the 'old school' actors weren't overjoyed by the rehearsal process.

I got in touch with Tim McMullan, who was 'Chief Weasel' in the original production. I asked him about the read-through.

The Wind in the Willows was quite a long time ago and I don't remember the read-through for instance, but I *do* remember Terry very well because he was so damn distinguished! He always wore a coat and tie, taking his coat off when necessary, but never his tie – which makes him pretty unique in modern times. That was an old-fashioned trait, if you like, when it came with a very considered, if occasionally gruff courteousness. I always felt, or rather feel, that these aspects of him were aspects of essential shyness; they had become part of a persona that helped him get through the world on his terms . . . if that isn't too clumsily expressed. It also meant he never fudged much. If he liked or respected you, you came under his civility and he shared confidences with you. If he didn't rate you, then he didn't. With most people you never know where you stand, because everything is equally casual . . .

He was so very classy in the rehearsal room, and you have a young man – me – who was rather in awe of him. I don't remember if Terry watched any animal videos. Michael Bryant famously refused to watch one, but I suspect Terry was too polite to have refused. I can believe that he went to observe Shire horses and I can imagine him having admired them and wanting to do them justice. Which, of course, he did. What I do remember very clearly was how perfectly Terry, usually in a blue checked shirt and red tie, achieved what we were all trying to do through observation of animal behaviour, which was to give the impression of being an animal, a horse, through weight, movement, reflex, gesture, etc., and come out with a fully formed human character: 'obstreperous Brummie'. Everyone loved his performance. And without naming names, there was at least one principal actor who was frustrated by Terry's success because they couldn't match him in terms of skill. He frequently got an exit round during performances because what he did was so delicious, and you could feel how pleased the audiences were each time he came back on. There was quite a bit of improvisation during the first week or so of rehearsal, and I don't remember Terry's part in that, but I suspect he would have done whatever was asked without complaint or comment. Perhaps he did, I really can't say.

He was a great ensemble player in the sense that he worked with everyone around him in the service of the play, and I never saw him do anything selfish, or showboat in any way, but it seems to me that he acted out his opinions rather than talking about them. He declared himself by working in a totally professional way under all circumstances.

It was on 22 December 1990 that I took my niece and nephew to their Christmas matinee treat. It was enchanting, and we were all completely captivated by the adaptation, the design, the direction, and the acting. Griff Rhys Jones as Toad was brilliantly supported by Rigby, Michael Bryant, Richard Briers, David Bamber, Carol MacReady and Mike Murray. Afterwards we went backstage to Rigby's dressing room. My nephew put on the horse's hat, complete with ears, and I tried on the tail, since Rigby reckoned I was wearing the right sort of cutaway coat and long boots. I was very touched that he had pinned the horse brass I'd given him as a first-night present on to his mane. He then took us to tea in the Lyttelton cafe where we met Griff Rhys Jones.

Reviews were glowing.

'To their credit Hytner and Bennett have rescued the story from the anthropomorphic jauntiness of the A.A. Milne adaptation . . . Bennett has also uncovered a whole new character in Toad's exploited Proudhon-quoting horse, Albert. He is beautifully played by Terence Rigby (the actor of the year who has moved effortlessly from Ibsen to Racine to Grahame) as a mournful Brummagem nag in battered felt hat. Mr Rigby is all lugubrious resentment at human misconceptions ("One carrot and they think you're anybody's") and full of quaint yearning to curl up in Toad's library with a spot of Tennyson. Delightful.' — Michael Billington, *The Guardian*.

I'm now in a position to have lots of people round my table – something I've always loved since I was a child. There were six of us at home in Llanelli and the kitchen table was the focus of our lives. It's where brass and silver cleaning happened once a month, when my mother would tell us about growing up in the village and how she met my father. And, during the war, we were joined by our 'three Yanks' (who lived in our attic because the drill hall, where they were billeted, was too draughty), whose mothers sent us treats from America. Rigby and I share similar memories since we both come from large families and many of our experiences run parallel.

My sister Liz is staying for a few days and we're preparing lunch. Rigby shows up and says he'd like to join us. He and Liz go up to the sitting room while I finish the cooking. After a minute or two, I hear a performance worthy of the National Theatre. What in God's name is he up to? I stand in the passage and listen.

'Let it be so – thy truth, then, be thy dower,' and so on. I go back to my cooking and the voice booms all round the house. Liz has told him she's re-sitting A-level English after failing it as a girl; one of the set books is *King Lear*, so Rigby, who has never played the part, quotes speech after speech to his audience of one. When they come downstairs for lunch, she looks shell-shocked. But it's often the case that Rigby will perform a speech from some classic or other. He rarely leaves without saying 'Don't become a stranger' from Pinter's *Homecoming*, or reciting that much-loved 'Bolsover Street' speech from *No Man's Land*.

Occasionally he accepts an invitation to dinner with my other friends and family. He gradually gets to know Tony Holland (now a frequent guest), the journalists Margaret Hughes and Richard Johns, David Cregan (playwright), Jack Atkinson (a civil servant in the Ministry of 'Ag and Fish'), and Richard and Ann, my brother and sister-in-law. Rigby mostly sits silent, taking in what's being said. As the wine flows and voices are raised, he excuses himself and begins washing up, and wiping down surfaces. Since he prefers to stand at the sink, I say nothing. He knows I've got a dishwasher but that doesn't matter.

When they've gone, we have tea and he tells me what he thinks of them all. He's taken a particular shine to Richard Johns, Margaret and Jack, and in due course will get to know them better. He finds Tony Holland too 'controlling', but I won't have it. So we quarrel gently into yet another late night. It doesn't matter, though, because everything is clean and put away.

Get Carter (1971) and
Man, Beast and Virtue (1989)

I was invited to the Tinniswood and Imison Radio Drama Awards at Carlton House, where the guest of honour, who would be presenting the awards, was film director Mike Hodges. With a bit of luck I'd be able to corner him and talk about Rigby. It wouldn't be that easy, but I was determined to try. In fact, I had met him once before, at a birthday dinner given by the designer Voytek to celebrate his sixtieth birthday. I remembered that he'd been an easy-going sort of man, but I couldn't recall what he looked like, so he was pointed out to me by a friend. A couple of glasses of wine and I felt I could approach him. He said he'd talk to me before the night was over. And he did – quite briefly, but it was enough.

In 1970, Rigby was cast in a very small but significant part in the feature film *Get Carter*, released the following year. He has two scenes as a gangland boss, Gerald Fletcher. In one of these he is watching a pornographic film with his brother Sid (John Binden), Jack Carter (Michael Caine), and his girlfriend (Britt Ekland). Rigby has his hand on Ekland's thigh and is smoking a cigar. His exchange with Caine is grimly suggestive, and also sets the tone for the scene – and film. It's short, but Rigby's authority is there, the menace is apparent but not overdone. It's a strong and subtle performance from such a relatively young actor. His immaculate pacing of the scene is outstanding.

Mike Hodges said that although they'd only worked together for one day, Rigby was a true professional and they'd always kept in touch since. In fairly recent years, Mike had wanted to cast him in a project, but Rigby was in the States. This was true to form: it often happened that he found himself on the wrong side of the Atlantic and missed out on what might have been interesting work.

Not long after this fortuitous event, David Cregan asked me to accompany him to the George Devine Awards at the Royal Court. I felt a bit like a fish out of water, at least until David introduced me to William (Bill) Gaskill, who had directed Rigby in Pirandello's *Man, Beast and Virtue* at the Cottesloe in 1989. My daughter Catherine and I had gone to a preview, as I recorded in my diary:

✎ [Diary]

26 July. Terry came round. We sat in the garden until quite late . . . Terry's working with Bill Gaskill, who is giving them improvisation and exercises that Terry doesn't feel comfortable with. Went through his lines. Read in. Hadn't done that for years. Quite liked it.

19 August. We worked on his lines. He works so meticulously. I think he's going to be brilliant. He has such integrity.

1 September. Terry's play, *Man, Beast and Virtue*, opens. Previews. Catherine and I went. Had a drink in the Cottesloe before the play. It is a beautiful theatre. The performance, for a preview, was impressive. I found Trevor Eve so frantic in the first two acts it made me feel uncomfortable, but when Terry came on stage the whole piece settled down and we enjoyed it very much. I did feel the director hadn't quite established the style.

4 September. Terry brought me a poster of the play. He talked through a scene or two.

In retrospect, I was probably being a bit harsh in my criticism of the direction, and I never offered an opinion to Rigby himself unless asked. The production was certainly favourably reviewed in the papers.

☰ 'There is no doubting, though, the wicked brilliance of this 1919 farce in which nothing is sacred . . . [The production] makes the captain a belching and bullying boor. Weather-beaten features usually further empurpled with rage, he lumbers round, in Terence Rigby's gloriously gross rendering, snarling at his quailing, berouged and décolleté spouse, "She got the whole lot on the slab . . . Close the shop, I'm not interested."' — *Independent* (September 1989).

In my conversation with Bill Gaskill, he said he'd seen Rigby in *The Homecoming*, and admired his performance greatly. He cast him in the Pirandello knowing he would do the part well and trusting him. I told him that Rigby didn't enjoy the rehearsal process – the acting exercises and improvisations. He said that some actors didn't, but he had trusted Rigby to come up with the goods.

Bill reminded me of the enormous cake Rigby had to devour at every performance. It bothered him for weeks before the dress rehearsal and he tried all kinds of combinations, in the end settling for a blancmange type of confection. But some nights it collapsed in the heat of the lights, or would be slightly off. Apparently, one night the cake was *really* off: Rigby ate it, and then immediately vomited the whole lot back on to the plate.

Rigby had to wear a half-mask for this character (another new experience for him), but as ever, he commanded the stage and the energy levels lifted at his first entrance.

❏ JULIET'S TABLE

It's a sunny Sunday morning and my plan is to have a lazy day pottering in the garden and catching up with letter writing. The doorbell rings and there is Rigby with a plastic bag full of sausages, mushrooms, and bread. He wants a cooked breakfast, but first he wants a cup of strong tea. We've barely sat down at the table when the phone rings. It's my journalist friend Richard Johns, who lives in nearby St Pancras, and before he can tell me what he wants, I invite him to join Rigby and me for breakfast. In no time he's here with bacon and black pudding and obvious delight at Rigby's presence – in fact, the delight is mutual. I rummage round and find tomatoes, eggs, and baked beans.

In due course, showing off a bit, I place a beautifully presented cooked breakfast platter on to the table. The fried bread is in crisp triangles and there isn't a broken egg in sight. I feel it's something I will never forget – three friends contributing to a meal worthy of the Connaught.

It's the time of Saddam Hussein's invasion of Kuwait, and Richard (for some reason known as 'Sloth') gives us his inside perspective as a renowned foreign correspondent and Middle East specialist on the *Financial Times*. He also tells a funny story about a Russian diplomat, MI5, and the carpenter who was fixing his front door – who happened to be the son of a famous British spy. So it's a lovely, lazy, gossipy day. Richard wants some ideas on what to wear for a fancy-dress party. Rigby offers to lend him his prized Wimbledon umpire's blazer. Richard accepts, glowing at the offer, and, when he's gone, I help Rigby with his lines. He's now due to reprise his Sir Toby Belch at the Lilian Baylis Memorial theatre at Sadler's Wells next Sunday.

Both of these wonderful friends eventually died on me – the bastards.

*

Softly, Softly (1966–76)

I used to enjoy *Softly, Softly*, and of course the opportunity it gave me to keep up with Rigby's career. The fact that I don't recall the dog Radar's antics must mean that Rigby managed not to be upstaged by an animal. He played the dog-handler PC Snow, his size-12 boots completely appropriate for the character. He had played a small character-part ('Brummie West') in two episodes of *Z-Cars* in the early Sixties, and that series spawned *Softly, Softly* as a spin-off, which began screening in 1966. Rigby joined the cast in the following year. His portrayal of the enigmatic, brooding PC Snow impressed a number of writers, including Alan Plater, many of whom would bear him in mind for later work.

I was now finding it very difficult to track down people available to talk to me about the series. Stratford Johns had died, Norman Bowler was somewhere in Asia, and Frank Windsor was too frail to meet me. I did manage to speak to Adele Winston, a PA on the show, who said that Rigby was a good company man but would generally disappear at the end of the day. She thought he might have had a lady friend in the East End.

But then, quite late in the day, I discovered that Simon Langton had met Rigby on the set of *Softly*. He was standing in as a PA when he noticed that the cast was ribbing Rigby, who responded by shouting and being very direct: this was apparently acceptable, ritual behaviour, and without malice. Later, Simon actually worked with Rigby in several episodes as a director. It was very early on in his directing career, and he soon realized he was working with an ensemble who knew the ropes and, crucially, knew each other's idiosyncrasies. He saw that Rigby was, once again, sitting apart from the rest of the cast. Stratford Johns drew Simon to one side and explained that Rigby always did that and to pay no heed. So when I spoke to Simon, I asked whether he was in any way put off by Rigby's approach.

No, he was wonderful. I came to realize that he was working within his limitations, but brought everything into a narrow wavelength. Very clever. Actors like that go as far as they possibly can and then stop before going over the top. Whatever that is, it's strong and powerful. He was clever enough to use his natural shyness – to exploit it – invest the right feelings into whatever he had to do. The cast admired him. He was an enigma and they were intrigued by him.

At the end of the day, Simon would ask where Rigby was and be told he'd gone off on his own – 'to explore the underworld', implying that he liked to see what was going on, what he could pick up by living slightly dangerously. 'Remember him in that *Softly* episode where his dog was killed?' wrote a journalist friend of Rigby's in the *Birmingham Post* in July 1975. 'More menace was contained in a moment of Snow's icy anger than in a whole episode of Barlow's bluster. Even his silences can produce a profound disquiet.'

'Actors are foolish to be afraid of silence,' Rigby was quoted as saying in the same piece. 'It can be so powerful. This is not something I learned from Pinter – it comes naturally to me and is probably why I'm used.'

Rigby was by this time drinking very heavily. On occasion he would join the cast for drinking sessions in the Salisbury and other pubs. He usually sat on a stool at the bar, staring straight ahead, downing glass after glass of vodka. He still frequented the Buckstone, though, where he met up with old chums – Michael Gambon, David Sinclair, Stephen Thorne, Noel Murray, and others.

v. Rigby as Sergeant Snow in 'Softly Softly'

Over the years, Rigby kept in touch with Frank Windsor and Walter Gotell (who played a top brass character). Rigby brought Walter to meet me. It was later reported that Walter told Rigby he'd got a good one in me and that he should go for it. I recently found a tiny cutting from a tabloid, in which readers were invited to tell 'which men send you out of this world'. A 'Mrs. H. Hargreaves, Walshaw, nr. Bury' wrote: 'Terence Rigby, *Softly, Softly*'s PC Snow is my ideal. He's handsome and cuddly.'

He got a more extensive write-up in the *Daily Express* (1976):

≡ 'The most compelling mysterious figure in British television serials was back at work filming a series this week. PC Snow, the dog-handler from *Softly, Softly* who no longer has a dog. As played by the actor Terence Rigby, Police Constable Snow projects a sense of desolation, a sense of a man who stands apart. Those eyes set in an impressive square face hint at emotions painfully contained. He neither smiles nor mixes readily. He is alone. His dog Inky was written out, shot at a scriptwriter's behest. His second, Radar, simply died. There was no replacement because everyone agreed that after the sundering of these ties, any real life dog-handler would have experienced symptoms of withdrawal from further emotional commitment.

Terence Rigby says: 'In television the camera is so sharp that you really have to use yourself as the core of the character.' In this case it's the actor knowing himself. For Rigby is such a man, possessing this quality of apartness.

When the familiar band of actors who make up the *Softly* team finish their day's recording, they usually amble along to the pub for a convivial pint. But Terence Rigby will have a taxi standing by to carry him off. He has an urgent appointment elsewhere. Most likely to a pub where he will have a pint on his own. He doesn't do it because he dislikes his fellow actors' company, or from arrogance or shyness; he does it simply because he appears to have been born with a sense of detachment.

'I would need to be on a psychiatrist's couch to sort it out,' he says. 'Actually I used to worry about it. At sixteen I'd go walking in the rain with five Woodbines for company and be quite happy. It was a dramatic period of my life and I suppose it led me into acting. Dramatics have helped – or made worse depending on your point of view – for heightening my feeling of loneliness and channelling it into useful purpose.'

With hindsight, if this account is accurate, it's easy to see that Rigby and Pinter, the master of the enigmatic play, were destined to discover each other.

Many years later, Rigby told his close friend, the actor/writer Douglas McFerran, about the only time anyone ever got one over on Michael Gambon, who was a notorious master of the wind-up. Douglas said that Rigby and Gambon met up in the Buckstone during *Softly*, and Gambon asked how things were going.

'I've had a great offer, mate,' Terry said. 'I'm going to Australia.'

Gambon asked what for.

'They've offered me my own spin-off show. PC Snow goes to Australia and goes into the Police.'

'What about Radar?' Gambon said.

'Nah, nah, they're leaving the dog. He's got a kangaroo.'

'What d'you mean, a kangaroo?'

'Well he's in Australia, isn't he? Instead of an Alsation – well it's down under, isn't it? It's a specially trained kangaroo with a lead and everything.'

'That's great,' said Gambon.

'No one ever gets Gambon,' Rigby said proudly when he told Douglas this story. 'But I did.'

It was around this time that Rigby's nephew (and godson) John first became aware of his uncle's burgeoning career. I talked to John shortly after Rigby's death in 2008, and asked him about his earliest memory of this 'glamorous' figure:

JR No specific first memory . . . just a general memory of him being around – except, of course, he wasn't really around. He lived in London and we lived in Stockport. I have this overriding memory of this fantastically glamorous figure who lived in London where exciting things happened. Coupled with the fact that he was an actor . . . And so from an early age I realized it meant he was in some way famous . . . Famous people did exciting things that other people were interested in. I really worshipped him from afar without really knowing him or having reason, except that he was far and away the most interesting member of the family.

JA Was he on TV when you were growing up?

JR Yes. I don't remember *Softly, Softly* when it first came out. I do remember when Inky was shot – Inky the dog. The first TV I may have caught was *Tinker, Tailor*, which I don't really understand still. I remember it distinctly. It would have been about 1978 when I was about eleven. There was a big fuss because Terry was acting alongside Alec Guinness, and I realized, because mother and father were talking about it, it must have been a big deal. I remember distinctly my mother confessing at some time during the run of *Tinker* that she didn't understand what was going on. He seemed to specialize in television programmes and films that were hard to decipher . . . I definitely remember *Airline*, and another series set in Birmingham about three brothers, one of whom was robbing the other two.

JA My kids reckoned I gave them street cred by working on *EastEnders*. Did that happen to you?

JR Something I do remember about Terry was this feeling that he never really made it big. I don't want to sound too harsh. There was always a feeling that there would be an *EastEnders* moment. In fact *EastEnders* was mentioned, because he was good friends with Barbara Windsor and Wendy Richard. The idea was mooted in some vague way and I guess we were all waiting for when he might become an actor who was instantly recognizable and who might be in the paper and on the telly all the time . . . and that never happened. I always wondered whether he cared about it. He was very devoted to his art. To the craft of acting. I suppose that side of him may have thought he could do without the real celebrity or stardom that comes with something like *EastEnders*.

My mother didn't really understand a lot of things that he did. She would quite often say that Terry was an act – all that brooding and trudging around London and being very dramatic and actorish, was him playing a character, was all a big façade – that he was playing a character all of the time . . . I think to a degree that may have been the case. He may have thought, 'That is my persona.' But I'm also thinking maybe that's just the way he was. I'm not totally convinced that every day he'd put on this mask and have to be this brooding, mysterious character, enigmatic character. I'm not sure how much effort he had to make to be that character. I think it just came naturally to him and it was just that my mother got frustrated and thought, 'Why can't he just be normal. Why can't he just open up, why can't he speak in normal sentences? Why does he have to be in these mysterious plays that no one understands?' And I think it is quite intriguing and we'll never know the answer about whether he was just like that, or whether this was part of the mystique that he deliberately created.

❑ JULIET'S TABLE

Bit by bit, Rigby and I fill in the missing pieces of the twenty-three-year gap in our relationship. I tell him about being married and living in Dartmouth and being heavily involved in the Royal Naval College; having two children, both of whom he's getting to know quite well; being alone and becoming a writer.

Rigby doesn't boast about his work; doesn't name-drop unless there's a funny or personal story to tell – anyway, it's only me – and it's becoming clear that we are going to be close friends.

He's met and fallen for a vicar's daughter, who happens to be an actress. That's the kind of quirky combination he goes for. When he's invited to afternoon tea at the vicarage, he is enormously pleased, as if it's a scene in an Oscar Wilde comedy.

In a rush of blood to the head, he hires a cab to take him all the way to Stratford-upon-Avon (where she's working) from London. I decide this must be love.

But here he is, eating a greasy kebab while I toy with a hard-coated, yellow fishcake that I've smothered in ketchup. We've done his 'women' list and of course the Vicar's Daughter has got the top spot. He complains that one of the others is stalking him. He insists that he keeps spotting her around and about Marylebone. Then he recalls a woman he met while he was on tour, who got herself a job as a tea-lady at the BBC in London, so that she could see him every day.

'Once you're married, they'll all leave you alone,' I suggest.

'It won't last,' he says ruefully. 'It won't last.' He repeats this several times through the night.

At three in the morning he looks at his watch.

'I'd better go. She's in the flat waiting for me.'

My mouth drops open.

'Treat 'em mean, keep 'em keen, that's what I say.

*

Friends and flatmates

Rigby's sister Catherine kindly drove me to Bognor Regis to meet Rigby's old friend, Noel Murray. We spent the day together and he lent me a pile of letters and cards sent to him by Rigby, that he treasured. I read them on the long journey home, and again, later. They demonstrated just how important Noel was in Rigby's life.

They met in the White Swan, Covent Garden (known as the Mucky Duck) in 1970. Noel recognized him from *Softly, Softly*. They barely spoke for the first month, but gradually realized they had a shared interest in theatre, film, and music. Noel wrote a little, but regarded himself as lazy. He didn't bore Rigby with any of his work, but they were both interested in the structure of plays.

Noel moved to Marylebone to work for Michael Tierney at the Prince Regent. Rigby showed up one day with David Sinclair, who had appeared in the musical *Robert and Elizabeth* in the West End. It was around this time that Rigby was cast in *Get Carter*, which Noel said didn't do him any harm.

'There was a real social buzz in Marylebone at the time. Lots of people from the Royal Academy of Music used the local pubs, including one of the tutors, Norman Knight, who was a flautist. Michael Tierney had little brass name plaques made for his regulars that were screwed into the bar, in line with where they stood.'

I realized where the inspiration for my brass plaque came from.

Rigby didn't appear to have many very close friends at this time, so Noel felt privileged to be regarded as one such. He was deeply impressed by Rigby's integrity, the tremendous sense of responsibility he felt for his job and towards people. Generally, he felt responsible *for* people. Noel got on well with Sinclair, who was arrogant beyond belief. Sinclair seemed oblivious to the thoughtfulness Rigby showed him. But maybe deep down he was dimly aware of it. They shouted at one another interminably, but ended up sharing a flat together in Chiltern Street. They rented it from Peter Crouch, a theatrical agent, and although Sinclair's name was on the lease, it was Rigby who paid the rent and most of the bills.

In 1976, or thereabouts, Rigby was going to be away for six months touring *No Man's Land* in the USA. Sinclair, similarly, was going to be touring Marcelle Maurette's *Anastasia* with Nyree Dawn Porter and Peter Wyngarde. Noel was invited to be a lodger with each of them in turn, and for a while, both together. Noel got to know them individually. He reckoned it was a happy time.

When he first moved in, the first thing he noticed was shelves full of empty bottles. The emphasis was on 'empty'. David Sinclair was an avid drinker. Rigby's obituary of Sinclair speaks volumes: They 'were the odd couple; so different; totally different'.

Sunday lunch at the flat was a ritual. Sinclair and Rigby cooked on alternate Sundays. It was always roast lamb. The big difference was that Sinclair liked gravy and Rigby liked onion sauce. There were often great wars. When Rigby was cooking, Sinclair wasn't allowed in the kitchen. On one particular Sunday, he was drinking in the other room. He suddenly stood up and roared, 'I see no reason why I shouldn't have gravy!'

Generally Sinclair played mine host and became more imperious the more he drank. Rigby did most of the chores, but if he ever complained, Sinclair would say, 'It's my name on the lease.' Anyone could be invited to the lunches, but not many women.

Noel said that Rigby was a misogynist. He had girlfriends, but treated them badly. On one occasion, he brought a girl to the Devonshire Arms. They were drinking steadily in a group, but the girl kept hinting that she was hungry. She became more and more insistent, so Rigby excused himself from the group and took her to an Italian restaurant in the High Street. He asked her if she fancied anything on the menu, which was posted in the window. She said, 'Oh yes, lovely.' So he opened the door for her and said he was going back to the pub and would see her later.

On another occasion, Rigby took Britt Ekland to Annabel's for lunch. His pals were envious and couldn't wait to ask him how it went. He said, 'The food was bloody awful and it was ridiculously expensive.'

'What about Britt Ekland?' asked Noel.

'Oh yes, she's a nice kid. Nice kid.'

Phyllis MacMahon agrees that Rigby behaved appallingly towards women. He would ask them out for a drink and if he found them boring or unattractive, he would excuse himself, saying he wanted a pee. On the table would be a packet of cigarettes and a lighter – or maybe a mac over the back of the chair. The girl would wait patiently, reassured by his possessions. But she would wait and wait until eventually she would ask someone to search the lavatories. And there'd be no sign of Rigby. He'd have scarpered, returning the next day for his belongings.

Rigby told Noel there were episodes of *Softly* that he couldn't remember doing, he was so drunk. And that wasn't like him, he was a professional. Noel knew he was a big drinker, but he never showed it. He was so strong, so solid, it didn't show. He recalled one occasion at the Groucho Club when they were with David Sinclair. Suddenly Rigby's nose started to drip and Sinclair said, 'I think Rigby's full up.'

The reality was that alcohol was taking over in a big way. He would start the day drinking with another alcoholic in one Marylebone pub and then begin his tour of all the pubs in the neighbourhood. He would wander the streets at night, often ending up at Langan's Bistro. At this point, Rigby admitted to Noel that he was on three bottles of vodka a day.

There's much more of Noel's story to tell, but having gone through the pile of Rigby's own words, I felt I should insert an extract of Rigby's account from towards the end of his time on *Softly, Softly,* which also includes a newspaper clipping on a propitious event at the National Theatre – which at that time was housed in The Old Vic.

☰ GOOD FORTUNE

'Terence Rigby, from Birmingham, is 39 and travelling light. But once again he has an immense stroke of good fortune in being able to put his own isolation to work. Several weeks ago, there was a backstage crisis at the National Theatre when an actor named Michael Feast fell ill 12 days before he was to perform a one-man play at the Old Vic. Terence Rigby, who had wandered in for a cup of tea, was handed the script. 'They told me it was 20 minutes long, the swines,' he says without rancour. In fact the script was 6,000 words long or a 50 minute solo. For 6 days, he paced Regent's Park mouthing the words and alarming the park bench habitués who were more accustomed to a more stoic Rigby. He spent 6 weeks with the director and last week gave his first 2 performances of *The Man Himself* by Alan Drury. It is a bleak, compassionate performance that Rigby will continue to give intermittently until he leaves with the knights for North America. He says slowly, 'I still have the key to my old hotel room on West 45th St in New York.' And then, so that we don't know where Rigby ends and Pinter begins, 'But they've knocked the hotel down.' — *Daily Express* (7 July 1976)

Alan Drury and Rigby became good friends together in the company of Jane Morgan and Peter Acre.

This first Rigby extract is about the years 1974–75, when he was coming to the end of a stint in *Softly*:

☞ [*Terence Rigby*]

The Police show meant I was never out of the rehearsal centre at North Acton and indeed the BBC White City Studios. One day I came across the tallest short actor I ever knew – Henry Woolf. He was a bosom childhood friend of Harold Pinter and was just slamming down the phone – he shouted to me, 'Harold's written another play.' 'Great,' I said, 'great' – truly pleased as I knew HP had not written a piece for some time. We didn't discuss the matter any further.

That chance moment, as it turned out, was to prove momentous in terms of my career – as the play was *No Man's Land*. For anyone who has not heard of Henry Woolf, apart from being a truly sound, professional actor, he is seriously one of the warmest, most affable people I have encountered both in or out of the profession and had been in the *Marat/Sade* with the RSC, Peter Brook's riveting production, at the Aldwych theatre which was, by then, the Stratford company's London home – around 1964.

❑ JULIET'S TABLE

He tells me that Maria José, his long-time girlfriend, is coming to stay with him in Devonshire Street. The Vicar's Daughter has literally disappeared; no one is unduly worried, according to Rigby, she's bound to turn up soon. Such nonchalance.

'So, I won't see you again. Will you invite me to the wedding?'

'Only if you behave yourself.' He gives me a quizzical look. For some strange reason, he's not brimming with excitement.

The day after she arrives, I pick up a message from Rigby – it's a long, amused giggle, then he puts the phone down. Not wishing to intrude I don't ring him back, but I am intrigued. A little later he rings to say he'd rung earlier because he needs to escape.

A couple of days later, I get another call from him, asking a favour.

'Do you think you could take Maria José to the theatre tonight? My treat, of course. I have things to do.' (He means he's bored.) And that's how I end up queuing outside a theatre in Shaftesbury Avenue with Maria José. The play is *The Madhouse in Goa* by Martin Sherman, starring Vanessa Redgrave and Rupert Graves. We've done the pleasantries but for some reason they won't let us in. And then we're told that the performance has been cancelled due to technical problems. So what now? Rigby's going to be so fed up if I let her go home. I suggest a meal. But this feisty Spanish woman demands to come to my house.

'I want you to cook me a typical English meal. Let's go.'

Luckily the Greek corner shop is still open, so I buy all the ingredients for shepherd's pie. I'm not doing roast beef and Yorkshire pudding for Rigby's girlfriend. What I don't know at this point is that Maria used to live in England and would have eaten hundreds of typically English meals. Fortunately, I don't have to entertain her. She rabbits on without pause while I peel potatoes and fry the mince and onions. I'm thinking, '*Madhouse in Goa*? Come to the one in Camden Town.'

We've just about finished when the phone rings. It's Rigby, wondering where his girlfriend is. I explain what's happened; he giggles. Within minutes he's on the doorstep demanding pie and tea.

Maria José takes photographs of me and Rigby with the elephant tea cosy on his head. Months later, she sends them to me.

Thinking back, I believe I actually enjoyed that evening.

*

Two days later a postcard arrived. I think it's meant to be a thank you. (There are usually tennis references.)

✉ [*Terence Rigby*]

Barcelona Balls   3   Camden Shepherds   4

Devon Delvers and Madrid Maidens, match postponed.

No Man's Land (1975)

☞ *[Terence Rigby]*

It was at the Buckstone Club that Michael Elphick rent the air, declaring, 'Sir Peter Hall – is there to be no end to this man's arrogance?'

He was referring, having taken the odd three or four, to the fact that myself and Michael Feast were chosen to support Sir Ralph Richardson and Sir John Gielgud in Pinter's new four-hander, *No Man's Land*. Essentially – utterly – a jovial, friendly declaration, but we all knew he meant, as apart from my own excesses, Michael had had an unfortunate brush with Sir John in a recent production of *The Tempest* – also at the Old Vic.

Having learned from Henry Woolf that Harold had written this new piece, it did not occur to me to pursue whether there was a relevant part for me. I felt I'd had my share of Pinter – and in any case, I was deeply involved for the sixth successive year with my police show *Softly, Softly: Task Force*, which was a big BBC TV smash hit. I played PC Snow, who had started off as a dog-handler but by this time in the series had already lost two dogs: 'Inky', who died dramatically, shot by the 'beastly' UK/ Canadian actor, Glen Beck (who more or less had to go into temporary hiding afterwards), and 'Radar', a star of Brazilian TV, we were told, who died a sad, natural death off screen. The passing of Radar was big national news, involving a star-attended funeral, with hearse and all the attendant trimmings – vicar plus cassock and prayer book, and final eulogy over the grave. The *Sun* newspaper gave it the middle page spread, relegating the dear old Prince of Windsor, who was buried the same day, to page 4.

But back to *No Man's Land* . . . I was genuinely astounded when Peter Hall sent the script around to my Chiltern Street home, offering me the role of Briggs. I was naturally very excited. It read like a dream and I finished it in one session. The music of it literally soared in my mind, and though my knowledge of music was modest, it reminded me of some great work by Bach.

A call from Harold quickly followed, an invitation to meet him at the Volunteer pub at the top of Baker Street. He was clearly still living in the family home at Hanover Terrace, though it was rumoured that he was going through an unsettled time. It was almost too much to take in when he confirmed that Sir Ralph and Sir John had, more or less, accepted. He also said he was puzzled, to say the least, that Sir John was taking his time to confirm the role, and asked me rhetorically whether the part wasn't

vi. 'He asked me the way to Bolsover Street': Rigby as Briggs in No Man's Land

'bloody big enough for him'. There wasn't anything sensible I could say on the matter, but later it came out in the wash.

> It turned out that 'RR' and 'JG' had been exchanging lots of phone calls, because the Spooner role included a reference to 'consuming the male member', about which JG was concerned and somewhat abashed – wondering whether it was detrimental to his image. Eventually, RR came across the wizard idea of declaring, 'Oh no, Johnnie – it's just a joke,' whereupon JG said, 'Oh, do you really think so, Ralphie? Well in that case I'd better tell Peter it's all right.' Harold was good enough to tell me that the final decision to offer me the role had been Peter's, which I thought was very generous of him.

Michael Feast, who was the original Foster in the London production, adds 'a few random thoughts and memories' of the first meeting with the director and cast.

> [Rigby and I] first met at the lunch given by Peter Hall at Rules restaurant in town. Also present were Sir Ralph and Sir John, Peter Hall, Harold Pinter, and John Bury the designer. I had met and worked with Sir John and Peter

Hall when I played in *The Tempest* a year or so earlier. But everyone else was new to me. Quite a line-up for a young actor. We sat round an oval table and were immediately asked what we would have to drink. I had recently gone on the wagon. Everyone ordered their pre-lunch drinks: a gin and tonic here, a glass of wine there – Terry, I remember, had a beer. I said quietly to the waiter, 'I'll have some water.'

Somebody, I can't remember who, asked me why I didn't want an alcoholic drink and I mumbled something about getting healthy. From my left, down the other end of the table, Sir Ralph said loudly, 'Never trust a man who doesn't drink.' I think he meant it with a degree of dryness, but given the situation and the company, I wasn't able to respond with anything other than a sickly grin. Terry, who was sitting opposite me, and who I had only just met, reached across and grabbed my hand, and said loudly, 'Don't worry, kid.' He always called me 'kid' after that, and I realized as I got to know him that the response was fairly typical of his kindness and ability to defuse difficult situations.

We did spend a lot of time together over the year and a half of *No Man's Land* and I got to like him and enjoy his company enormously. There was always an uncle–nephew protective nature about his relationship to me, and given that I had a certain wild child tendency at the time, it was strangely appropriate. I know he was disappointed that I didn't go to New York with the show. And he wrote a long and very caring letter saying how much he missed me.

☞ [*Terence Rigby*]

At this time the National Theatre on the South Bank was still in the process of being finished but had suffered setback after setback regarding its opening date. Consequently there was a long list of productions which had been meant to open the building which subsequently played at the Vic.

No Man's Land was set to open on 23 April (St George's Day/ Shakespeare's birthday), so it would have been a definite candidate for the official opening of the Lyttelton – but it too was to be passed over as the theatre still wasn't ready.

'Day One' eventually came, and we met in one of several Nissen huts attached to the Old Vic to boost their administration space, Nissen huts which also let in the rain, demonstrated by several buckets placed strategically around the room. In addition to Sir Ralph and Sir John were Michael Feast and myself (being the entire cast), Peter Hall the director, Jackie our lady stage manager, and John Bury the designer. It's amazing to think I can't remember if Harold Pinter was there or not, but I do recall that he was being hounded badly by the Press at the time, concerning his new friendship with Lady Antonia Fraser, and over all we certainly saw very little of him. Way back, during *The Homecoming* rehearsals, he seemed a frequent if not constant presence, but then his wife Vivien Merchant had been the leading lady in that play. Michael Hallifax, the company general manager, was also present – but the excitement of it all makes the event curiously distant. Clearly I shook hands with everyone but the details have not stayed with me.

We had settled and Sir Ralph was about to speak the first magical line – 'As it is?' – when I realized I hadn't got a handkerchief, so I dashed across to my overcoat to get one, thus creating an hiatus, which Sir Ralph 'marked' quite heavily, and after I had settled I heard Peter apologizing to him, as it were on my behalf – and we settled again. Not a good start. The play read well, as one might imagine, and I remember 'PH' telling me that Sir Ralph had enjoyed my 'Bolsover' speech in Act Two. It was then announced that we were to have lunch at Rules in Covent Garden, and then to have two full weeks off to enable the knights to study their lines. RR was already doing *John Gabriel Borkman* and JG was possibly doing a play too, since the company was operating the full repertoire system. Rosemary Beattie, our stage manager, somehow got us all over the river for our slap-up lunch.

I had started to grow a moustache for the role of Briggs as it had come to me that the character could well have been in the RAF – perhaps as a medic. It also happened that RR had a moustache. At one point he said, 'I see you are growing a moustache.' I said, 'Yes, Sir Ralph, I thought perhaps it would suit my character.' He replied, 'Well, as you see, I already have a moustache – and somehow I don't think this play is about moustaches.' It must have been the euphoria of the event, creating a touch of madness, as I found myself saying, 'I tell you what, Sir Ralph – I'll toss you for it.' He didn't respond, and I don't think he smiled – but just got on with his lunch. Another lurch in the wrong direction. I am glad to say we both kept our moustaches, and I was able to convince the great man that Briggs would only have a plain, straggly one, and had merely grown it as a kind of tribute to his master whose moustache would have a fine military clip about it – quite superior in all ways. Sir Ralph finally bought it.

As might be imagined, a new play, started in such illustrious company, and with the added bonus of two weeks off – well, it was, for the actor, wa-hey-hey time, and local hostelries in and around Cecil Court, the Round Table and the Salisbury, plus no doubt the Kismet Club in Newport Street, were duly visited – with the final call at 11 p.m. being the old favourite the Buckstone Club to put the icing on this day of celebration. Present that evening was my flatmate Sinclair, plus many of the usual suspects as well as the BBC sound producer Bob Craddock (essentially a pal of Sinclair's, whom I had met many times). He had in fact frequently stayed overnight at our Chiltern Street flat, as he had difficulties with his family. If we chanced to return from an evening out at the same time, I would pull out the mattress from under my bed and dump it in the sitting room, and that is where Bob would slumber – after having put his shoes outside the front door for the non-existent night porter to polish up. This odd little habit came to light on the occasion we turned the flat upside down looking for Bob's lost shoes.

There follows here the memory of a most traumatic and deeply saddening occasion. Bob came home with us that night and eventually took his place on our sitting-room floor and just never woke again. His laughter, his expertise in his work, and affection for all mankind were lost to us for ever. Sinclair had the task of calling up the BBC Management, who duly spoke to his wife, and I myself called the police. Later, both of us, shaken to the core, went to visit Mrs Craddock and their children to try and explain what had happened. Some weeks later we were required to attend an inquest – and neither of us for several weeks was able to sleep in the flat.

The rehearsal process when we got back to it seemed to be an effortless matter – there were no dramatics, only quiet, gentle progress. There was one moment where I had to command Sir Ralph, as Briggs, to 'Get up' – which I clearly did too roughly. RR suggested quietly that he thought my character would be more gentle with him, which I took on board, and it did work much better his way.

Sir John decided to call me 'Pussy Cat' (I was sporting a 'bouffed-up' head of hair during rehearsals) and always seemed to compliment me on my shirts, which in fact were nothing out of the ordinary – but it made me very careful not to ever wear the same one two days running. 'Ralph and John' were deeply affectionate towards each other, and Michael Feast was clearly a great favourite of Sir John since their recent Old Vic/NT *Tempest*. The tea breaks were sensational – simply listening to these two great loveable actors, just talking.

Nobody ever cuts lines from a Pinter play since they are already so skilfully honed, with all non-essentials ripped out, by the time the finished play is released. Nevertheless, as can happen, I can bear witness to an exception to the rule: one cut in *No Man's Land* of a couple of lines' length which Sir John decided were uncomfortable. The lines taken out were something like: 'to embody in essence von Kleist's retreat from the Caucasus – the wittiest, and most subtly systematic withdrawal known to man.' I felt sure there was a lot of to-ing and fro-ing behind closed doors at the Old Vic and Hanover Terrace respectively, but eventually they were removed. I remember getting hold of a World War Two photo of General von Kleist, on which I wrote the absent text, and with the help of a lovely lady in the Press Office and sent it to Sir John as a first night card. It may need to be checked for accuracy – but my understanding is that von Kleist was shot for his 'witty withdrawal'. Pinter's reference here was related to an historical fact: at some point during the war, the German general and his regiment were entirely cut off, surrounded by Allied forces. Perhaps aided by fog and bad weather generally, one night they escaped to a man. By the time the Allied Forces woke up, von Kleist and his regiment had *gone*.

When the play had settled into Wyndham's Theatre (which is where I saw it), Rigby was forever anxious to keep his performance as sharp as in its opening days. It was never an automatic process: he never allowed technique to carry him. And he always appreciated a director who kept tabs on a play.

A letter sent by hand to Wyndham's Theatre:

✉ [*Terence Rigby*]

A few worries that I promised to jot down for you.

The removal of the chair has to me got technical. It lacks force, lacks violence.

I spoke about the 'Must be wonderful to be a poet' section. Too elaborately slow.

I think the telephone conversation is now mistimed. You used to pick up the phone and listen to what the voice said and while looking at Sir John say 'Yes Sir' quite firmly (not tentatively) so that it was clear that the instructions referred to him. You then hung up smartly. I find this better than what's going on now. I can't understand the haziness of what is currently happening.

Couldn't you give yourself more chance on 'Want for nothing'? It needs framing. And it certainly needs a longer beat before it if you're going to get that large laugh on '*The Times*'.

Small points these. Your level of work last night was magnificent.

Best wishes,

Yours ever,

Dictated by Peter Hall

By the time the play was remounted for a tour of Canada and the United States, Michael Feast had been replaced by Michael Kitchen.

❏ JULIET'S TABLE

'There's a new addition to the list,' he tells me. 'She could be the one, mate.'

God, not *another* one, I think. I know he's rather hurt that Maria José wasn't particularly sympathetic when he told her about Zagreb, and the Vicar's Daughter being engaged to someone else, but isn't it a bit soon?

'She's a radiographer, I've known her for some time, but I've asked her out a couple of times and she could be the one.'

Thereafter, she is known as 'X-Ray', and she occupies the top spot on the infamous list. It doesn't preclude the occasional dalliance, but he's clearly smitten.

Reading between the lines, I gather that he is behaving more sensitively towards X-Ray than anyone else in his life. In fact, when one of the 'Cup-of Tea Ladies' warns him not to hurt X-Ray, he is so angry, he vows never to take tea with her again. The estrangement lasts for a very long time until he is persuaded that it's all a bit silly.

I thank the Lord that I haven't yet put my foot in it, but it's so difficult because he asks impossible questions.

So tonight he's arrived with a tricky topic.

'What is passion?'

I drain the vegetables and make gravy, stalling for time. What can I say without offending him?

'Could you lay the table, please? Use the place mats – the tablecloth is in the wash.'

For the moment he is preoccupied.

'I burnt a hole in X-Ray's posh tablecloth. I had to buy her another one. Cost a fucking fortune. Excuse my French. Over a hundred pounds.'

Blimey, that *is* posh. Mine come from a bloke who opens the back of his van in Inverness Street market once a week, and sells all this stuff from India, China, and Japan.

'When I gave it to her, she said she'd had the other one invisibly mended.'

I laugh, but he's not amused. After a few mouthfuls he says, 'So what is passion?'

'Passion is like the time you hired a cab to take you to Stratford to see the Vicar's Daughter.'

He thinks carefully. Then he shakes his head. 'Nah. That was a spur-of-the-moment decision. A whim. I just wanted to surprise her.'

I tell him that passion is something that can't really be described. It's something you feel – that you have no control over – it overwhelms you. It's a rush of blood to the head – it's loving and hurting and hating and it's very painful.

It's tempting to say, 'D'you want me to show you and leap across the table and ravish you?' but I know he'll either think I'm being serious or be deeply offended. He persists with the topic and I just go round and round in circles until I'm bored with the whole thing.

Eventually he sighs tragically before saying, 'I'm not very good at this.'

And I feel genuinely sorry for him.

*

After a short break, Noel Murray was eager to share more memories with me. It became clear that his love for Rigby was unconditional, despite having seen the old rogue at his worst:

There was a balcony in the flat in Chiltern Street that overlooked the yard of an Indian restaurant. They were frequently annoyed by the noise and the curry smells. In their turn, Rigby and Sinclair used to flick their cigarette ash over the railings. I said, 'Isn't that disrespectful?' Sinclair responded that they were only keeping the place tidy, and that they threw empty bottles down there as well.

Rigby had a pet tramp that rested on the doorstep several times a week. He would fill a tonic bottle with vodka and leave it on the doorstep together with a cheese sandwich. One night, on his way out, he shouted back, 'Don't forget to feed the tramp.'

One day, Samuel Beckett, Harold Pinter, and Lady Antonia Fraser turned up at the Prince Regent. They asked if there was somewhere quiet where they could talk. I took them upstairs to the restaurant. Michael Tierney showed up and asked who was sitting in his private dining room. When I explained who they were, he just asked what they did! I told them they were about to open a supermarket lower down the High Street. Rigby always liked that story.

Rigby hated Christmas. He never went back to Birmingham and rarely accepted invitations from friends. But one year he agreed to accompany David Sinclair to Mrs Roddy Hall's house in Hampstead for Christmas lunch. They found it very difficult to get there, but finally, after catching a succession of buses they arrived hungry and cold. As they were late, they were shown, immediately, into the dining room. There at the table sat an American actor Rigby loathed. He was furious. He shouted out, 'You didn't tell me that fucking cunt was coming!' Then he stormed out and walked all the way home.

He was kind but had a vicious side to him. He was very hard on himself. He was a very private man.

There were several cheap exercise books in the pile of Rigby papers. I noticed that one of them was a mix of two separate accounts that would have to be dissected and then put back together in chronological order. It took a while to work out that when he was writing the first account he'd leave spaces when he didn't have the time to write – meaning to catch up later. Which, of course, he never did, and as he was extremely careful about paper wasting, he used the spare pages for an account of a different occasion. I cursed him on a regular basis.

I couldn't understand why, in 1976, he decided to keep a journal of the *No Man's Land* tour of Canada and the United States. Then I found a letter from a journalist friend of his at the *Birmingham Evening Mail*, dated 21 October 1976:

✉ [*Terence Rigby*]

Dear Terry,

It was good to have a line from you. As it happened, Snow had disappeared from 'Softly Softly' a week before your letter arrived, nevertheless we carried a story about your latest travels. I like your bit about Woodward and Bernstein, but there is plenty of corruption at the moment in your native Brum!

Quite seriously it does occur to me that you might like to consider trying a spot of journalism yourself from the States. Something on the lines of PC Snow on tour in Washington and Broadway with the two famous knights. There are probably quite a number of amusing and illuminating anecdotes that could bear telling. Having said that, I should perhaps add the 'dear old Mail' never paid a fortune and anything that reached us of that nature is necessarily on an accept or reject basis.

I leave the thought with you – and in any case I must owe you a jar or two on your return.

Yours sincerely,

Jack.

A newspaper cutting is attached to the letter, dating from the previous day:

 'Stalwart PC Snow is missing from *Softly, Softly*. Snow, Birmingham actor Terence Rigby, who plays the enigmatic constable, is now to be found staying at the same Watergate Hotel, Washington, where the seeds of President Nixon's downfall were sown.

He is touring with Sir John Gielgud and Sir Ralph Richardson in the National Theatre production of *No Man's Land*.

If Snow gets any whispers of scandal and corruption, I'll have to give the *Mail* a buzz. He could do for the *Mail* what Woodward and Bernstein did for the *Washington Post*, he says.

So, for the first time, Rigby writes a journal. Much of it is incomprehensible. Here are some heavily edited extracts.

🖋 [*Diary*]

Hotel Toronto. Day One. 8 September 1976

Flight to Toronto. [Michael] Kitchen helpful. No fear, no eats for me. Two and a quarter bottles of champagne and packets of fags. Preparation for landing. Asked Sir Ralph about perks in 1st. Class. Said he always travelled 1st.

Day Two. 9 September

Bought map from Chinese girl and heard radio say Mao was dead. I wondered quite what that would mean. Went into 3 churches and heard organ. 2 repair men screaming at each other. Peace outside and euphoria

broken by a man pissing against church wall. 2 p.m. first rehearsal –
lights awful. JG [Gielgud] talking of his Hamlet in '37 and Guthrie. RR
[Richardson] and JG a bit fluffy perhaps due to good press lunch. RR still
on English time. Lights gave me trouble. Wondered if I would recreate
former problems.

11 September
   Slightly later up: 8.30. Walked down to harbour and took boat around
Toronto Islands – worth looking at. Met first PC Snow spotter. We have a
sort of public dress tonight. It happened. I am told only 100 or so but it was
an indication – I felt good – the lights were better.

12 September. Sunday
   There was something of a personal hiatus later as Toronto on Sunday is
dry. I did sleep well but the next day woke at 8-ish feeling very whacked –
and it was the Opening – not a good omen. Did very little of interest except
visited very interesting Queen Street – rather reminds me of England.
Helped Pat a bit with bottles (First Night presents) and went to theatre. I
got thru it but it is now very dream-like and sometimes worrying – the only
consolation seems that I have worried before. Of course I had some cables
[...] Vodka from RR and whisky from David Warner.
   There was a reception at Royal York which was crap. I shall try to avoid
any such further. Later at the hotel I was hungry – room service took about
50 minutes – eventually a young black boy came – I could not be angry and
gave him a dollar for his trouble. The BBC (Geraint) are due to telephone
me in the morning about sending tapes – I do not care enough – I feel this
next few months will not be easy. [4]

14 September
   Geraint did ring around 11 – helpful and said to contact Danny Wilson
who is BBC rep in Canada. His sec told me Series 7 sold to Canada. I was
pleased but reflecting now – don't suppose actors will get much. Failed to
arrange lunch. Is he a cunt or not? Seem to have done well with postcards
and the odd letter. Went to Woolies and bought a hairbrush. Notices
very good in *Toronto Star* and *Globe* and *Mail* – *Star* said Kitchen and I
'depicted a couple of sinister lower class homosexuals' – we should worry.

15 September
   Rose late – developing a rotten cold and it's fruit crunch day with a
matinee. Got through them OK – finding a little odd improvement in my

---

4   Back in the UK, Clive James, who had become the 'must read' television critic in the
    Observer, was heralding the autumn season with reviews of both *The Brothers* and *Softly*:
    'Back too came *Softly, Softly* with a passable episode about crooks and terrorists . . . PC
    Snow has put on weight, which gives, in combination with his moustache, a Victorian
    appearance, befitting his latter-day role as one of the grand old men around HQ – which
    is a splendiferous new building dubbed "Thamesford Hilton" by the wily Watt.' (The BBC
    rehearsal rooms at Acton were dubbed 'the BBC Hilton'.)

performance, but a mountain to come yet in that direction. Had a late night snack. Only half an hour wait on this occasion.

16 September
Up around twelve – cold awful. Weather bleak.
Later – Bought a pair of silly scissors from Woolworth for my moustache, 43 cents or so – Am fairly pissed as I write, on lager – would you fucking believe – mind you the lager is OK. Did the show – it went well on a cough drop from Terry who is RR's man in Toronto. Have now done 5 shows which helps. Got paid by Pat. Have tried room service again. It would be nice to know what acting is all about – perhaps one should go on dry for rest of life and take a chance at finding out and being disappointed.

17 September
Went to a store to buy a hat – bought a Canadian one. Pretty bad cold and it is raining bad. Did show after lunch with Sebastian, JG and Kitchen. Fucking awful food but JG good. Lots of good stuff.
Called room service and got record service, but bit pissed so will not claim world record.

18 September
This was the day I was scheduled to do two shows and then visit my sister [Caroline] who lives near Montreal. Paul the husband was to pick me up and drive me there. Later I arranged a ticket to the show and Paul came – and it seems we had not met for 10 years although it seemed like nothing.
Later – Paul and I drove to Montreal – long – lots of fog, horrible, got in around 7:30 – met beautiful children and Caroline. Finally went to kip, woke 12:30, had two bacon sandwiches with ketchup. Didn't have a bath but did have a shower, reasonable. Met Wanda – fancied her quite a lot. Her hubby was out shooting. Spent the day in the garden drinking lager – bit pissed – had good beef, Yorkshire pudding, etc. in evening cooked by Sis.
Took Rapide back to Toronto, 11:07, arrived an hour later. Had letter from Phyllis and Maria José's address. Did show – pretty good. Pat asked for drink after, pretended not to hear. Went to Shakespeare. Pat turned up pissed, having had some Grandad from RR. Took her home to her hotel. Went out. Bars shut down early. Went back to hotel and had two blues. Back now in room. Called service for a bit of soup and sandwich. Television on. Waiting now. Exactly 30 mins – gave that black youth another dollar.

22 September
Have ordered a fridge for my room. Matinee and evening done – feeling overall and mentally improved – must stop living on energy nerves and calm down.
Looking back on NYC '67, booze creates false energy.

23 September
Late start around 12. Had breakfast – trying to persevere with black coffee, no milk, sugar.

After show had fish supper with JG on us, Kitchen, Firth and myself – $36 each – good but a near take on. John is nice but not sure could take too much – bless him.

Becoming obsessed with money I'm earning – very stupid really. Had late coffee with Kitchen and watched some rotten television.

26 September
Met Kitchen at Royal York at 12:30 and had generous bloody Marys with RR, L[ady Muriel] R[ichardson], JG in suite, very nice. Then had ride to tower in limousine and were met and taken to restaurant. Wine and meal OK, company great – scenics too, too much – just ridiculous – and frightening.

Now back at hotel, asked again about fridge – wrote note of thanks to RR. Sent it by taxi. Feel tired. Wrote to Sinclair.

Lady R was superb at lunch. 'Take your pipe out of your mouth, dear – we can't hear what you're saying.'

JG was fairly quiet during the meal – although he did manage 'Terry dear – your lashes are awfully long – are they yours?' RR went on at some length to Kitchen about the dangers of gliding and how a colleague had been killed – also told a very funny story about Concorde pilot and Bill, his No. 2 (listening for nervousness in voice as they landed). Also muttered about how certain actors, Cedric Hardwicke and others, had fallen to Hollywood airs – 'Even the great Laughton.'

3 October. Sunday
We met in lobby with Pat and set off to Niagara – about an hour-and-a-half ride and we were there. Quite impressive – very strong. Had a fair amount of PC Snow treatment, and went under Falls, which was not pleasant – we all looked like penguins. Ate in German restaurant and signed book, sort of chatted up a young German student. Young birds are a bit worrying.[5]

Later. Sitting in the lobby after all had gone, who should stride in direct off plane but Colin Blakely, to film *Equus*. We had dinner together – and there was this beautiful young Bulgarian waitress [. . .]

5 October
[...] later in two minds whether to pick up a rather pretty black bird but waited too long and she was gone. First signs of potential tension with Kitchen. Slept fitfully.

6 October. Wednesday
Breakfast Osgoods, had a baby at the matinee – RR corpsed me rotten with his 'Christ'. Pouring down like England.

---

5   A British tabloid of the time had a 'Celebrities I Have Met' column, where a reader writes: 'I met my celebrity at Niagara Falls. Turning to speak to my husband, I found myself standing next to Terence Rigby who played PC Snow in *Z-Cars*. His autograph reads "Snow in Niagara" '

10 October. Sunday

Gave the maid who I used to chat to $15, which I hoped was fair – had last breakfast and waited for transport to airport. We had been told we would break our journey in NYC so I wasn't pleased. However the 2 flights were I suppose as good as flights can be and I even felt a twinge of enjoyment. I had decided foolishly or not to stay at the Watergate – I found I had a very good room. Later that evening I went up to the Kennedy Center and reckon it to be pretty magnificent. Had a few drinks with Malcolm, Sir John's man.

11 September. Monday

Up late – did little. One senses Washington to be a clean, up-to-date city with lovely white monuments to their past and dead. I have a fair little kitchen which could be of value, but I shall be choosy. The show opened and there were quite a lot of minor upsets – mostly lighting, which I suppose were expected. I had a few drinks at a party given for us which was a first-class do – Sir John's man got plastered and raised a few eyebrows. Later, I went off with Miller and eventually finished at my place eating, me drinking and talking some sense and some rubbish about America. I suppose as Mike is AA, I was talking most of the rubbish.

12 September. Tuesday

Late up 1:30. Read reviews which as usual are good. Kitchen and I got reasonable mentions but there seems to be no way to get more.[6]

I walked to Arlington to the Military Burial Ground and saw JFK and Robert K. and felt a little bit weepy – although politics is a bit foreign to me – I liked JFK very much and said a prayer.

Also saw changing of guard at Tomb of Unknown Soldier – the guards seem like almost 'puffy' puppets. Walked back and did show. Had disaster with the curtains – completely my fault. Later mooched off by myself and relaxed.

14–15 October

Seem to be spending a lot of time in bed resting – not really keen to do much. Friday audience first reasonable one so far – the rest are rotten. Feel gruff this morning. End of week crunch now in US. There are a lot of pretty birds in Washers – pity the way things are avec moi.

17 October. Sunday

It was great to have a whole day off – got a bottle of wine in to spoil myself and a fridge of lager and some chicken pieces. However, as it turned out I didn't have a drink until 4 – didn't open wine. Went out for a couple

---

6   In fact, the *Washington Star* praised the 'ominous restraint' of these 'unsavoury servants': 'Their command of timing and tone is so exact that even a mundane exchange sounds like poetry and casual insults come across as keen comic fencing.' 'The two manservants are subtly frightening,' wrote Terry Coleman. 'It was an added and fortuitous nuance to recognize Mr Rigby as PC Snow from *Softly, Softly*, a very honest policeman. That was not something for the Americans, but it added just another layer to this play of layer upon layer.'

of hours and was thoroughly pissed by 8 – completely misjudged the whole day.

19 October. Tuesday
   Sir John has started giving a few niggly notes which no doubt PH [Peter Hall] will undo when he arrives. I hear HP [Harold Pinter] is ill in NY with glandular fever. He is also with Antonia Fraser whose husband is divorcing her – an unexpected step. What fireworks! [William Archibald's] *The Innocents'* notices appear to be poor – they open on Broadway Thurs 21st. I hear whispers that JG is to redirect [Simon Gray's] *Otherwise Engaged* as HP is unwell. VM [Vivien Merchant] now holds a few cards. What a game.
   I slipped off after the show – got chatting with fair French lady at 'Le Grand Scene'.

23 Saturday
   Last Night. Sir Ralph vocab very scratchy tonight. Avoided Marlene after matinee. Might try to make contact tonight with slender young woman. Did so – she was not prepared – K proved to be a nuisance. No way – no call – helped.

24 October. Sunday
   Lounged about and wrote letters – raining. No call as I said. Getting to dislike myself physically.

26 October
   Had lunch with Pat. Nice long walk – then in evening had dinner with JG and Kitchen – on us – $66 sans plonk which JG kindly paid for ($22). Sir was on good form and I asked him about several old actors – good evening – finished up talking piss balls with Miller.

27 October
   Had sore head. Met at Guest Quarters to go to Embassy for lunch with Brit Ambassador Ramsbottom. Nice day. Greer Garson – Emlyn Williams – Greer Garson and John Gielgud made little speeches – it was terribly English and GG made me drop a tear. Not often that happens. She seemed great fun.
   I thought the ambassador was very impressive – his wife femme fatale – a bit wicked. A very good day – kipped it off for a couple of hours before show.[7]

29 October
   Today received script *de Londres* from RSC. [Peter Nichols's] 'Privates on Parade'. Difficult – fairly solo role but hardly a notice role. Will be a bit tricky to decide, have asked RR to take a peep.
   RR shook his head rather a lot. Also muttered something re: NML [*No*

---

7   I note that on the back of Rigby's invitation he's scribbled 'Dear Miss Maid – have a beer – T Rigby'.

Man's Land] – January, London perhaps. Gabrielle came to show – took her to Georgetown then dropped her off. Pleasant enough evening.

30 October. Saturday
Final crunch before big uphill to NYC. Kitchen's birthday tomorrow – agreed to lunch. Saw Gabrielle and asked her to call me Sunday.

31 October. Sunday
Halloween Day. Had good breakfast. Gab rang and arranged for her to join us for lunch. Saw JG at lunch. Had walk – went to Alexandria in Virginia – rather poor – finished at Nathan's and took Gabrielle home. Talked quite a lot.

2 November. Tuesday
Going nowhere on a personal level – just want to stop doing it – but what do I really want? Went walking along Potomac and bumped into Gabrielle.

3 November. Wednesday
Writing this at Washington Station en route to NYC. Went to visit Congress and old Senate buildings. Stood on Kennedy spot where he made his speeches. Met Speaker – he's just retiring – seemed a nice bloke. Visited Folger theatre based on Globe.

4 November. Thursday
Part of long Washers haul – was supposed to meet Gabrielle but ducked out. Peter Hall due but now not arriving until Friday. Anti-climax.

5 November. Friday
Went to give talk at Catholic Uni. Very, very pleasant bunch got me doing my one-man [Alan Drury's *The Man Himself*]. Did small bits from *The Homecoming* and altogether really took off a bit. With patches of nerves. Carol Fleming was there (this train is fucking awful). I am however tucking into Heineken. PH arrived, good to see him, had fairly long chat – spoke of part of young Stalin and man himself. He saw show. He's on to K[itchen] already as I expected. Notes tomorrow.

6 November. Saturday
Peter notes fairly heavy but will have to steel myself. Acting HP is agony – very few kicks but thanks to Mary [8] my spirit seems still strong. Sent Gab some flowers out of guilt I suppose – saw her briefly at Grand Scene – she meant nothing any more if she ever had. (By the way had drinks with Penny Moore, 17, Japanese-American, who had seen the play 10 times and mostly sneaked in – she was pretty. On final perf she was in the front row.) I left bottle Jack Daniels for local men. Got pissed and saw Hazel – that was a bit shattering – a good woman – 11 bucks down the drain. Had

---

8   Unexplained. A reference to the Virgin Mary?

77

final drink with night porter and his 'friend' – knowledgeable on theatre and films.

7 November. Sunday
Free coffee in lounge – waited to go to NYC.

My first week in NYC
The train was bumpy – not much to see but remember passing through Philadelphia. On arrival the pace changed suddenly and fought for a cab – eventually walked and finally got a cab and went to Longacre. Eighth was pretty horrid.
Marshall saw me to the flat – it seemed OK – a bit sparse – and I wondered quite where I was. Later I had dinner with Lee, who looked marvellous.

Frustratingly, the journal abruptly stops there. I'm sure the *Birmingham Post* journalist wanted the Broadway experience most of all, but Rigby disappoints him and us. From snippets of conversation at odd times, over the subsequent years, it sounded to me like more of the same, except that he was reunited with Lee Hooper, who had been his girlfriend during the Broadway run of *The Homecoming*. He was constantly drunk during that production, staying out half the night and wandering the streets. He behaved very badly towards Lee – by his own admission. It was something he regretted because he was genuinely fond of her.

I met Lee in New York in 1995 but she was loath to talk about the time she spent with Rigby. I sensed sadness tinged with bitterness. She was anxious not to repeat the experience, so that when she came to London she was with a friend. She only agreed to see Rigby once on her own.

Some – albeit a minority – of the American reviews of *No Man's Land* were glowing. 'Terence Rigby and Michael Kitchen are splendid as the smoothie thugs,' wrote Clive Barnes, the *Village Voice* critic Michael Feingold comparing Rigby's performance with an earlier generation of greats: 'Terence Rigby, as in his performance for Pinter in *The Homecoming*, communicates a marvellous sense of lower-class pudge pathos: a Mack Swain with Chaplinesque delicacy.' I think 'Chaplinesque delicacy' perfectly sums up Rigby's own behaviour. There was always a sardonic edge to his black, lumbering movements.

Rigby enjoyed Sardi's, the famous Manhattan haunt for actors, and over the years took many visitors there. I suppose he felt at home. In one clipping I discovered that while the play was panned by most of the critics, no one doubted the quality of the acting: 'Terence Rigby and Michael Kitchen, who played supporting roles, were both warmly applauded when they walked into Sardi's for a celebration party.'

After reading (and editing) this journal, the most important element I see, apart from his alarming intake of alcohol, is his developing possessiveness of Pinter's work, along with Peter Hall's understanding of what Pinter wants in the presentation of the plays. He mentions Richardson getting 'fluffy', Gielgud beginning to give fussy notes, and Michael Kitchen obviously displeasing Rigby in his performance. He can't wait for Peter Hall to arrive so that he can pull the play back into shape. Much later in life, he kept hoping that Peter Hall would make an appearance to rectify any lapses in his own performance – whether in Pinter, Beckett, Wilde, or Shakespeare.

Although he makes the effort to visit important places and landmarks, I get the sense that he remained very much the loner. He spends day after day alone, getting drunk and questioning the meaning of it all – Does he want to be an actor? Is he really any good at it? There is also evidence in the journal for Noel's assertion that Rigby was a misogynist. He seems to crave a girlfriend, and there is no shortage of young, pretty women keen to get to know him. But he dismisses them all, treating them badly along the way.[9] I wonder whether, on arriving in New York, he read through the journal he had made thus far and decided that his friend in Birmingham would find his North American adventure rather less than starry and glamorous.

❏ JULIET'S TABLE

He puts a foolscap envelope on the table, laying his hand firmly on the surface. It's going to be a 'topic night', I say to myself, but I wait for him to introduce the subject – whatever it might be.

---

9   This reminds me of the poem I found transcribed in his own hand at the back of his 1985 diary. I thought for a while he had written it – it's exactly the sort of poem that would have amused him – but I later discovered that the actor Freddie Jones had recited it to him (and its true authorship dissolves in the mists of time):

'Thank you for the flowers you sent,' she said

As she shyly blushed and bent her head.

'I'm sorry for the things I said last night.

I was wrong and you were right.

Forgive me' – and so I did.

And as she strolled through moonlight hours

I asked myself, 'What fucking flowers?'

The fishcakes are particularly disgusting tonight. I've left it too long to say 'Please don't bring me any more – I hate them'. Perhaps I can say I'm on a diet and that he should only bring one.

'Keeping you up, am I? I'll go if you want.'

'Sorry, I was miles away. Curiosity killed the cat. What's in the envelope?'

He reluctantly opens it and shows me a small pile of pages, some of which are paper-clipped.

'These arrived in the post this morning,' he says. 'Harold sent them. His latest sketches.'

'Wow. God, that's wonderful,' I say, picking up the pages and flicking through them. Imagine having Pinter send you some scripts, personally. Have you read them?'

'Only about a dozen times.' Rigby is looking gloomy. He's clearly bemused by what I regard as a privilege. 'Can't make head nor tail of them.'

He pushes his plate away and begins to read to me. They are very short. There aren't many laughs and I think I need to hear them again. Maybe, second time round, I'll see the significance, see the political undertones or some ominous meaning. What I feel is shame that my intellectual prowess – if ever I had any – has deserted me. I'd grabbed the pages eagerly – I am handing them back defeated.

He seems to understand. 'You feel the same as me,' he says. 'Let's read them together'.

So we do, over and over. We try out different possible meanings, I wonder why one man has a paper bag over his head – that must be symbolic of something. Torture, perhaps? That seems too easy though. I'm always scared of showing my ignorance. Best to keep shtum. Rigby knows more about Pinter than I ever will. I find some rather old Cheddar in the fridge. It'll do to cover my inadequacy.

We are both disappointed. Harold Pinter has been let down by our lack of erudition perhaps.

At the end of the evening, Rigby says, 'I'm sending them back, mate.'

*

Friends old and new

Michael Gambon was due to appear in Beckett's *Krapp's Last Tape* at the Duchess Theatre. Rigby often spoke fondly of his friendship with Gambon, and there was a famous story that I wanted to corroborate. I wrote to him, care of the theatre, and was very surprised to get a phone call the very next afternoon. He was happy to talk to me in person. What a privilege: the chance to meet one of my favourite actors. I prepared my interview as best I could. I arrived at a small cafe right next to the theatre on time and he took me on the labyrinthine journey to his dressing room. My usual apprehension and nervousness evaporated and I sensed that he would be easy to talk to. I gave him a copy of Rigby's account of the Buckstone, and the story about Gambon and the kangaroo. He didn't remember that, but said he loved the Buckstone.

'We used to have this trick that if you could walk around the Buckstone without touching the floor you'd get a free drink. I watched Peter O'Toole doing that.' He stopped for a moment, wanting to know what Rigby died of. I explained, but he wanted more detail of where and when. So I began with the collapse on stage at Yale and everything that happened subsequently. He was visibly upset, angry that he wasn't aware of the funeral.

'We must stop now. It's too late.' But he was already in tears.

He apologized for having a bad memory, but over the next hour, with gentle prodding, he told me much. It was clear that the Buckstone had featured largely in his early days as well. He told me that he was explaining to someone that he had trained as an engineer before acting; that he worked for Wilmot Briggs, which made locks and other mechanisms, and that he used a micrometer which measures the density of metal very accurately. Rigby, who was nearby, said that he'd also begun an apprenticeship. Gambon thought that was their first encounter and at a later date, Rigby had turned up at the Buckstone with his micrometer.

Gambon told me that he and David Sinclair were at the RSC at the same time:

We used to muck about together, understudying, learning lines. It was through David that I got to know Terry. I met him several times, but he

81

didn't say much. We went to a gig once. It was a very posh place in Surrey. I drove him down there. He was playing in mixed doubles! Pro-Am. He was playing Björn Borg. I sat in the restaurant bit and Björn Borg sat next to me. I said, 'What do you do?' And he said, 'I'm a tennis player.' Then Terry and a disk jockey from the BBC went out – they were the amateurs – and Björn Borg and some other bloke.

Gambon broke off from the story for a moment to ask, 'Is it right he worked at Wimbledon – as a linesman or something?'

I told him that he was an umpire, and very proud of his green blazer.

'I remember,' he continued, 'we were sitting there, and one of the big players asked Terry if he drank and he said, "I drink vodka. And I drink two bottles a day." The other bloke looked shocked. He said, "Are you playing today?" "Oh yes," says Rigby, winding him up.'

It's true to say that Gambon is a self-confessed liar: he embellishes and teases. The most famous Gambon/Rigby story has become a theatrical legend and even appears in print. Apparently, knowing that Rigby had a fear of flying, Gambon suggested that he take him up in his private plane and give him a gentle spin to boost his confidence. Rigby reluctantly accepted the offer and they took off. It seemed to be going well with Gambon pointing out local landmarks. Then suddenly Gambon appeared to be having a heart attack, plunging several hundred feet. Rigby sat, passive, according to legend – looking straight ahead, probably rigid with fear. But of course, Gambon was messing about.

'Was it true?' I asked him. 'Rigby told me the story but would never tell me whether it was or not.'

Gambon thought for a moment. 'The flying story. I used to take David Sinclair around. And I think I feigned the heart attack on David. But Terry . . . I took him up once in the aircraft, I don't think he enjoyed it very much. He was very shtum. We went to Ipswich – somewhere I know really well and we had a cheese sandwich.'

'He really was very afraid of flying.' I persisted. 'Shall I leave it as a myth?'

And typically, Gambon said, 'Yes. I don't mind what you do.'

When I asked him about working together on the 1999 film *Plunkett and Macleane*, Gambon couldn't remember much – or whether they had worked together on anything else. He said he felt guilty for not remembering.

I only knew Terry through the streets of London – the pubs. We used to laugh like drains. But he was an actor-mate. Lately when I've been in plays in the West End, he's been there. He came to the Duke of York's. I was in another Beckett. He liked Beckett. He used to come round. He was very plain speaking. He'd give his opinion. He'd say exactly what was wrong. I've got a letter at home from Terry – but I don't suppose I'll find it. It's from New York and the acting he'd seen there. He was a very straightforward man. But he would give me advice.

I asked if he liked that, and Gambon said yes, he did, since it was from Terry. 'We're swimming in the same water aren't we? I didn't mind that at all. He knew what he was talking about. I saw him when he was with Ralph Richardson at the National in *No Man's Land*. He loved that. I think those were his favourite years, somehow. Did he go to New York with *No Man's Land*?'

It was good to have him ask me questions because I was able to fill in some gaps for him, tell him about the journal, and that Rigby was a prolific letter writer. The more I talked, the more he remembered. He told me stories about the Buckstone, about Robert Stephens and Antonia Fraser, about Pinter and Lord Longford, Elaine Stritch's husband John Bay and Sir Peter Hall. The trouble is, none of the stories was directly relevant to Rigby – except that Rigby would go to the Open Air Theatre in Regent's Park and remonstrate with Robert Stephens over Antonia Fraser! With some difficulty I steered him back to the subject of Rigby and Sinclair.

'They were always falling out. I spent a lot of time in that flat. There were times when they wouldn't speak for days. David wouldn't go back for days – he was so fed up. They had a continuous tug-of-war. Terry would have friends there, not so much David. We went to Sinclair's brother's school once – he was the headmaster there. It was a big public school down in Bournemouth. Rigby and I were impressed. David was quite posh, wasn't he?'

'Stephen Thorne,' I said, 'says that Rigby was afraid of BBC Radio and Broadcasting House. Thought the place was run by intellectuals – "All those public school chappies".'

Gambon agreed that Rigby wasn't very posh and was possibly afraid. I said I thought Rigby was, nevertheless, a grand figure. Gambon smiled.

'He would stroll around London with that judgemental walk. He would stand at the Stage Door and give you notes on your play and be very proper. He was very classy. He dressed well. I never associate him with women. Never saw him with any girlfriends – he was always alone whenever I met him. I'd arrange to meet him in some pub up in Marylebone . . .' He stops suddenly. 'I'm not saying very much about him, am I?'

I tell him it's my fault and he says his memory is a blur. I move on quickly to *The Caretaker* and the fact they both played the same part – Davies the tramp. I asked if his version was directed by Peter Hall.

'No. My version was by the director/playwright Patrick Marber. I was in the West End with it for three months and I hated it; I was not good in it. Rigby came to see it; he came round after, but he didn't have much to say about it. He said he enjoyed it. But I went up the wrong road. I played it as if he was dying. I played him covered in shit. No man would walk the streets like that. I went too far with it. I was going to play him Welsh. Someone says, "You're Welsh, aren't you?" and he says, "I can't remember where I'm from," so I played him with different accents all the time. I got bored. I'd like to do it again. Anyway, I didn't see Terry's performance. Where was that?'

'Bristol'.

'He was the caretaker. Wasn't he? He would have been excellent as the one who sits on the bed and gives that long speech . . . slimy.'

'I didn't see it either,' I tell him, 'but an American friend of his from RADA saw it and she said he was magnificent. He'd got the underbelly of it, she said. He used to wander the streets of New York at night, and London too, and got to know people.' Then I tell him about Rigby's pet tramp, but that when I asked him what he thought the play was about, he said he didn't know – he just knew his part.

Gambon understood perfectly. 'He used his intuition,' he said. 'That's right.'

I wanted to know whether they ever discussed working methods.

'Whenever I saw Rigby, I was pissed. And in later life when he used to come backstage, I used to listen to his notes and he was very good. He would simplify what you were doing. I'd like Terry to see this [*Krapp's Last Tape*]. It annoys me sometimes that he's not here. He'd tell me where I was going wrong.'

If ever Gambon was in New York he'd meet up with him, but Rigby rarely spoke unless he had something important to say. According to him, Rigby's fellow actors and directors thought he was 'solid'; they respected him; he was an actor's friend – 'always on your side. I loved being with him. He was very funny. His jokes made me laugh – he had a funny laugh – and you never knew what that laugh was.'

For some reason, I had got it into my head that Rigby sometimes felt inadequate in comparison with some other actors, and that it probably stemmed from the old public school, academic background that he had missed out on. So I asked Gambon whether he remembered Rigby's performance in the BBC's *Tinker, Tailor, Soldier, Spy* (1979), and of course he did. He said that Rigby had loved it – he loved jobs that were good quality. Nevertheless, he had told Noel Murray that he didn't measure up.

Gambon disagreed.

'Of course he did. He was as good and as knowledgeable as anyone else he worked with. He just had the same insecurities'.

I said that were times when he felt that the other actors had a greater understanding of the piece. Gambon reckoned it was a class thing – and that he'd probably have found it difficult to play a lord – someone who lived in a stately home. I pointed out that in recent times Rigby had played two genteel clerics in the Wilde comedies *The Importance of Being Earnest* and *A Woman of No Importance*, the former directed by Sir Peter Hall.

We talked about the sometimes stormy relationship Rigby had with Sir Peter and it reminded Gambon of another famous Rigby story.

He wanted to wear a wooden leg in something Peter Hall did at the National, I think it was the Scottish play. He was playing Second Soldier, or something Shakespeare. He came on with a wooden leg because he wanted to make something of his part and Peter Hall said, 'I don't think that's right, Terry.' So Terry replied, 'But why can't he?' And Peter Hall said, 'Because there's nowhere in the text that intimates that he wears a wooden leg.' And Terry said, 'There's nowhere in the text that says he doesn't.' He never did wear it, but he had one made up for him. He was a good tryer, Terry, wanting to try something out. Peter Hall was a lazy fucker.

When I told Gambon that Rigby had problems with iambic pentameter, he dismissed the whole thing, said he took no notice of it, he just spoke the lines intuitively – 'It's what you do.' I wish I'd said that to Rigby all those years ago. At some point I realize that 'Tryer' is an anagram of 'Terry'.

❑ JULIET'S TABLE

'Nearly everyone I know rings before they want to call in. You don't. You just turn up – whether it's early in the morning or the middle of the night.'

'So?'

'I'm just making an observation. It's a very Welsh thing to do. In Llanelli you just turn up and you always get a welcome. Well, nearly always.'

'You want me to write and ask to come a week next Thursday at tea time?'

'It's always tea time with you, night or day.'

I get the tee-hee laugh. Then he thinks about it. 'Mother would have a meal on the table in no time. A cup of tea at the very least.'

To make sure he knows he's welcome, I refill his cup and tell him again how much I like people to drop in. He nods in agreement.

'I've always done it. Over the years, I've called in to see Harold – in

Hanover Terrace. Not so much these days, mind you. We're much more likely to have a lunch.'

But I know that if he's near the Paddington Sports Club, he'll call in on Jane and Peter; in the West End, he'll see if Phyllis is in. If he happens to be getting off a train, he'll drop in to see Mr Mustapha in his King's Cross restaurant. Mr Mustapha used to be a printer in Marylebone and Rigby has tracked him down. When he was doing *The Wild Duck* in York, he found out where my son lived and knocked on his door, to the delight of a household of students, who then watched the play – courtesy of Rigby.

So 'dropping in unannounced' is tonight's topic. Rigby laughs.

'I called in on Sir Ralph once. He'd got this beautiful house in Regent's Park. He ushered me in – "Come in, my dear fellow." Mu [Lady Richardson] was coming down the stairs. She stopped and said good evening rather starchily. Then he calls for the lift – he had a lift that went up to his study at the top of the house. And he says, "We'll go upstairs, I think." He pours me a Scotch, then he says, "Sit yourself down, my boy, make yourself comfortable, here's the bottle, help yourself. I've something to do – shan't be long." So I sit and I sip my Scotch. After half an hour I pour myself another one. And I sit and I wait. Three hours later, he comes back. "Ah, good. You've helped yourself to the Scotch. Let's have another one." Sir Ralph and Mu had been out to dinner and left me to my own devices. Can you believe it?'

Rigby thinks it's very funny. I tell him I'll try that one for myself.

*

The Road to Zagreb

Noel Murray told me that Rigby was a huge fan of Robert Mitchum so that when he was offered a part in the American mini-series *War and Remembrance* (broadcast 1988) he jumped at it. It was the turning point in Rigby's life – he was determined to be the consummate professional and to that end, he decided to give up drinking. By this time he was on two bottles of vodka a day. The series was being filmed in Zagreb in Yugoslavia; Rigby, because of his fear of 'the iron bird' (as he called aeroplanes), decided to make the journey by train. Sinclair and Noel accompanied him to Waterloo. Rigby looked dreadful.

I knew the Zagreb story really well (it had been a 'table topic'), and maybe because I was so interested and sympathetic, Rigby once asked me whether I would consider writing it up as a screenplay. He felt it would make a surreal Buñuelesque movie. I probably didn't sound enthusiastic enough (more likely I was overwhelmed), and the subject was dropped until about a year later, when he told me he'd asked Douglas McFerran to write it. I wasn't in the least offended – at that time I was never out of work and would have found it difficult to clear my desk for the project. He told me that Douglas had already done several hours of interviewing and recording.

One evening, Douglas turned up at my flat in Hanson Street and sat at the ubiquitous table (now far too big for the small room) and spoke eloquently of his friendship with Rigby. When he quoted him, his impersonation of Rigby was remarkable – as if he were in the room with me again. What follows covers their friendship, the time they shared together at the National Theatre, and the journey to Zagreb where Terence Christopher Rigby finally gave up the booze.

Douglas first encountered Rigby when he was a shop assistant in Marylebone in 1977. He was about twenty years old and a theatre lover. He'd seen Rigby in *No Man's Land* the previous year and was a great fan. Rigby walked in one morning, smartly dressed in a Crombie, and the first thing he noticed was that when Rigby spoke, he stank of booze.

I thought, 'This is a proper actor: nine o'clock and already on the sauce.' The shop sold an odd collection of items and Rigby bought two fake onyx ashtrays, one of which I now have. While he was paying for them, I told him how much I'd enjoyed his performance. As he left, he said, 'Are you in acting, mate?' and when I told him I was, he said, 'Best of luck.'

About ten years later, when Douglas was understudying Pozzo in the 1987 *Waiting for Godot* at the National, Colin Welland injured himself and had to leave the production. It was announced that Terence Rigby would be taking over the part. I asked whether this was a Peter Hall production, but in fact it was directed by Michael Rudman. It was Douglas's first play at the National and John Alderton, who was playing Estragon, organized a little drinks and cake party in his dressing room to welcome Rigby. Douglas saw this from his dressing-room window, several floors up, so he raced down and burst into the room and said, 'Terence Rigby, ten years ago you wished me lots of luck and I've achieved absolutely nothing in my career.' Rigby apparently enquired if Douglas was stage management, to which he replied, 'No, I'm not bloody stage management, I'm an actor!'

Douglas, who was in the understudy company, helped Rigby prepare for the play by helping him with his lines. It was all a rush. They went to Glasgow for a week, after which Rigby invited Douglas for a drink. They went on to his flat, but he suddenly stopped and said, 'I'm not sure I'm ready to have you in my flat yet, mate.' So Douglas said, 'Well, that's all right,' and left. 'But over the years,' he remembers now, 'I became a permanent fixture, and I would sit in that magnificent flat, which was a waste of money, because, as you know, you never went into any of the rooms. You just sat in the kitchen – which over the years, I decorated twice.'

By this time, Sinclair and Rigby had parted company and Rigby bought the mansion-block flat in Devonshire Street, W1. Douglas was clearly moved by the thought of sitting in that kitchen: 'I even papered the ceiling,' he told me,

and we would drink gallons of tea and smoke. When I told him I'd been impressed by his smelling of booze, he found that ironic. But one time, we actually sat in his living room and he asked if I wanted to smoke. He went to fetch an ashtray. And he returned bearing this ashtray, as if he was holding a communion plate, and it was the cheap replica onyx ashtray I'd sold him all those years ago. We never used it again. But I did ask what he was doing that morning, all those years ago, and he said, 'I was probably up all night, mate, and I fancied a walk – went into the shop and thought I'd better buy something.'

I think when he finally invited you into his flat, you'd crossed the line, you'd crossed the final hurdle – we met in that intense cauldron.

I understood precisely what Douglas was talking about, and felt we would talk more about it later, but I wanted to get back to Rigby's first tussle with Samuel Beckett.

When he came to *Godot*, it was already up and running, and he was given no time to properly prepare the role. But I thought that because he was famous he'd sort it out. As a young actor, I could see how difficult it was for him, so I asked him if he'd like me to run his lines with him. It became a regular thing over the next two weeks, during the lunch hour. And of course, without realizing it, it became a very bonding experience.

But the first night was disastrous; he dried all over the place because he wasn't properly prepared. The prompting system in the Lyttelton is that a girl gives the prompt offstage, but the speakers are up in the proscenium arch – you can hear the prompt in the audience. The actors can't hear it. It was catastrophic. He was unnerved and kept asking for the same line, over and over, and the girl kept repeating it. In the end, the audience were calling it out. It was horrendous.

I'd never heard this story from Rigby. It must have dashed his confidence for a while, but Douglas said he pulled it together and in retrospect, although he didn't realize it at the time, that first performance had been an extended dress rehearsal. I wanted to know whether Rigby was slow in the rehearsal process, as people had said, though of course his method would build into a solid performance.

He was an easy man to underestimate. His persona was not dynamic: it was ponderous, in a way, but there was a lot of deep thinking going on, which a lot of people would realize or anticipate. But I know that whenever I went round, I'd notice that there would always be – propped up – some script or other. It would be a manky old script he'd picked up from somewhere.

I felt it was time to tell Douglas that Rigby had asked me to write the screenplay of the Zagreb episode and then changed his mind and asked him to write it instead. I also told him about Rigby wanting the taped interviews back from Douglas.

He'd got to know my work – he'd read some of my film scripts and he read my *Godot* . . . I wrote a third act of *Godot*. We made these tapes – they went on for hours – and then he changed his mind and asked for them back. I didn't keep copies, by the way. But the last time I saw him before he died, he showed me the Zagreb script and asked if I'd like it back. I said I didn't want it and that he could do what he liked with it. I thought he would throw it away. As always with Terence, there was no reason given as to why the project was abandoned. One day he just said, 'I don't want to be doing this any more.' He never gave the impression that he was upset or that it was distressing – or anything.

Sometimes I would stop recording and ask him something and he'd say, 'No, no, you've got it all wrong, mate . . .' And I'd say OK. Then he'd say, 'No. Let's start again. I . . . got . . . off . . . the . . . train . . .' He was very particular about getting it right. I can't remember it properly now, but I remember saying to him, 'What you've got here is the perfect three-act structure. The journey there, to Zagreb. The actual asylum episode –' which was full of horrors, as you know – 'and then there's the journey back and dealing with doctors telling you what's wrong with you.'

And in those days, it was conceivable that that sort of story could have been made – not now of course – by Peter Greenaway or someone. But that was it. I'd done all the work. The interviews were twenty hours in all. I was disappointed.

I asked Douglas whether he had fictionalized it, but he reckoned the material was so dense he didn't have to. It was just a case of 'ordering' it.

What a good word: it's really what I'm trying to do myself with the mass of material I've gathered about Rigby's life and career.

Douglas gave me permission to use some of the script to tell the story of Zagreb. That will be a separate sequence below – but first, I want to continue with Douglas's account of his friendship.

Broadly speaking, the one thing I would say is that you had to have a friendship with Terence very much on his terms. And you didn't have to mind that. And in fact I didn't mind, because I thought that it was the only way that this guy could do it. It's not selfishness, it's not mean-spiritedness, it's some sort of guarded caution in his personality where he is able to express himself openly within certain contexts and parameters. I don't think I ever asked him anything directly. I asked him things obliquely, or came at it with a question which was not about him, but would lead him to drawing it out of himself.

Years later he told me the reason he did the job in *Crossroads* was not because he was a Brummie (which is what he'd told me years before), it was to show the business how he was: 'Because everyone would have heard what had happened to me in Zagreb and that I was drunk, and I wanted to be on telly every other night and people would see I was still functioning.'

That was twenty years ago.

That made sense alongside what Rigby's one-time agent Peter Charlesworth had told me about life after Zagreb.

I asked Douglas about the time he decorated the kitchen and Rigby became his employer.

I never saw him! He was either out or in his study, except for tea time. There was an immense amount of work to do – especially the first time. Stripping down the wood, papering, etc. – and he said he'd see me all right. But when

I finished I was taken aback at how little money he gave me. I was there for about three weeks and he gave me £200. And again, I never said anything. I knew it wasn't meanness, it was a complete misunderstanding of how much one would pay for these things and how much work had gone into it. There was a complete unworldliness there.

Someone rang the doorbell once. It made me jump and I fell off the ladder. He was furious. Not with me, but with whoever was ringing the bell – 'I've told these people not to ring in the mornings' – and he had this mysterious coterie of women friends who would pop round, and he'd say 'Don't answer it' or if the phone rang he'd say 'Don't answer it'.

The funny thing was, the last time I decorated, there'd been a leak from upstairs and nobody could get to the bottom of it. He would stare at the stained ceiling, in his slow way, working out how to tackle it. Like when he wanted to get his Green Card. It had been about two years, and he hadn't done anything practical towards it. It took him five years. But eventually he announced, 'Oh. I've got my Green Card.' And with the flat. He was talking about selling that flat for so long. But that was his tempo – and eventually, of course, time ran out.

I recognized these examples of Rigby's procrastination so well. So often, he would leave my house, having wrestled all night with a problem and finally made a decision, only to announce the following day that he'd gone with the opposite option.

It seemed the right moment to talk about the years of silence between them. 'I would ask after you, and Rigby, sitting at my table, would say you'd disappeared from his life. He felt very hurt.'

'I'm astounded by that. Astounded to hear you say that. Because there was a period of years when I felt he had dropped *me*. So to hear you say that . . .' Douglas was visibly stunned. 'I was hurt, I really was. People commented on it because we were like a double act. 'One day one of us rang the other – I can't remember which way round it was. It's ten minutes to Baker Street so I said I'd go round. But I sat down at my kitchen table and fell into a daydream, a reverie – I couldn't leave the flat. But I eventually arrived and I was really very late. I realized I'd been very rude. And somehow, after that, the phone calls dried up.'

I commented that it was all right for Rigby to turn up late, or sometimes not at all.

'In the months that followed I thought that this was very harsh punishment. Having said that friendship with Terence had to be on his terms, he was now divorcing me. When we got it together again, it was never quite what it was before. I suppose it was a more mature friendship.'

I wonder whether the friendships that undergo breaks and then continue are the friendships one can trust, despite the distance and the hurt. Perhaps

Rigby, during this time, believed that because Douglas was becoming a success in his own right, he didn't need him any more?

> No. No. He had this big shouting match with me. I can't remember how it ended, but I just know he never rang me again, ever. I was in my early thirties then. It was all rubbish, wasn't it? What brought us together, in some ways, was that we were similar in disposition. Slightly different forms of eccentricity – we could relax into eccentricity – he liked that.

So many times, in talking to people, I have been able to answer questions that have puzzled them about Rigby – and vice versa. As ever, I wanted to know about Rigby and acting – his approach to a part, and to a play.

> He would talk to his lady friends in a particular way. To his male friends, the talk would be very 'male', if I can put it that way. We would never have talked about the artistic approach. We could talk about a specific problem with a part. He would say 'This bloke is just a cunt, mate, and that's the whole fucking problem.' We would talk in a kind of shorthand: 'What d'you think of . . . ?' and he'd say, 'Cunt.' And that would be it. Nothing more would be said. Nothing more was needed. Fair enough.

I couldn't resist asking Douglas about Rigby and Pinter. I knew that Douglas had worked on several Pinter plays over the years and had played Joey in another Peter Hall production of *The Homecoming* and later Foster in *No Man's Land*, but I didn't bargain for the answers to many of the questions hanging over Rigby when we talked.

Douglas told me that Rigby had put him up for the part of Joey and Gillian Diamond, the casting director, had apparently said, 'Oh God, it's going to be one of his pisshead friends from the past.' She was surprised when Douglas walked in.

Most evenings, Douglas would go round to Rigby's to talk about the rehearsals. I can imagine him listening intently since he had created the character in the Sixties. Apparently there was one scene that wasn't working properly. As John Bury, who designed the original set, had also designed this one, Rigby would have been familiar with the arrangement of the furniture.

Douglas said that the scene where Joey and Ruth get it together on the chaise longue and end up rolling on the floor just wasn't working smoothly and they couldn't get round the problem. Rigby was puzzled until it dawned on him that the chaise longue was in the wrong position on stage. Rigby had a similar chaise longue in his study, so they practised together, sitting, lying and then rolling off on to the floor on top of one another.

The following morning in rehearsal, Douglas told Sir Peter and Harold

Pinter about the previous night's meeting with Rigby and how they might have solved the problem by setting the chaise longue on the other side of the stage.

'We tried it out on his chaise longue together and we practised rolling off it on to the floor.'

Peter Hall turned to Pinter and said, 'That's a photo opportunity missed.' Pinter wasn't amused. (He was having an 'off' period with Rigby, which I will save until later.)

Rigby watched Douglas's performance with great interest but he didn't like Douglas's interpretation of some of the scenes. 'You can't play your Lear when you're playing the bloke in the background,' he said. But naturally, Douglas had his own ideas.

That's what he thought. I saw his performance on film and it was very good. Mine was different. What he did was to play Joey as a visitor, he played him without a spark of animation. But my view is that quiet people, when they are poked in the wrong way, are the most explosive. So basically, there's one moment when the men are discussing 'playing with' this woman, who Joey is in love with, and at this point I simply let go and explode. I felt that if this man who has been quiet then tells them he'll kill them if they set one finger on her, it would rev it up a bit. And that of course was the Lear bit. Harold loved it and said so in his notes.

Fired up by the memory of his version of the part, Douglas remembered another sequence:

Lenny says, 'Take a table, take it . . . but once you've taken it, what are you going to do with it?' and Joey says, 'Chop it up for firewood.' I decided to laugh, then to cut it immediately, because I don't want to reveal myself . . . So there was this twisted sense of humour in Joey, which again Terence didn't like. He felt I was nicking moments from the part that I wasn't entitled to take. But the big explosion, I felt, was justified.

But a few years later, Pinter rang me up and asked me if I'd cover Douglas Hodge in *No Man's Land* which Pinter was appearing in as Hirst at the Comedy Theatre. So I did twenty performances. Harold said to me, 'I know you'll do it without rehearsal or anything' – which I did. Of course, *No Man's Land* was Terence's favourite play – and mine. He was fantastically complimentary about my Foster. As far as that went, he thought I was terrific.

Things were beginning to fall into place. Rigby was extremely certain that his interpretation of Pinter was the only one that was true to the playwright's intention. Douglas as Joey could never hope to get it right, but Douglas as Foster didn't put a foot wrong. This was probably when Rigby became the self-appointed guardian of Pinter's work. Gawn Grainger, according to Douglas, was waylaid by Rigby on several occasions, because he wasn't getting Briggs 'quite right' in the same production. He laughs fondly at the memory.

> Gambon asked, 'Did he give you notes?'
> 'I got fed up with him,' Gawn said. 'He kept saying "You can't play that part like that, mate".'
> Gawn is a very nice man. He's very laid back. He set up a bar in his dressing room and Terence kept popping up. He went to the Almeida, and then when it went to the West End he would come and see me when I did the odd show here and there. So my Joey wasn't so good, but my Foster was terrific and Gawn's Briggs was not good. Gawn was lovely as Briggs, but Terence *was* Briggs.

I ventured that Pinter probably knew that. He might even have written the part for Terence. However, they all listened, and took his notes on board.

I asked Douglas if he thought Rigby was a purist as regards Pinter. He said he thought so. They spent hundreds of hours talking about Pinter, not so much as a playwright, but about incidents that each of them was party to.

> Terence knew Pinter when they were both younger and he premiered in both plays. I think he felt possessive of him. Proprietorial. He wasn't alone in that. To go back to *The Homecoming*, there were other aspects of this show. He had this bee in his bonnet about Vivien [Merchant]. He loved her. He really was devoted to her. And the chap who played Max in the first show – John Normington – I know that Terence spoke to him, and he said he couldn't come to see the version I was in, because it – the original – had been such a beautiful thing, he couldn't bear to see it in another way.

So maybe Rigby wasn't alone in thinking that the 1965 production was the definitive one. But now I wanted the Pinter anecdotes, including the story of the socks . . .

Apparently Rigby stayed at Hanover Terrace one night and the following morning Pinter said, 'You'd better have a fresh pair of socks. But I want them back.' For some reason Rigby didn't return them. Pinter rang wanting know why. Rigby fobbed him off saying they were in the wash. There were several more phone calls by which time the socks were inexplicably lost. Rigby was so embarrassed he stopped returning Pinter's calls. Martin Shaw had a similar bust-up with Pinter over a pair of socks. Douglas thought they may have been silk ones, and rather special.

Douglas then told me the infamous story of the chairs.

I don't know whether one is allowed to talk about the chairs now that Pinter is dead . . . that saga about the chairs in New York! They were on Broadway, Harold rented a big suite somewhere. It was snowing. Everyone was very drunk. The understudies were there as well. Everyone was there. It was packed. Swish. Knock on door. The janitor came up and said, 'Could you stop throwing the furniture out of the windows.' They were fifteen storeys up. Someone was throwing chairs out of the window. And Pinter said, 'Look here. It's got to stop.' But it didn't.

I have to be careful, because there are so many versions of this story . . . But the next day, Harold called a production meeting, and said, 'I want to know who's responsible for this . . . I want to get to the bottom of it. And if someone doesn't confess –' and this is typical Harold – 'I'm calling the FBI. And then he called everyone in to be interrogated. It was like a Pinter play . . . But the thing you're referring to [Rigby's fight with Pinter] . . . It all fizzled out and they were starting to go home, to their own digs. It was very cold outside. And Harold was drunk and he started throwing peanuts at Vivien and insulting her . . . calling her a cow and worse. She was used to this and was saying, 'Oh, stop it.' And Terence was very upset by this . . . and I always believed that he was in love with Vivien. 'And finally, I couldn't stand it any more, mate,' he told me later. And Terence wasn't a man of violence . . .

'Harold, Harold,' he began, 'you've got to stop doing this . . .'

'She's my fucking wife. I'll do it if I want to.'

'If you want some, you can have some!'

'I thought I was finished,' Terence said later. 'But I kept on until Harold told me to get out. And I couldn't find my way home. It was snowing.' And the next day he thought he would be fired.

At some point one of the actors wrote a play about the whole thing which he sold to the BBC. But Pinter served an injunction on him – and it was the first play that he'd sold. He emigrated to Australia. I think Michael Bryant was there. Everyone who was there had a different view of it.

On another occasion, Harold and Terence were in a pub in Drury Lane one night, waiting for Vivien. An Irishman came up and said, 'You're Harold Pinter, aren't you?' Harold said yes. And the guy said, 'You're a cunt.'

'Outside.'

So there they are outside . . . Pinter, Terence and Vivien, and this Irish fellow starts going at him. And Terry said Vivien was getting upset – 'Oh, Harold, please, stop it.' So Terry thinks, 'What can I do to stop this?' – and the idiot gets hold of Harold from behind, gets his arms trapped so he can't do anything, at which point the Irishman kicks Pinter in the bollocks and floors him. The Irishman runs off and Terry thinks – 'Oh no. This is *my* fault, mate.'

Then Pinter got up and dusted himself off, and said, 'Terry. What did you do that for? I was just getting on top of him.'

He's met a nun at a party in Hampstead and she's rung him up a couple of times.

'Shall I add her to the list?' I say jokingly. He can't resist little forays into Catholicism – much as he professes to loathe his religious background.

'You may mock,' he says, 'but I was going to become a priest once. When I was a teenager I nearly went to a seminary. One of my mates became a priest. I still see him.'

'*I* was going to be a missionary,' I tell him. This curate came back from Africa and I had a huge crush on him. He was called Jones Uganda.'

Then he starts chanting from the Catholic Mass, in Latin no less. So we get a rendition of the Nunc Dimittis and I respond with the Magnificat. Down comes my Book of Common Prayer and between us we chant and sing our way through endless prayers and canticles. When it comes to my favourite, 'Benedicite, omnia opera', we begin improvising our own version:

'O ye Stars of Heaven praise ye the Lord, O ye Stars of Screen and Stage praise ye the Lord, O ye Beckett and Pinter, praise ye the Lord, Praise Him and Magnify Him for ever.'

He wants the Bible now and my jumble-sale tape recorder. He settles on Job, finds what he thinks will be a powerful piece of Old Testament wisdom, and begins reading. But it's one of those repetitious 'begat' chapters and it takes all his concentration to keep a straight face. Nevertheless, halfway through we have the Rigby giggle and I vow that I will have this recording played at my funeral.

*

It's always lovely when one hears another view of the same story – or the outcome from an earlier situation which had been left unresolved. I learned from Douglas McFerran that he had been involved in the Pinter sketches Rigby had shown me. He was working in Pebble Mill in 1991 and was alerted – by Tannoy – to the fact that Harold Pinter wanted a word with him. Heads turned as he rushed to the office.

Pinter explained that he had written a curtain raiser for *Death and the Maiden* at the Royal Court: *The New World Order*. He told Douglas that although he had no lines and would be wearing a paper bag over his head, his performance was crucial to the play and Douglas, he knew, would do it justice.

Douglas spoke to Rigby about it, who claimed to have no knowledge of the play. Douglas asked why Pinter should have asked him to play the non-speaking part. Rigby's response was classic: 'I can only imagine that Harold thinks you'd look good with a bag over your head.' (Ironically enough, Pinter evidently thought the same of Rigby.)

The play, which (according to one reviewer) ran for 480 seconds, meant that Douglas was free by 7.15 p.m. while being paid the full rate for his performance. Of course, the play had a deep, political resonance and was a perfect prelude for the Ariel Dorfman play that followed it.

Rigby was becoming more confident in his opinion about Pinter's short plays of that period. He thought that there was another full-length piece to be written. 'What Harold has to learn, mate,' he said after seeing *Mountain Language*, 'is that you've got to put on an entertainment. Bloody dire, mate.'

This in no way detracted from Rigby's admiration of Pinter, however, and he continued to watch out for any infringement of the rules of performance in his earlier work, even though such prestigious actors as Douglas McFerran, Michael Gambon, and Bill Paterson were happy to perform in anything by him.

Zagreb

Leaving Waterloo for Zagreb, Rigby embarked on the most horrendous journey of his life. He was ill equipped for the process of going 'cold turkey'. He had no medication and only a couple of bottles of water. In no time at all he was seriously dehydrated and beginning to lose all sense of reality. Somehow he changed trains when he was meant to, but each was an impossible adventure filled with surreal characters who presented an enormous threat to him. To go from two or three bottles of vodka a day to absolutely nothing at all would surely have killed a lesser man.

The script Douglas McFerran fashioned charts the train journey brilliantly, using all of Rigby's own laboriously recorded words.

At the hotel in Zagreb, the production team were understandably concerned by his strange behaviour, but probably thought that a good night's sleep would do the trick. But from Rigby's own recollection, when he got to his room, he was tormented by large beasts, monsters, his mother, and weird situations, until he was completely traumatized and so delirious that a doctor was called. By this time he was wandering along corridors in the hotel, shouting and screaming. He was immediately restrained and taken to a mental hospital.

Here are a few extracts from Douglas's screenplay. The actual train journey is very tautly written, showing the effects of alcohol withdrawal and lack of water. Thomas (i.e. Rigby) comes over as strange but not yet entirely out of control. At the hotel he orders two glasses of orange juice before walking down endless corridors and encountering a goldfish which alternately swims around an aquarium and lies on the floor. In his room he finds three men, huddled up in the wardrobe.

 [*Filmscript*]

THOMAS

Hold on, piglet.

Thomas's expression on his face somewhere between a sigh and a grimace. He squeezes his eyes closed. He opens his eyes.

INT.

The piglet is still standing there. Motionless. [The piglet ends up lying across his feet before disappearing. He is then shocked by the appearance of two women standing just inside the bathroom. One of them is elderly and it becomes obvious that she is Thomas's mother.]

INT.

The two women. They have stepped completely out of the shaft of light now. And in the shadows we see the most extraordinary thing: the elderly woman looks awfully grotesque – her arms seem to be made of wires – her hands are plastic pads – her lungs, visible through her chest are awful, grotesque plastic lungs. It is a horrifying apparition. Thomas is upset by what he sees. He helps the woman to lie down on the spare bed and rings room service. He orders two large brandies.

In the following monologue, taken verbatim from the tapes, I think we get into Rigby's subconscious. He had been behaving appallingly towards his mother for a long time.

⊗ [*Filmscript*]

THOMAS

I've ordered some drinks . . . I've ordered some brandy . . . you like brandy . . . anyway it'll pick you up a bit . . . you'll feel better . . . you've you had a long journey . . . I know how . . . tiring it is . . . you need some rest . . . need sleep . . . anyway you can both stay here . . . sleep here . . . this is my room . . . I'll be going to work very soon . . . You don't look well but everything's going to be all right now . . . I mean . . . I've been meaning to speak to you for a long time and well . . . it's been on my mind that . . . you know . . . maybe in the past I . . . I didn't pay as much attention to you . . . I didn't . . . that I should have done and . . . you see I'm always so busy . . . and you put things off . . . and the years seem to fly by and suddenly . . . suddenly . . . time has passed and . . . it's gone and . . . but look . . . I want you to know . . . everything's going to be different from now on . . . that's all finished now . . . let the past rest . . . we can . . . we can . . . forgive and forget . . . I'll make it up to you . . . and as soon as you're feeling a bit better . . . because I want you to know that . . . I . . . I care for you . . . I've always cared. It's just that . . . that . . . I want you to know that   I . . . I . . .

99

The last extract, where the old woman has been attacked by a large cat, is horrifying.

⊗ [*Filmscript*]

THOMAS

Bastard! Bastard cat! I've got you. You fucking cat! You bastard fucking . . . you've . . . you cunt fucker! I'll fix you. I'll kill you, you fucker . . . you've desecrated the . . . you fucking cunt . . . you've eaten the body.

INT. HOTEL ROOM. THOMAS'S P.O.V.

The hotel room is in a state of great disarray.

There is no body.

There is no cat.

There are no sounds.

Having been told the story in great detail on another occasion, by Rigby himself, I am convinced that the above scenes are verbatim. It was clearly etched – engraved – in his mind, and if I am right, the piece demonstrates the guilt Rigby felt about his treatment of Trixie, about whom he had been both harsh and dismissive – though it's also true that when he sometimes talked about his occasional stays in his mother's house during the *Crossroads* months, he did so with fondness.

His account of his medical treatment is equally shocking. The hospital looked more like an austere prison, he said, or Dracula's castle. He was alone in a damp basement room that had perhaps been a dungeon. When he woke from a drug-induced sleep, he realized he had been strapped on to an iron bed with leather restraints and chains. He was practically naked and covered in his own excrement. He says he was left in this condition for several days. In fact he thought he would be incarcerated for the rest of his life.

Noel Murray remembers David Sinclair getting a phone call from the producer to say that Rigby was hallucinating. His brother Joseph, who then worked for Granada Television, was at a conference in Cannes when he got the message that Rigby was in a seriously bad way in Zagreb. He made his way to Yugoslavia as quickly as possible and had to fight his way through considerable red tape to achieve Rigby's release both from the hospital and the country. He never forgot the kindness shown to him by Joseph or the effort it took to bring him home. Back in England, Rigby spent several weeks in a private clinic, drying out in a controlled atmosphere and rehabilitating.

As a postscript to the whole Zagreb episode, I discovered a poem written by Rigby with the simple title '1986':

1986

Trust you're well. I have
An improbable tale to tell
Of horses, dogs and elusive men
And whether I'd ever be loose again.

Of dark sea trips, iron curtain trains,
A beautiful face with Bible primed,
Tyne Side sounds ordained,
A search in snow, pure orange neat.

Sit drifting by, white-coated Slavs
Doing for me but not by halves,
Shite-caked walls, clicks of locks,
The nightly room for bursting bugs
And strangled feet till morning becomes

Pale loony fellows in part-pyjamas,
Sweet icy teas slaking the heat,
A dulled mind, no visiting feet.
Then a face I know, a brother too,
Came through snow, flew through snow –
Task undone at Monte Carlo.
Valium downed, we left that ground
And that half-light pain.
England again. Beloved rain.
Farewell snow. Beloved rain.

TCR

101

Beiderbecke and *Crossroads*
(1984–88)

After Zagreb, Rigby never drank again. He avoided food marinaded in alcohol and only occasionally risked cooked food where the alcohol content was burnt out. Every one of his friends respected this restriction. Nevertheless, he continued to frequent all his old haunts, and could be seen in his favourite pubs in Marylebone and the West End. He would buy bottles of wine for friends and at the table would pick up a wine glass, swirl the contents round and take a sniff, giving an opinion on it. I only ever saw him drink tea or water. He was never tempted by non-alcoholic beers or fruit juices.

Sadly, he never could apply the same iron will when it came to smoking. He managed a year or so from time to time, but always returned to tobacco. He reckoned it was easier to give up booze than smoking. Other recovering alcoholics, in my experience, have the same problem. Over the years, he had suffered severe heart problems and had a triple bypass, a heart attack and dangerously blocked arteries. No amount of lecturing or nagging ever did any good.

Working on *Crossroads* meant that Rigby saw more of his family. His mother lived in Erdington, and brother Patrick close by. He renewed old friendships and mentored the teenage daughter of a family friend. Angela Bull spoke of his kindness to her, following her journey through drama school and into the profession. She was one of many young people who were nurtured by Rigby, including Julia, one of his Canadian nieces.

He had completed the first series of Alan Plater's *The Beiderbecke Affair* before Zagreb, and worked on the next two after *Crossroads*. I made contact with Alan shortly before his death in 2010, and he answered a series of questions I put to him via email.

Rigby played the character of Big Al in the series, who became a great favourite with viewers. He and his brother Little Norm (played by Danny Schiller) run an unorthodox, barely legal business, justified by Big Al as a way of saying 'Bollocks to the system'. He is more dominant than his brother and given to strange philosophical views.

Alan Plater wasn't sure whether he was involved in Rigby's casting, but he certainly had de facto casting approval and his response, he told me, would have been a resounding yes. He had no idea how Rigby approached the character because he was a law unto himself: 'In rehearsal he was quiet and contained. In performance astonishing. He had a quality of not being in the real world.' Alan thought that could be why Pinter loved him so much – he had a sort of existential quality. When I asked him whether Rigby brought something new and unexpected to his role, Alan answered, 'Absolutely: Like Max Miller used to say, "There'll never be another".'

I wanted to know whether he ever turned up on Alan's doorstep out of the blue:

> I don't remember him doing that, but I do remember phone calls – after a five-year silence!
>
> 'Rigby. Fancy a game of snooker tomorrow, Al?'
>
> So we'd meet up at the Paddington Club, have a game of snooker, vow eternal friendship and five years later . . . There's a bit of hyperbole here but he was like that.
>
> I checked into a hotel once and a taxi pulled up outside. Terry leapt out and said, 'Joe Stalin!' Turned out he was playing Stalin at the National, needed a left-wing historian and figured (correctly) that I could find the right person.

I didn't watch *The Beiderbecke Affair* when it was first transmitted, so it came as a shock when I looked at it quite recently. When Rigby and I resumed our friendship in 1987, he wasn't the man I knew in the Sixties, nor did I expect him to be, but seeing Big Al – with the emphasis on the 'Big' – was disconcerting. I asked Noel Murray if he thought Rigby would take on some of the characteristics of a part, or whether the writer wrote specifically for the actor. Noel said he sometimes did have a tendency to do this. He would take on the air of a philosopher or a great thinker, he said. It was inevitably cloaked in humour, so that you were never quite sure what was real and what wasn't. But maybe that was yet another tool to cover up his uncertainty.

On the other hand, Alan Plater might have subconsciously registered the quirkiness of Rigby and written it into Big Al. This is, needless to say, the one question I forgot to ask. But in answer to my question 'Why do you think he was a one-off?', Alan replied, 'No idea. But imagine trying to recast him. That's your answer.'

vii. Rigby at the Crossroads

❏ JULIET'S TABLE

So I've been working hard all morning, and reckon I deserve a break, when Rigby turns up, out of the blue as usual.

'Can I wash my feet?' he says. 'I've got a costume fitting at Angel's and I'm not sure they're in a fit state.'

I give him a clean towel and put the kettle on. He's bound to want a cup of tea before he goes. When he's finished, he sits at the table and I give him his tea and a sandwich. There's something different about him.

He says, 'What?'

'Have you got cotton wool in your cheeks. Your face looks very fat.'

'Don't be so fucking rude. Excuse my French.'

Then I realize he's shaved his beard off but left a broad, thick moustache. He's been cast as Stalin again. Last time it was a Robert Bolt play at the National – *State of Revolution.*

'Tony Palmer's making a film. Wants me in it. Did you know that Stalin was a very small man?'

'You're perfect for the part then, aren't you?'

When he's gone to Angel's, I think about his odd request. Would I admit to dirty feet, to a girlfriend, say? Probably not. But Rigby has rung up in the past and said, 'Can I come for a shower – my bath's leaking?' And of course he can. He's always welcome. One night he rang and said he'd lost his keys and wanted to stay over. Several hours later, he told me he'd found them but had wanted to come round anyway.

*

Testimony (1988)

Sorting out 'The Rigby Papers' was immensely difficult. In sifting a jumble of material, there'd be bits of letters, bills, and pages of parts he had played and therefore written out, over and over, as part of the line-learning process. There was even a letter from Harold Pinter, torn in half by mistake. By the time I'd pieced it all together, I found the following correspondence illuminating.

Rigby must have been to an early viewing of *Testimony*, as Tony Palmer's film was called, and was disgruntled by his place in the credits. His agent, Peter Charlesworth, wrote to the director:

✉ *[Peter Charlesworth]*

Dear Tony,
    I write on behalf of my client, Terence Rigby, who is distressed and puzzled by the radical alteration to the agreed billing matter and position of his name in your film of Shostakovich. Maureen Murray's letter of the 15th December to me clearly agrees that the billing should have been below the main title with 'Terence Rigby as Stalin' and should have appeared on a separate card on the screen [...] I understand now that whilst he is still the first name under the title he shares the card with another actor and the additional 'Stalin' credit has been dropped.
    Maureen Murray has explained to me your attitude regarding this. However, both Terry and I feel that it was very cavalier to make these alterations without at least discussing the matter with me [...]

Having had a similar experience, I sympathize with Rigby, but I'm sure he would have been at least partly mollified by Tony Palmer's direct and personal response, dated 6 October 1987:

✉ *[Tony Palmer]*

Dear Terry,
    Please take this letter in the spirit that it is intended.
    First, I discussed with Peter Charlesworth ages ago the problem of what to do about your credit. I explained, that although, at the time of signature, it seemed like a good idea to give you a single credit 'as Stalin', as the film developed (and I think as you will have seen), this

credit became nonsense. There are *five* Stalins in the film, not including you, but including the genuine article (at least I'm not quite sure which is the genuine article, if you see what I mean, so overwhelming is your performance). So I could not have 'Terence Rigby as Stalin' without saying 'Other parts: Stalin . . .'

Then: it seemed out of place, given the ensemble nature of the piece, that (with the obvious exception of Ben Kingsley) anybody should be separated out from the others. Although it is my normal practice to list the Stars alphabetically, I realized that I must (as well as wanted to) put your name first. Which is where it is.

But the real point at issue is more obvious. Usually, in my experience, actors want to have credits along the lines of 'Fred Smith as Adolf Hitler', because they are concerned that otherwise their performance will get lost. I can assure you, absolutely no one, unless they are blind, asleep or dead, is going to miss your performance. Indeed, one of the astonishing things about the general reaction to the film, including two hard-bitten Americans we showed it to, was that everyone seems unaware that there are *any* 'performances'. It is assumed they really are watching Stalin and Shostakovich. Greater credit than that you cannot have, even if I had begun the film with 'Terence Rigby', 'starring Terence Rigby', 'with Terence Rigby playing the part of' and 'with special participation of Terence Rigby'.

Your place in cinematic history is assured. Don't worry about that, and make sure you are there on the 15th.

Yours sincerely,
Tony

Searching through newspaper clippings, I came across an appreciation written by Tony Palmer after Rigby's death, which confirms the blurring of identity that audiences made between Rigby's depiction of Stalin and the real thing. It says more about him, and his skill, than any of the reviews I read about his performance:

'Terence Rigby had the extraordinary – and in my experience unique – quality of being able to inhabit the characters he portrayed with awesome power. When I made my film about Shostakovich called *Testimony*, with Ben Kingsley as the composer, although not in fact based on Solomon Volkov's memoirs of the same name, Volkov was personally most helpful in authenticating many of the details of Shostakovich's life. After the filming, Kingsley and I and several of the crew gathered for supper at our hotel, with Volkov and his wife as our guests. Volkov sat on my right looking towards the door of the restaurant. Suddenly he dropped his glass of wine and, white-faced, began to tremble violently. I was sure he was having a heart attack and I began to rush for the door in search of a doctor. Then I noticed standing in the door was the actor who was playing Stalin in the film, still dressed in that murderous villain's costume. That actor was Terence Rigby.

The irony was that Rigby was one of the gentlest of men, whose personal kindness knew no limits. But 20 years later when Volkov and I were together at a Shostakovich festival in Rome, Volkov told me that the image of Rigby standing in that Wigan doorway still haunted him.' — *The Times*, 13 August 2008

And of course, when one takes into account that Rigby was a towering presence with size 12 feet, and Stalin was very small, it's all the more remarkable.

❏ JULIET'S TABLE

Late one evening, Rigby arrives with a shuffling old man.

'I've brought John Heaward to meet you, Lady Camden.'

He always refers to me as 'Lady Camden'. He's bestowed similar honorific titles on many of his friends ('Lady Clarendon', 'His Excellency' Stephen Thorne); a potted hydrangea arrived for my birthday one year, and I had to sign 'Lady Camden' for it.)

They sit at the table. Rigby plonks down four cans of beer and asks for a glass and a pot of tea. I am intrigued and a bit miffed that this might turn into a Maria José situation. I pour myself a glass of wine and having made the usual small talk, realize that I am sitting opposite a legend.

John Heaward was a dancer and choreographer. He had been a stalwart member of The Players' Theatre in the Fifties with Hattie Jacques and others, and had choreographed the original production of Sandy Wilson's musical, *The Boy Friend*.

'I remember seeing it in the West End when I was a student at Rose Bruford,' I tell them excitedly. 'And coincidentally, my friend Tony Holland was in it for a while, a bit later on in the run.'

And so begins another magical evening with a man who, after oiling the system with a couple of cans, tells us stories of his exploits in theatre and film. He actually choreographed the 'Hot-Box' dancers in the film of *Guys and Dolls*, he says.

I realize that this is another Rigby quirk, or gift: he brings people together; seeks out an old man, who by this time is living a rather secluded life somewhere up the end of Camden Road, and then sits quietly by, allowing the evening to develop.

Before midnight, a minicab is ordered and John is safely dispatched with strict instructions to the driver to see him into his house.

As usual, the minicab controller suppresses a giggle when I give my honorific name. 'Devonshire Street?' he asks in a knowing way. We have fantasies about what's being said in the cab office about our friendship ('What goes *on* in that house until four in the morning . . . ?').

Introducing colleagues and acquaintances is one thing; however, Rigby doesn't like my meeting up with any of his close friends. He understands that I know Stephen Thorne and Jane Morgan independently, through my work in radio, but he more or less instructs me not to talk about him.

I respond indignantly: 'We've got more important things to talk about than you. Who d'you think you are?'

Mutter, mutter, mutter.

*

Richard III (1992–93)

Rigby played Buckingham in this early revival of Richard Eyre's production, starring Ian McKellen. It was not a fulfilling experience for him. He didn't feel part of the ensemble, that the production was really a vehicle for the recently knighted Sir Ian. I recall his concern that some scenes had apparently been conflated, which then didn't make sense of Buckingham's role. He therefore found himself on stage when, logically, according to him, he shouldn't have been. I thought long and hard before deciding to include my own diary entries from this time. They show my loyalty, misplaced or otherwise, and occasionally an arrogance beyond belief. But that's how friends are, I think. Right or wrong, we declare our bias.

✎ [*Diary, J.A.*]

1 May 1992

Terry, after the first week of rehearsals of *Richard III*. He has come into a company which has performed this Richard Eyre production before. It all sounds a bit unsatisfactory for an actor coming to a play that already has an established style. Rigby says of Ian McKellen: 'God knows he can be forgiven . . .' (for his attitude?) '... but you can't tell when he's acting, coasting, or regarding the proceedings as a waste of time. He varies pitch, tone, etc. all the time –' uses tricks presumably, technique – 'to such an extent that you don't know what he's doing – where he's at.'

'As an actor', Rigby says, 'you don't know where and how to blend in.' He's such a hard worker he will find his way, providing his confidence isn't diminished. It seems to me that Ian McK. should take this opportunity to re-evaluate his own performance – a good actor must always be ready to explore, to be flexible, to let in new thoughts, new ideas. (Who do I think I am? Good thing this is just a diary.)

2 May

[...] then Rigby rang. He's having problems with Ian McKellen. He wanted to come round but I was too tired.

'I'm worried about my teeth.'

Rigby bares his gums to show me what he means. I've never been impressed by his teeth: they've always looked a bit worn down and uncared for. Now, at least, some of them look very white and even.

'They look all right to me.'

'I'm making too many slushing sounds. Have you noticed?'

'Let me listen for a bit.'

So he carries on talking while I listen and scrutinize the offending choppers.

'Seems to me you've got a problem with your *s*-sounds. And now you're being too careful.'

He listens to my expert view, so this encourages me to chance my arm and give him my thoughts on the current trend of covering all your manky teeth with porcelain – a fashion I don't approve of if it's just for cosmetic reasons.

'They're all at it,' I tell him, 'when they've got a bob or two to spare. Even Thatcher's had it done, and she can't cope at all. They're too big for her mouth.'

I'm clearly on a roll because he then asks me what he should do. I tell him he should look into the possibility of a wired bridge, not a plate – *definitely* not a plate. Perhaps a false tooth supported by a bridge. OK, so I'm a dentist now, but he knows I mean well. And what's more he doesn't say 'Bollocks!', which is what he usually says if he thinks I'm spouting garbage.

He's so depressed about *Richard III* that I take him to the new Thai restaurant in Camden High Street. He finds the food 'titivating', a word he once used to describe some marmalade.

*

✎ [*Diary, J.A.*]

3 May
    Went to see Rigby in *Richard III* at the National Theatre. The play was interesting. Rigby wonderful. Ian McKellen rather mannered. The women mediocre.
    2 June
    Rigby came round. I took him to a Thai restaurant in Camden High Street. The food was exquisite. Terry liked it.

Later in June
    Farewell to Rigby before he goes off on his tour. He was upset by
Jane Morgan and Peter's remarks about *Richard III* and Ian McKellen's
performance.

I find it interesting, rereading my diary, that although Rigby was himself
very critical of both the actor and the production, he somehow could never
tolerate unsolicited comments.

    Richard Eyre re-rehearsed the play for Broadway, and I received a
postcard from Rigby on 11 June 1992:

✉ [*Terence Rigby*]

Found a down and out caff for my cuppa fix near Ruth's place. R. Eyre's
last night and he and I danced. We did it my way together – quite fun.
My perf tonight sh'ite and got down – reviews due today – but know it's
within me and not press notices. Several layers of desparu (French I think,
or sort of Latin). Just wish I was 40, then I'd get hold of this bastard
– still one can't be so c'est la vie (more French). Hope your writing is
inspirational. Sorry about this fairly precarious note. It'll brighten up.
Thinking of moving out of Ruth's – the place is always empty – they are
busy people – talking rather a lot to Daisy the dawg.
    Lord B'Lyn de Harlem

✎ [*Diary, J.A.*]

20 July. A lovely (belated) birthday card from Rigby. He says that Sir Ian
McKellen is a selfish actor and is after everything. It's worse than *The Wild
Duck*.

Tim McMullan (who played Tyrrel) was able to throw more light on the
production. Over a period of months, Tim became quite close to Rigby, and
he described some of their meetings and conversations during that tour.

Richard III was a very different experience from *Wind in the Willows*, but I
got to know him a bit better. He was very disappointed to discover that his
part of Buckingham had been heavily edited. It was a part he had always
wanted to play, and he had learned it before rehearsals began, and he told
me that he never quite found the 'edited' character, having once learned
the complete one. He just couldn't fit it into the more immense thing he
had prepared. He also had terrible trouble with his teeth, which he was on
medication for, which affected his moods and behaviour a lot, and which no
one knew about. It meant that he didn't get on with everyone, and had quite
an unhappy time, I believe. He particularly didn't get on with Ian McKellen.
They sort of despised each other, although I can't really comment much on
that as I didn't involve myself in it. He was happiest in New York where he

had friends. I remember that lots of autograph hunters particularly wanted his autograph at the stage door – and in New York, they only want the star.

I remember him telling me, quite early on, that he was Secretary of the Equity tennis tournament, which surprised me as he didn't look very athletic, but I soon discovered that he had been a very good player, which raised him in my estimation! There were also rumours of the many beautiful women who paid court to him, which made him more mysterious.

I remember talking with him about working in rep in the Sixties and a bit about his telly work, and I also remember him talking about Ralph Richardson, whom he had clearly adored.

I sat in bars with him while he drank water, and other soft drinks. He explained to me that he had given up drink when he saw animals and birds flying or walking through the walls of his room and out the other side. He asked me what I liked to drink and what it did to me. The experts tell us alcohol is all the same, but dedicated experience will tell you that different drinks do different things, and I remember discussing that with him. As you will know, he drank two or three bottles of spirits in a day, and that he had given up without any kind of help. I heard other stories about his drinking later on. In spite of the trouble he had on that tour, he was loved by many of us, particularly the younger actors, for his uniqueness, his honesty, his humour, his cussedness, and much else. He also seemed to prefer the company of the younger lot. I suppose he could be monosyllabic at times, but I always liked being with him. He was private, but curiously open at the same time – or if he wished to be. And importantly, in my eyes he wasn't choosy about who he sat with at lunch, unless it was someone he didn't like, and was just as happy with the wardrobe or stage management as with anyone.

I don't know if this is something I should refer to, but he had a girlfriend with him for several weeks, and they slept in the same rooms, but not together, it transpired. She was a lovely woman, a radiographer I think, obviously in love with him, but driven to distraction by him and their friendship, which he always steered away from where she wanted it to go. I hesitate to mention all this as it is an observation merely. Anyway, she gave up eventually.

I did keep up with him afterwards, and he wrote me the odd postcard, and we talked a little from time to time, but I never knew him again as well as I did to begin with. Our paths never crossed that much after that, but he always seemed to be interested in what us young actors, at least the ones he liked, were up to, and he was always delighted if I had any particular success. Like many people I have known who have died, I would love to see him again and talk to him about his life as an actor, and about mine too. He was a singular man. I have never met anyone else like him, and I didn't make the most of our acquaintance by a long chalk. The last time I met him was at your house, actually . . .

❏ JULIET'S TABLE

It would seem, to judge by the letters and cards that arrive during this tour, that poor old Rigby is not having the best of times, and the mutual dislike between Sir Ian and the future 'Lord Marylebone' is never resolved. But there's nothing I like more than to have a mug of coffee at the table and read and reread the Rigby letters. It's always with reluctance that they are eventually added to the pile which is growing apace – evidence of the increased amount of time he's in the USA. The Green Card looms and I'll see even less of him.

*

✉ [*Terence Rigby*]

Arlington, Virginia. Tues. 14th July
   Birthday Greets to her Ladyship Camden – I hope and feel certain that the shindig was an overwhelming success of post dawn proportions . . . The weather is such that one instructively allows (say) only one expedition of any sort during any one day – there is a show to do in the final analysis. As for that – I have settled on a performance of some sort – with perhaps one scene still being a major problem and quite bored with some scenes – a sense of constriction and Sir I. is frankly even more boring and irritating than the Wild Duck problem actor. He is quite clearly an insatiable megalomaniac anxious to gobble up all the fish in the pond and is on the lookout for anyone giving anything like a strong performance – even if you start to travel well in a short section – he will drop you a slow cue or break a line into pieces, plastering one with egg. Quite enough of him.

The next letter has me falling about with laughter. For some reason I see him in the Jack Lemon character, pinned down by 'nymphets' (including Marilyn Monroe) in the sleeping compartment in *Some Like It Hot* . . .

✉ [*Terence Rigby*]

7th August 1992. St Paul
   Hotel Radisson is swarming with nymphets aged 11 through 70, here for Daughters of Job Conference – lists are not in it – it's Volumis Bedlam in Eternum. However let me be calm and think of cups of tea and England. Thank you for your latest epistle bearing bits and pieces of delight. By some fluke we've just had two days off but now settle down again to finish off our stint here, preceding Colorado from Monday. I have spoken to [brother] Joseph twice since his operation and all would appear to be proceeding very normally. Thank you for concern. As a rarity we

are rehearsing p.m. today, due to a different stage space at San Francisco which of course is after Denver. The climate is fine good English weather, so that humidity seems not be present here. So glad Faith [Kent] does the job well – always give my love – in my youth she was honey pancakes ma'am, sure thing, baby doll. What-what. Thinking back to your letter – glad you've seen something of Ned – he does seem very special – sorry to hear of his malaise – hopefully, that can be changed with all this advance in laser research and usage that is current nowadays. As Lear/Kent – there's far too much nonsense about your obedient servant suitability of this and that. But – maybe thank God there is. As I am sitting writing at the poolside – there are dripping nymphets and screams of ecstasy quite putting me off my strokes. I suppose I could move.

The Washington woman has sent me a gift of an American commemorative medal and some Stars and Stripes braces and Lady Ann often stares provocatively towards me and presses some odd smooch – but that apart, St Paul has been very much DIY. Hope my risqué mood denotes the coming of some sort of second wind. So your radio series is up and running – congratulations – I hope the coffers are building against rainy days – hopefully there will be none. I think it's been a destructive year for you. For a while it wasn't all beer and skittles – but slowly it broke and it always will. Do tell Richard [Johns] the World Weekend Financial Times is really an excellent read – I do hope he is bearing up being confined to base, that some dazzling assignments will suddenly pop up unexpectedly – I believe I mean unexpectedly. Some madcap actor turned director has offered me Max in Pinter's 'Homecoming' in LA – you will recall, the Paul Rogers [i.e. the original Max] recently played awfully by Warren Mitchell. A lot will depend on getting the rights and clearly he wants me on board to and for this end. I'm not much interested but I did know this fellow years ago – and my bones tell me that Harold Pinter will decline permission, but as of now – that stays in the pot. However I am thinking again of applying for resident alienship – Time will tell.

The nymphs have shimmered off – to travel down – must be careful of the ticker. What-what! Popped into the bar and now sitting with a calming cup – at least they do serve tea here – and have been quizzing a splendid nymph who tells me that she is the daughter of Job from Wisconsin and is a princess of this Bible order. Oh well. She has been dragged away by others – just as well. I do the Mississippi boat ride every so often and have seen down town Minneapolis, twin city with St Paul – which has amazingly futuristic skyscrapers – truly a very glorious spectacle.

I would like you to tell Ray [Jenkins] that The Sea Surgeon books are really fascinating me – I finished the Sea Diaries and am three quarters of the way through his land adventures. It's a very long time since I was captivated in the way I have been. The horrific life, being at sea and the fascinating life of the young surgeon in the 18th century London – with so many references to streets and places that still exist and the way people lived and behaved – immense amount of potential for drama. However

115

I am not necessarily convinced that I would be his man for the job. But please thank him for a wonderful diversion. I'm certain it will cause me to read more sea travelling subjects of which I recall at Greenwich, there is a huge library/shop. I had nine daughters of Job in the lift coming up to my room – four of them dripping, clutching tiled surround sound bathing suits – it's all hell I tell you. For the record, age [*of consent?*] here is 18, so it's not all beer and skittles.

Back home from the *Richard III* tour of the States, our friendship begins to change into a series of catching-up sessions. Our learned short-hand makes this an easy transition.

A tribute to a flatmate

H is close friend David Sinclair was by now – the early Nineties – back on the scene and had moved into a flat in Covent Garden. Rigby was very solicitous towards David, who had calmed down very considerably over the years. Being a parent was extremely important to him and Rigby was always regarded as godfather to Alexander – David and Christine's only child (although he wasn't prepared to make the full formal commitment).

David got an understudy job in a Chekhov play in the West End. He asked Rigby to help with line-learning. They worked for days at a time, but no matter how many different tactics Rigby employed, the words would not embed themselves in David's brain. I recall that Rigby was as apprehensive as David – both praying that the actor he was understudying would not fall ill. Tragically, David was then diagnosed with cancer and moved back to Hove, where Christine nursed him for his remaining days. Rigby visited many times and was deeply affected by David's death in December 1996.

Rigby came round after the cremation and told me it had been standing room only. I wrote a letter of condolence to him. He was very involved with the funeral and wrote an obituary for the *Guardian*. Stephen Thorne, who was away at the time, asked Rigby for an account of the funeral. I include both accounts here, if only to demonstrate the singularity of Rigby's voice, whether for private or public ears. The funeral first:

☞ [*Terence Rigby*]

The hall was full, about a dozen perhaps, standing, squeezed into corners. Michael Gambon among them. I found out later six or seven were in the entrance hall. The Rev. Henry Birgin, who I got from All Saints Blackheath – famous by chance for his Terry Waite TV worldwide appeal – told us of being once a singer/actor – and did a shrewdly good rundown of all Sinc's career, ending with his *Dombey* credit. There were prayers – then we sang Psalm 23 – accompanied – reasonably well – Young Alexander then spoke from the podium: 'In my father's house are many mansions' – clearly, no pause, no fault – quite wonderful. I then made tribute – which I started by thanks to the Rev. Henry and then spoke about the many regrets for absence from many close friends. That there was little new I could tell them about

117

David – perhaps no story being left already untold. How I had known all his family with the exception of Don, his painter father, whose paintings he admired so much. His dying mother asked me – as mothers do, to look after him. That Crouch Peter had given us a flat. That I became Warrant Officer to his Wing Commander. How understanding he was of my modest Grammar School education and my Birmingham background and was quick to assure his classy pals that I was, nevertheless a damn fine cove. And stories of Sunday lunches and Langan, and them falling in, and then playing Golf rather badly together and agreeing sometimes to retiring at the fourth or fifth and heading off to the 19th. Of many charming lady visitors and my function as morning tea boy. How I was going to be called from my bed to push-start the many Morris Minors he went through. But during all our time in the flat, there was no anger and many of the 10th, 11th, 12th years, so much in need of one of the rooms – and my departure and wedding bells – that although I started to see less of them that I was present when Christine rang from the clinic to tell Sinclair she was pregnant. But I met occasionally thereafter to console him regards loss of his bachelorhood. Later, in his Covent Garden years – I realize how much I missed seeing and nattering with him and started to seek him out in pubs and clubs and how we sometimes found it difficult that I didn't drink any more – but that eventually we did occasionally enjoy what had been for us, in old times. Although a lot of darkness had descended on him and less control – but radio work and voice-overs now and then came along, but he seemed no longer capable of making upward steps, and his overriding motivation was love of Alexander. I spoke of seeing him a handful of times in the Middlesex and how he told me he did not fear death – only was angry that there was not enough time for him with Alexander – and my last 2/3 visits to Hove and finally being with him in a coma, of how brave and loving Christine was during his Hove days – that I had sensed he half wanted, for some while, to have been back there with them – but that he had not been able to deal with such a difficult question. I ended abruptly. There were more prayers and the curtains closed around him. There was a good pile of us in the Queen's Tavern upper room, drinks and food.

Affection to you both. Terry.

Now the *Guardian* obituary:

☰ PUBS, CLUBS, AND A BRASS BED

'In the 1970s. I had the luck to share a Marylebone flat with a fellow actor, David Sinclair, who has died aged 62. It was a whirlwind arrangement, spent mainly at the Buckstone Club – in the Salisbury pub – or at Gerry's Club, which was then in Shaftesbury Avenue. He was a remarkable and loveable companion and when I did well and he did not, he hit me for several large ones.

We had first met in 1964 in a pub. Sinclair was then appearing in the musical *Robert and Elizabeth* at the Lyric theatre. He had a magnificent voice and had won the baritone prize at the Guildhall School of Music in the late 1960s. Despite training as a singer he wanted to be an actor, but put the voice to good use in musicals like *Carousel*, *My Fair Lady*, *Windy City* and *Oh What a Lovely War*. And at the cusp of the 1960s he toured America in Tyrone Guthrie-directed productions of *HMS Pinafore* and *The Pirates of Penzance*.

Sinclair was a good actor. He was also somehow out of his time. Very understanding about my modest Birmingham Grammar School background, he would explain to his public school pals that I was, nevertheless, a first-class chap. I had indeed come from a rougher provincial arena, and while we were approximate contemporaries, the theatrical times were offering rougher-hewn parts. He was trained in an older school, and did not so easily get the bookings. But in the mid 1970s he worked with John Clements and John Gielgud at the Chichester Festival Theatre for two seasons: he did two Royal Shakespeare seasons for Trevor Nunn and Sir Peter Hall – replacing Michael Hordern, he played opposite Peggy Ashcroft in the RSC production of Edward Albee's *A Delicate Balance*; his television work included Jonathan Miller's *King Lear* and he performed more than 100 plays for BBC radio drama repertory company.

As a flatmate – and human being – he was audacity itself. He once sold the brass bed in which I slept to a comparative stranger, for 50 quid. After all it was his, he explained with a tinge of regret. His mother had left it to him.

Because of his passion for music, I learned about opera. It wasn't necessary to buy a ticket to hear him sing, he would pump out 'Ol' Man River' at the drop of a beer mat. At his 50th birthday party, he rose, unannounced, and rendered the song to a packed and startled Langan's Restaurant in Mayfair. I feared he might clear the place, but Peter Langan led a standing ovation.

He played a very ordinary, often wild game of golf with Langan, and was always pleased when his 'opponent' decided to chuck it in for the day at the third or fourth, as they tended to do. Thus would they happily drive off together to the 19th. For more relaxing matters. I can verify this. I marked for them.

The absence of a fourth room had caused us to break up after the 1970s. We went our ways. When we met again, he was much changed and life was thinner for him, although he continued to pound himself mercilessly with late hours. His final performance was in Radio 4's *Dombey and Son*. He faced his demise with most baffling courage. His overriding love and joy in his last days was Alexander, his 13-year-old son. His former wife Christine's attention during his last weeks was gold.

It's interesting, I think, that Rigby nowhere mentions the ferocious arguments and rumbling silences between them. Nevertheless, what shines through, is the undeniably strong friendship that existed all the time they knew each other. In his self-deprecating description of the status each had in the relationship, Rigby shows how much he revered David Sinclair for his confident, arrogant *joie de vivre*.

I had given Rigby a pocket version of Shakespeare's Sonnets, which he took with him on his walks in Regent's Park. Many months after David died, Rigby told me he'd lent the little book to him when he was in hospital – a typical Rigby gesture. He asked me to get him another one. I tried everywhere to find one and had just about given up when I accidentally came across the very edition in the Barbican Bookshop. I'm glad to say he hung on to that copy.

The Green Card

After crossing the Atlantic on numerous occasions to perform on Broadway, Rigby finally decided to go ahead with his dream of having the Green Card that would enable him to work in both countries without bother. So in 1997, he began his application – following all the correct channels, filling in the countless forms, and eliciting the help of influential people in the profession.

Letters in support of Rigby's application came willingly from the great and the good: Sir Peter Hall, Sir John Gielgud, Nicholas Hytner, Sir Richard Eyre, Alexander Cohen (one of the most prolific producers of Broadway plays in the US), Roger Stephens, (founder of the Kennedy Center for the Performing Arts in Washington) and Vincent Dowling (who had directed Rigby in his Abbey Theatre days, and now wrote an eloquent letter on his behalf). Eugene Foley, who eventually presented Rigby's application, described Dowling's letter in particular as deserving of 'serious attention' – 'written from the point of view of a highly distinguished theatre veteran who recognizes exceptional or extraordinary ability as distinct from stardom'.

Extraordinarily enough, even this mighty pedigree was dismissed as being too personal and biased: independent statements of Rigby's expertise were required by people who do not know him personally. Bernard Levin and Michael Billington, who knew Rigby's work but had never met him, were therefore approached. Here are the testimonials they wrote.

✉ [*Michael Billington*]

21 May 1997
    Dear Sir/Madam,
    In my view as a theatre critic, Terence Rigby is a quite exceptional actor. He has worked with most of the major British Theatre Companies. He has appeared with great distinction in the classics. He has created new roles in plays by Harold Pinter and Robert Bolt: most famously in *The Homecoming* and *No Man's Land*. In 1990/91 I chose him as my Actor of the Year, against fierce competition, for his varied performances in plays by Ibsen, Racine, and Alan Bennett. I have no personal connection with him whatsoever: indeed, we have never met. I simply regard him as

one of the best actors in Britain: he has weight, authority, and a palpable integrity that shines through everything he does. If I were a director, he is exactly the kind of actor I would want to have in my company: he has great physical presence and vocal power.

Yours faithfully,
Michael Billington

✉ *[Bernard Levin]*

TO WHOM IT MAY CONCERN: MR. TERENCE RIGBY

Although I do not know Mr Terence Rigby personally, I have been impressed by his performances in a variety of theatrical roles.

My interest in the theatre is both personal and professional. I have been Dramatic Critic for the *Daily Express*, the *Daily Mail*, and more recently for the *Sunday Times*, and was for many years a member of the judging panel of the annual London theatre awards, The Evening Standard Awards.

As a regular theatre goer, I would particularly recommend Mr Rigby for his extraordinary versatility as an actor. Through the years he has proved how easily he can adapt himself to work within television, theatre and film, moving from soap opera to musical, from children's theatre to plays by Ibsen, Pinter or Shakespeare. This amazing flexibility is also reflected in and worked successfully with so many of the great theatre directors and 'great and the good' within the acting profession.

I wish him continued success with his career.
Bernard Levin.

Levin appended some reviews of his work, including this piece by Russell Davies, dated Sunday, 10 April 1988:

☰ 'The closing of *Crossroads* removes a sizeable blot of embarrassment from our national ledger . . . Lately there has been Terence Rigby, bellowing and grating away at a pitch of commitment not often encountered in British acting outside of *King Lear*. In his quieter moments the Rigby character still sounded like Donald Sinden imitating a motor-bike. Had he really been as splendid a solid copper as we remembered him in *Softly, Softly*? When he partnered Gielgud and Richardson, no less, in *No Man's Land*, had he been cast not for his positive virtues but because he supplied without knowing it, the uncouth and boomy whiff of the soap opera? Unworthy suspicions all round, of course, but *Crossroads* couldn't help encouraging them. I can't think of anyone, whatever their present distress, who isn't better off without them . . .

Despite such damningly faint praise, Rigby was in due course awarded his Green Card and began (as he put it) to 'commute' across the Atlantic. Some of us are of the view that achieving his new status was a mixed blessing.

He was on the wrong side of the Atlantic so many times when new projects were being mooted, that it meant he missed out on what could have been high-quality work on stage, in film, and on television. And after all the effort, he often felt put out that British actors who did not have Green Cards still performed in the States when he could have been used. Nor did he ever find an American agent that suited him, either in New York or Los Angeles.

However, the upside of his decision was that being in New York suited his lifestyle. In London he was known to wander the streets night and day, dropping into pubs, cafes, clubs, and in to his friends'. In New York, his circle of friends was wider and more consistent, such that he could always rely on meeting out-of-work actors in a particular cafe at a specific time. Cafes and bars seemed to be open much later into the night and he got to know several families and bar owners as a consequence. After surviving in digs and cheap hotels for some time, Rigby eventually found a small studio flat.

It occurs to me that it was during this period that Rigby effectively re-invented himself. Douglas McFerran refers to it as a sort of 'costume change', but I think it went deeper than that. It must surely have been a breath of fresh air to walk out in New York as a relatively anonymous man – with no one knowing much about his background, his drinking years, or the fact that he was TV tabloid fodder in Britain.

Tomorrow Never Dies, with Pierce Brosnan playing James Bond, was released in 1997. Rigby was cast as General Bukharin. He was pleased to be in a Bond film but found it ironic that he got more fan-mail for this cameo role than for any other performances in his career.

A postcard sent in October 1998:

✉ [*Terence Rigby*]

Juliette darling,
    Another quite wonderful morning – fish cakes and chatter – and your gown, charming. Tell me, are you sneaking off and getting them in Paree! Do hope my Norfolk tweeds weren't too bizarre but came post haste from the Royal Links. So clever of you to give the gardener the night orf. Never can understand a word he says. Is he Welsh? Tikitiboo.

❏ JULIET'S TABLE

God-daughter M. is getting married. She wants me to speak at her wedding and to wear 'bizarre' clothes. Is this what I am – a batty old aunt, reminiscent of my own great-aunts who still wore grey lisle stockings, Louis heels, and cloche-type haircuts in the Sixties? The turquoise tunic and harem pants will do very well, but the headgear is a problem. Catherine has a long scarf in the same colour which I can borrow as long as I don't cut it. I buy a turban-shape hat in Oxfam, and then ask dear friend Jack to help in what has become known as 'The Making of the Hat'.

We're having a light supper when Rigby shows up, shares our meal and insists on helping. There follows much pinning and tacking and trying on. Photographs are taken at every stage in the process.

'Give it to me,' says Rigby. 'You need to see what's like it from the back.'

He puts it on his head and poses to the front, sides and rear. Jack and I make adjustments. Then he poses again. We sew on a turquoise feather and fix two ornate hatpins like crossed swords. It looks exotic. Rigby puts it on again, having found a pair of clip-on earrings; he pouts provocatively and lowers his head over one shoulder like a sultry model.

It doesn't stop there. The hat becomes the basis of a party game and the three of us collapse in hysterics, tears pouring down our cheeks.

When Jack leaves, we calm down and I begin to realize why Rigby came round in the first place.

He says ,'It's all up, mate.' I raise my eyebrows in puzzlement.

'It's all up. She's stopped coming round.'

'Old X-Ray? Give it a week. She'll be back.' But he huffs and puffs before blowing out an enormous sigh. 'Not this time. I can't get her out of my head.'

Now is not the time to ask about the list. He's deadly serious . . . but we've been here before. He walks away. She walks away. The recurring topic is 'Commitment'.

But he can't resist telling me that the Nun has been packed off to the Lebanon and he's relieved about that. The mind boggles.

On the morning of my god-daughter's wedding, as I slip into the side door of Llansteffan Church – so as not to attract attention – someone in the crowd by the lychgate calls out, 'Oh look, there's a Sikh.'

*

viii. (Right) 'The Making of the Hat'

Waiting for Godot (1998–99)

I'd been searching for Struan Rodger for some months. I'd look out for him in the French pub on the off-chance and we did exchange the occasional phone call, but somehow it was all rather difficult. Eventually we met up at the Groucho and were allowed to sit in the empty restaurant for a while. I wanted to hear another actor-friend talk about Rigby's rehearsal methods and his approach to an extraordinary Beckett character.

In a production of *Waiting for Godot* in 1998–99, which was promoted by Bill Kenwright for the Peter Hall Company, Rigby reprised the part of Pozzo and Struan played his companion, Lucky. Sir Peter had first directed the play in 1955 – its first British production, and therefore a significant one both for him and Samuel Beckett himself. Pozzo is an impossibly demanding part, but Rigby paced himself well and gave his usual impeccably observed performance in a revival described by Robert Hewison in the *Sunday Times* as 'riveting'. 'Re-casting has done nothing to dent the immaculate clarity,' agreed Michael Billington in the *Guardian*: 'The Pozzo, Terence Rigby, is in fact better than before; he makes the character a comically insecure tyrant forever straining to see what effect his words are having. And Struan Rodger treats Lucky's tirade less as a tour de force than as a vain search for philosophical coherence.'

Struan said he hadn't worked on stage with Rigby before. He remembered Rigby with fondness and reckoned their first meeting, like so many others had been at the Buckstone, but had met up with both him and Sinclair in Soho.

Rigby was rather taciturn and gruff, but I quite like people like that. No easy smile or sneaky eyes. He was gruff, slightly morose – and I got to know him better and better. I got to know him more through Jane Morgan, who was a great friend of his. I worked with him on the wireless, I think, but never in television. He would pitch up when he was drinking. He was omnipresent.

I remember once – I was seeing this girl who invited me round to her flat in Marylebone. I rang what I thought was her bell and a window opened and Rigby stuck his head out. And I thought – Has Rigby got there before me? And then another window opened and there she was. She was in the flat above. This was in Chiltern Street. So we ended up on Rigby and Sinclair's kitchen floor and we demolished a bottle of whisky.

He'd done Pozzo many times before. He used to have great trouble with the rope around my neck. We used to practise with a clothes line. Alan Dobie (who played Estragon opposite Julian Glover's Vladimir) said, 'You just pull it like this –' and nearly broke my neck. But Terry was more sympathetic. We were both very heavy smokers. We'd nip out of rehearsals for a cigarette. If anyone complained about it Rigby would tell them to 'fuck off'.

I was anxious to know whether Struan and Rigby enjoyed working with Peter Hall on this *Godot*. He thought for a moment before answering.

I've worked with Peter a lot and I respect him greatly. I actually like him. I really do – and I've done a lot for him. I suppose we were slightly in awe of him. But . . . Peter did a bit of it, but then went to America and came back to it. He was never quite hands-on. And when Beckett himself had rehearsed *Godot*, he always started with the Lucky speech – I ended up doing the Lucky speech only three times before the preview. It took a long time to get it under my belt – but I only had three weeks – four, max.

I couldn't resist saying that that seemed to be par for the course and that Hall's assistant director would take over. Because this was to all intents and purposes a remounted production, this was perhaps perfectly in order? Struan agreed.

'She was very good. I just had trouble getting it under my belt. I was bloody awful in it.'

I had to disagree – Struan was *splendid* in the role – but I persisted with my need to know about the read-through and the rehearsal.

'It was just a normal read-through. We then just worked it. We skipped the Lucky scenes. I might get half an hour at the end of the day. I would use the time to learn it. He concentrated mainly on Estragon and Vladimir. Not on Pozzo and myself. Terry had done it before – and I wasn't off the book. The Lucky speech is like an aria.'

I wondered whether he and Rigby worked together independently.

'Yes. But we weren't always together because he had scenes with Estragon and Vladimir. But we would run it together. I kept myself to myself until I'd learned it a bit. I remember on the first night, Rigby said, "Are you going to do it like that?" And I said, "I got through it. That's all I care about." In the end we got standing ovations for it.'

I told him that Stephen Thorne regarded Struan as an expert on Lucky.

'God, no! I knew Beckett. I knew the Irish and I could tell you stories about that. I'm not an expert, but I did know how to do it. You can split the speech into three. It's eight pages long. You could split it into 33 lines – that's three lots of eleven. And they go right across an A3 sheet of paper.

So I got them duplicated and stuck them around the rehearsal room – so I could jog my memory and learn it on the hoof. The other thing Peter did was to fill the bags I was carrying with sand. I didn't mind that. It was real. They were weighted . . . so you had to salivate – Greg Hicks used to do that. It was very hard work. It's been likened to a slalom where you are at the top of a ski jump and then about halfway down, you're interacting, in and out, and then in the second half you just went on. Thank God it was in repertory . . . I've played some heavy roles, but that was the hardest.'

I was astounded. 'When Rigby said "Is that how you're going do it", was that *it*? Did he ask any questions after that?' I told him I knew how he used to give Michael Gambon, Douglas McFerran, Gawn Grainger, and others complete notes on their performances. But Struan said they had complete mutual respect:

> He never did that with me. He saw *Medea*, and said nothing. Just long silences. I was very fond of him. But it all blurs – it's like half a dozen oysters – you have a warm memory. Sorely missed. You can tell that by his funeral – how highly thought of he was . . . Peter [Hall] thought he was great. But he thought he was barking – 'barking'! But once you'd crossed him [Rigby], that was it – with some people.
> I recall that in conversations there would be Pinter-like silences.
> I think we were both glad when *Godot* was over. We were counting it down. It was so physically demanding. And he was supportive in that sense. Oh, yes . . . Rigby gave me a Zippo lighter as a First Night present. We were in a pub, and he just tossed it across the table and he said, 'Here you are. It cost me twenty fucking quid to get that engraved.' And on it – heavily ironic – was: *He capered for joy. Piccadilly Theatre 1998.*
> When I was in New York, he was living there. He wasn't drinking by then. It was in 1992 and I'd been touring with *Medea* and we ended up in New York and Dan Bradley reviewed it – he was so acerbic he makes Nicholas de Jongh sound like Enid Blyton.

I told Struan that in a letter to me, Rigby told me he thought it was wonderful.

'Did he? Lovely. He never told me that. One of my oldest friends, Frank Morgan, was living in New York and Rigby would wander into a bar for a cup of tea. He just seemed to know where you'd be. I don't know how white-knuckle it would have been to give up drink . . . I don't know why he stopped. I never saw him drunk.

It seemed important to tell Struan about the brass plaque on the kitchen table, and how he was put off by any new friendship I might have.

'He was very possessive of his friends and kept them apart. He was really part of that era – that tradition of characters like Wilfred Lawson and Robert Newton . . . In *No Man's Land* – that was one of the greatest performances I ever saw. Rigby was part of that tradition. He had a great presence. He had a wonderful presence.'

After this conversation, Struan took me to the French pub for a drink. By chance we met Frank Morgan there, who had known Rigby in New York. He said that they were never really close and Rigby only met him on the odd occasion. Struan then introduced me to an old friend of Rigby from the early days – Dorothea Phillips – who said she loved Rigby, thought he was a wonderful actor, but that he was definitely gay.

❏ JULIET'S TABLE

Another friend, actor Philip Sayer, has died: a tragedy since he was so young and yet was already regarded as a prestigious figure in the theatre. While he was in school in Swansea in the Sixties, he used to come backstage after every Saturday matinee to chat to us in our dressing room. He was going to drama school but had to wait until he was eighteen. One of the ASMs was sacked so I told him there was a job going if he was interested. The following Monday he joined the company and when he eventually came to London, he had a room in our flat. Rigby, of course, was around at that time.

I've been asked to speak at Philip's memorial at the Aldwych Theatre – a huge privilege. I've written a piece based on Dylan Thomas's reporter, young Thomas, from 'Return Journey'.

Rigby says he'll coach me, something I'm not expecting.

Oh, Lord. I have to stand by the kitchen sink and speak.

He stops me almost immediately.

'You can't say "And with apologies to Dylan Thomas". You say "And with thanks to Dylan Thomas". You're always so fucking self-deprecating. Excuse my French.'

I get lessons in projection, when to pause, how to build to a climax, then I have to do it again. And again. He says, 'That piece is too soft.'

He's brought a couple of Kinder eggs which we eat, then make the miniature models and play with them for a moment.

He wants to know what I'm going to wear, but I haven't got that far in my thinking. Before I know what's happening, we're on our way to Long Tall Sally in Chiltern Street, where he picks out a suitable long-sleeved blouse and skirt. When I come out of the changing room, he nods his approval. So I'm all set.

Oh no I'm not. When he's not around, I go to Laura Ashley's and buy a black velvet suit and feel a little less like Eliza Doolittle.

His coaching pays off because the audience roar with laughter in all the right places, the casting agent Mary Selway pursues me, and the guitarist from Queen tells me how much he liked my bit. Rigby, when I tell him, is deeply unimpressed. All I hope is that lovely Phil would have approved; after all, it's his big night.

*

Great Expectations (1999)

In April 1999 the BBC presented a new dramatization of Dickens's *Great Expectations*. Tony Marchant wrote the 180-minute screenplay, which could be broadcast in either four 45-minute or two 90-minute episodes. Julian Jarrold directed, and it was produced by David Snodin.

Rigby was cast as Uncle Pumblechook, and after reading the book was very clear how his character should be played. This was typical of his rigorous research and reading of the original text. I recall helping with lines and how he would question his own interpretation, go back over the text until he was properly immersed in the character.

David Snodin was anxious to give the drama a 'modern edge', an idea embraced by Tony Marchant. Sadly, Rigby's approach was regarded as out of kilter and many of his exchanges were cut during the edit. (In a later 'Master Class' Tony gave to the BBC Radio Drama department, he apparently confirmed that Rigby's performance was not in keeping with his ethos.) In the Press package, Rigby doesn't even appear in the cast list. He never referred to this omission in my presence.

So it's ironic that the one thing that Rigby took from the experience was the phrase 'What larks, Pip, what larks', which he often used in conversation and in letters, despite it being Joe Gargery's catchphrase rather than Pumblechook's. I see that in my diary for 12 April 1999, I wrote that the production 'was okayish but I'm afraid I dozed'.

A few days before this, Rigby heard that Sir John Gielgud's long-term partner Martin Hensler had died. In typical Rigby fashion, he persuaded Phyllis MacMahon to drive him to Wotton Underwood near Aylesbury, where Sir John lived. Although they presented themselves at the door, they were not received.

A letter from Sir John arrived, dated 9 April 1999:

✉ [*John Gielgud*]

Dear Terry,
    I had no idea it was you yourself at the door. You had taken all the trouble to seek me out.

When I begin to feel more human I will try and get in touch with all my friends who have got in touch with me and been so charming about Martin.

I do not know which of the two of you is the cleverest. Everything you do is so skilful and professional.

My love and thanks as ever.

John Gielgud

From time to time Rigby had what he described as a sudden rush of blood to the head. At these moments he would get on a train to Edinburgh or the Outer Hebrides, dash to Stratford by taxi, or a boat to some distant land. Sometimes the flight was to get away, alone, from himself and his internal muddle. At other times, a woman was involved. My diary records a 'very companionable' day with him working in my garden in May: 'He still hankers after X-Ray, but he's keen on a French widow in Paris. Plus ça change. Made a nice supper.' Et plus c'est la même chose. In the Summer of 1999, he met a young Norwegian actress whom he mentored, before deciding to respond to her advances. On 17 August 1999 a postcard arrived from Norway.

✉ [*Terence Rigby*]

Dearest Lady – With hope that you are all well and essentially comfortable ('bloody cheek – treating me like his granny') – and writing. A great deal of almost improbable tale to tell at some moment. There is currently a lady Nina Elisabeth von Kuttner – we share a chalet up a mountain – the daily climb is absolutely daunting to get provisions but I'm getting quite fit. The view from the chalet, 2nd highest on mountain over lake, is nearest to bliss one could hope. Was due to fly back today but am playing truant officially. I cannot describe this situation and do it all justice. Enough – no more.

Love of course to you and Sir Taff and children.

Lord Marylebone

That September, he went off to the States for ten months.

❏ JULIET'S TABLE

'Hello, stranger,' I say in a rather starchy tone. His visits have become less frequent and I think I must have offended him greatly. He's brought two Indian ice-cream things from Mr Mustapha's. He grunts as I make tea and search for a bottle of red.

It drips out, bit by bit. He was offended when my daughter Catherine rang from the basement flat to tell him to shut up when he was doing his Henry V way after midnight. He doesn't want my offspring to think that he is my man. He doesn't like being here when my bloke is in situ.

'You didn't tell me he was coming round. I prefer to be *à deux*.'

'Really?'

'Well, that's how it is.'

'That means you'll have to ring to tell me you're coming round. And you don't like that.'

He grumbles in response. 'I nearly came round the other night and turned back at Warren Street. I don't like other people being here when I'm here.'

'Yes, *sir*.'

'I've got a van at the corner waiting to pick up the carpet.'

At this point I know that all's well. He's managed to say what's bugging him so we can carry on as normal.

But it's all so complicated. At Christmas when I was alone and everyone was concerned for my welfare, he showed up on Boxing Day and we walked along the canal to King's Cross and then along the wastes of York Way. I told him we could have turkey salad when we got back.

And there at the garden gate stood my son and daughter, back a day early from Devon. My (by now) ex-husband was about to get into his car, but I asked him to join us for a snack. Rigby took over. He sharpened the carving knife and stood at the top of the table asking who'd like which bit of the turkey. He was playing the role of head of house – but I have no doubt he would have gone home thinking he'd overplayed the part somewhat.

That's why he's been keeping away, in part. I am not to get the wrong idea about his place in my life. Do me a favour. I'm perfectly happy with my bloke, thank you very much.

But then he says, 'I dreamt I ravaged you last night.'

'Sounds more like a nightmare to me.' I pause. 'Well, what else am I supposed to say?'

Part of me thinks he's testing me. Is he still worried that I might throw myself at him, get into bed with him when he stays the night, or when I stay with him in his place? I ponder as to whether the other Cup-of-Tea Ladies have this problem.

*

Amadeus (1999–2000)

Rigby sent a card to Stephen and Barbara Thorne in October, before the opening of *Amadeus* in Los Angeles:

✉ [*Terence Rigby*]

. . . the mist has risen a centimetre or two – but it seems that whoever played the role before – got himself into some silly corners – pack drill. Vastly inauspicious card from colourful LA but there we are – it's not just anybody that gets 2 missives almost abreast. My feet are killing me – squeezed into very silly high heels – and the podiatrists will grow fat with my visits. That apart all seems to proceed well, overall. There have been quite some text changes as Peter Shaffer is around constantly and also his twin Tony turned up from Australia. A handful of crisps and some salsa and a cup of tea has just relieved me of $18. A Japanese man I chatted to has invited me to Tokyo – so if the worst comes to the worst . . . It's a very large theatre 2–3,000 I believe. We wear mikes in our wigs – perhaps they will introduce stilts before we open. Officially on October 10th – when sadly I shall be temporarily homeless due to a convention. I promise to make further text more palatable. What I'm getting from Peter Hall is 'faster, funnier'. But it's reasonable fun. Love of course,
    Terry R

The remounted *Amadeus* didn't get universally positive reviews in the States, and Rigby rarely gets a mention. But there is a nice quote in *Newsday* (16 December 1999): 'Terence Rigby, as Count Orsini-Rosenberg, clearly enjoys getting to announce that most-believed putdown by powerful philistines, that Mozart's music has "too many notes".'

As before, when touring the USA, Rigby kept a journal. This particular one was extremely difficult to decipher because, having left blank pages during the *Richard III* journal (presumably to fill in later with missed days), he used them for entries in his account of *Amadeus*.

✎ [*Diary*]

Flew SW to Burbank – Oakland – met by Maria Paco. Maria loud due to English – It became a very pleasant time. We spent day on Bay and in San Francisco. Walked Geary Street. Lack Dinner. Saw Ollics old Paris City

Bar. Maria talked – may come to NY during opening times. The whole situation is very disquieting and with luck may even now work out. *Retrospective.* The flight back as we came over the mountains to Los Angeles was very eerie rather like looking down on No Man's Land.

Los Angeles. Biltmore Hotel. 'Amadeus', *Day 20*
Woke at 0310 as it became clear that we were having – what they all used to talk about – an earthquake. It was disturbing in a cold quiet way – not daring somehow to hope anything, almost as if supplication might not be favoured. *Hamlet.* Retrospectively might have 'The fall of the sparrow' – 'If it is not now . . . yet it will come!' [...] It was unsettling for at least a couple of weeks – but the show ground on.

Wednesday. Day 52. 17 November 1999
Having had a letter from Ida B. regards room [...] I then called Ida – to hear the sad news that the artist who I had met in NYC has died. For Ida it had been a terrible shock – and I was sad. I'd seen her wonderful sculptures. Made appointment to see someone about my ingrowing big toenail. The Amadeus shoes have a lot to answer for.

On Amtrak beyond El Paso. *28 November. 1999 D-Day*
The final matinee was the ghastly culmination of three matinees in a row due to Management nicking our day off and giving up Thanksgiving. On that day Thank God Mike drove to an excellent place where daily we had turkey, pumpkin with Bob Terry – and onwards to Beverly Hills Hotel for 'Cocktails' and tremendous feting by the staff. I went off to see the tennis complex. Somehow I managed the packing. Jane G. came round to Grand Promenade at 7:30 – and we left for the sensational Union Station for the 9:55 p.m. Mike was already there and manhandled the baggage and provided a very large bag of goodies – plus a video of the Holyfield–Lewis fight – for Anthony. Lots of photo opportunities and left waving my straw boater – Jane and Mike stranded together to work out whatever they wanted. The goodies bag was crammed with goodies. The generosity of Mike and Bob Terry is quite fazing.

29 November. Amtrak train 2
Slept badly – a bone-shaker – reminded me of my uneasy time on last year's Queen Elizabeth trip. The trick seems to be – become exhausted – then sleep. Was not up to much at breakfast – and didn't suffer the beady academic. Been chestial stingy. Ate well. Several trips into the Black Hole Penitentiary Style Cig Bin on lower decks. Lovely bunch – mostly receiving. Sure it must offend USA regulations. Past California we were into Arizona and then New Mexico – endless amounts of space and scrub and mid-distant hills and small mountain ranges.

Tuesday. 30 November. Houston, Texas
Pulled out 10:25 a.m. – warm sunny. I did Houston – on the platform. Mood more relaxed – avoided the breakfast Academics. Ashley the

135

travelling attendant – a pleasant woman. Upgrade to deluxe would be $200. About 24 hours to Jacksonville. The small room for smoking is like I imagine a mini penitentiary space – highly colourful characters sit around there – as well as staid middle-aged and older folk. At New Orleans some police got on with a sniffer dog – they say – two were held and taken for questions. Had my steak dinner – all complimentary – and hope I'll sleep. Tomorrow is Jacksonville. All my bags of sweets I've given to Ashley my room attendant. The showers aboard are very good. Lots of smoke-room opinions on state of the state and the President and Hillary [Clinton]. Calm anarchy.

Rigby's brother Patrick wrote him a newsy letter to wish him a Happy New Millennium. He gives a round-up of family news, but I suspect this letter was kept because Patrick says there:

✉ [*Patrick Rigby*]

. . . Have finally started to put all your Post Cards over the years into albums. Trying to get them into some sort of date order. You now put dates on most of them, but some not dated and postmarks are often obscure. Post Cards now reaching 180. Would have made a good book. Must be a few thousand words. The earliest one is dated 1991 – don't know what happens before then. Perhaps I didn't save them – or perhaps we weren't speaking, though I don't think that was the case.

Patrick ends the letter, 'Sorry I can't compile a letter like you. Lack of practice and lazy and getting tired. Yours as ever Best Wishes, Pat.'

✎ [*Diary*]

12 February 2000
We're passing by Gulf of Mexico in one nocturnal ride – Bay St Lewis! It happens perhaps with more frequency – perhaps was to do with [*his dresser, turned biographer*] Lovat's Olivier script arriving sent Royal Mail, redirection by Phyllis MacMahon, my Irish actress friend of yonks, with quite a story to tell of her own. A strengthening realization that putting down words gave me – well, more than simple pleasure – I felt 'better' doing just that – than anything that otherwise comes to mind. Certainly right now – acting was strenuous and as elusive as ever – but it was the way my economy worked. I am on Broadway in *Amadeus* – Sir Peter directing. It seems I last recorded some passing notes in this book, way back around Millennium Eve or Day. There will have been reasons – I know – there have been reasons. 'Too late for the Met,' I said after la-la-ing my way down the stairs to drop my dressing-room key off. 'I'm afraid so,' offered Ms Dahling. Did she have to say that? I queried her – feeling really rotten about her response.

Sunday

Dan Mason coerced me as ever to come to Brendan's home for a meal – with Fidelma – where I met Antonio – a Sicilian film actor who cooked excellent pasta – and was a good human person – Brendan is a fine host – and Dan proves to be more and more an interesting man. The 'Olivier Files' has arrived due mainly to Robert's prompting and I was surprised to find that dear Lovat had actually completed his version, and it seemed at face to be a full work. Dan was very complimentary about my professional attitude – much appreciated – *Essex Boys* shown at Warners, Leicester Square. No billing for me – what a shower . . . Where can all that end up? My letter to Kilve Feb 2/3 has not yet got the village postcard I asked for and the mind is racing again.

St Valentine's Day 2000

I strolled mid-town and went into Morgan's Bank – then took a nap – the phone, Ida, woke me around 7 p.m. and I had a good chat with loving affectionate one-off Ida – later I rang and went over to E24 where this so-dear person filled me with food delicacies and I met Marion – later we walked to E23 and saw Marion's very wonderful laid-back den. More laboratory bills arrived so now the medics have taken $345 and $189. Sorra [*consultant*] still has to confirm outcome of one test. Tonight the curious burning tops of chest and left flank plus both lower sides was back in play. Got off letters [...] as well as speaking to Noel in London. Earlier this week, finally wrote to Ray Jenkins and declined Sea Surgeon play – though I'm not sure I'm seeing straight. Also card to Taggs Island. Caroline T. card still lies staring at me.

Wednesday, 19 April

My week's dash to London/Birmingham now over and fading. Spring is rain so far. Snow back on St Patrick's Day parade, and pretty severe, and parade disruption but the band and the cold, cold majorettes played on [...] In NY now, I visit the New Garden Family on 9th twice, thrice, a week and that is a rejuvenating experience. I've been asked to go fishing – at night – when Summer arrives – Don't think I have ever fished. My return heralded my 10th/11th podiatrist trip. Lady Richardson (Mu) died April 7th and also Charles it seems has gone – they were all very, very special. Finally a letter to Sir John which I got done at the 42nd St Library. Last evening met Barbara Caruso, had supper to catch up and a lot of [actor] Bruce [Purchase] talk – later discovered loss of expenses envelope. Shades of '66/'67 at the same theatre when I sent $1,000 to the cleaners. Three awards (nominations) from Outer NYCC for our 'stars'. World Cafe (Raoul) rang to say something had been found. Perhaps my 'Give me a break, Anthony SS!' had got through – will see. Had joke with Michael Sheen. Told him to ease off on the nominations – we want out. He couldn't agree more. His wife has landed a large Hollywood role.

Thursday, 25 May 2000

What a ten days or so. Pat rang to say Sir John died in Wotton

Underwood. I stood under the Longacre lights at 8 p.m. and witnessed the Broadway lights being turned off to mark his Immense Service. Wednesday I attended a memorial at the O'Neill for Alexander H. (Horshit) Cohen (much laughter from assembled), who had produced *The Homecoming* '66/'67 at the Colonial Boston and The Music Box. 4 Tonys, Hal Prince, Robert Whitehead among speakers (*No Man's Land*) – nobody to say thanks on behalf of England. I spent long hours with wonderful Jill Tanner At W14. And turned down $1,000 to play a Bishop in a NYC day soap – 10 pages. Far too little! Nothing further on the big Prague venture – much too rushed video – day after the *Amadeus* closing. Question is – what does one do and not do – for how much?

❑ JULIET'S TABLE

We sometimes go to the Paddington Sports Club where Rigby has been President for many years. He reminds me of a visiting priest doing his rounds of the parish. He shows me the indoor bowls, the outdoor tennis courts, the changing rooms, the snooker tables, and the bar. Everyone treats him with great warmth. There's a sneaky back gate where actors and directors working at the BBC Maida Vale studios can hurry in for a welcome drink. I realize, more and more, how big a part tennis has played in his life. He talks fondly of Summer breaks at Lou Hoad's tennis school in Mijas in Spain and insists I make a special visit when I have to do some research in Fuengirola.

His big achievement is the creation of the annual Equity Tennis Tournament. It always features in *The Stage* and is very popular with actors.

This afternoon, however, he's fretting. The tournament is tomorrow and nothing is ready. I leave my accounts spread all over the table and rush round to Devonshire Street. Rigby is polishing silver cups and still working out the seeding. Actors keep ringing up making last-minute decisions to play.

'You shouldn't have to do all this,' I tell him, outraged on his behalf. 'Give me a duster.'

'The caterer's let me down as well. They'll be lucky to get a glass of water.'

It's too late to find another caterer and he's too proud to ring up members and get them to rally round. Before I leave, I manage to persuade him to ask two people to help. Someone promises a Victoria sponge.

Much later I ring him up to see whether he's made any progress on the catering front. The pathetic little answer is no. I foolishly offer to do what I can.

At the crack of dawn I go to Sainsbury's and buy several dozen scones, sliced bread, jam, butter, sandwich fillings, baking ingredients and cream. By lunchtime I've made a couple of cakes, some jam tarts, and several rounds of sandwiches, and persuaded a friend to give me a lift to Paddington and help set it all up.

They're already playing matches when we arrive. Rigby, smartly dressed in his blazer and flannels, nods in our direction and points to an upstairs room where trestle tables covered in white tablecloths have been set up. The crockery is already laid, in the middle a solitary Victoria sponge. We get to work and eventually make the tennis tea look more or less home-made and welcoming.

All this time, Rigby has been standing with other committee members on the balcony overlooking the courts. He's going to give a papal blessing any time soon. When the tea is brewed in a giant urn, I take two cups out on to the balcony.

Rigby turns in my direction. 'Put it there, would you?' he says in a Ralph Richardson voice. So I do.

'Come on,' I say to my friend. 'I'm out of here.'

That's what he says now, whenever I give him a cup of tea. 'Put it there, would you?'

*

Friends in New York

Rigby, who wandered the streets of New York, made friends with very many people, and if he liked them he would seek them out – often turning up out of the blue, as he did in London. In particular he got to know a Chinese family who ran a small takeaway restaurant near 5th Avenue. The owners spoke very little English and often relied on their small daughter Jocelyn to communicate with the customers. I believe she was about ten years old when he first met her. He helped her with her schoolwork – her English and Spanish. It's obvious from the following extracts from her letter how fond she was of her unlikely mentor – and maybe also how she'd noticed his 'tee-hee' laugh.

✉ *[Jocelyn Chan]*

26 September 2000

Dear Terence Rigby,

¡Hola! ¿Como estas? [*Hi! How are you doing?*] Today, I just receive your letter at 4.30. Right at lunch time. Thank you for sending me the Spanish book. Also the stamps for my father. I am very happy!

At the first day of school, my teacher was there. I told her you went to England. She say she had missed you so much. She also say she had called you, at home. Voice and phone number. No one picks up. She had trys to contact you again but then I told her you went to England . . .

I really liked your hand-writing. Very long and neat. I like how you write. I hope you don't mind my spelling . . . Also, I want almost forgot to add some more paragraphs, before stopping the letter . . . Sorry! I almost forgot to ask a question. Have you heard of the Olympics? I heard them all over the TV . . .

I'm really sorry to hear you had to change your ticket to go back to London, because of the flood that happen at your house . . . I never get to write neat and straight in lines or not lines. Hopefully you won't mind me writing big or small. Not neat and straight.

So . . . I'm pretty much looking forward to seeing you in New York. Nice writing to you. I do have a recorder to play the tapes. Don't worry! Also, they are really helpful! I'm gonna learn more words than my friend! He He He! And good wishes to you in LONDON.

Yours truly,
Jocelyn Chan

P.S. Really Really Really Really Really are looking forward to seeing you!

Enclosed is a complicated multi-coloured origami flower. (This is one of relatively few letters that Rigby kept and – I'm certain – treasured.)

 [Diary]

Wednesday, 1 December 2000
    Into Jacksonville at 2 p.m. Hitched cab to local shopping centre. All black population. Bussed back to get 4:19 (at 5 p.m.) the No. 98 – SAV-NYC. Stopped smoking at 5 p.m. until 8 p.m. – then OK – 8:30 etc. Several faces on similar journey, though none from LA. Called Anthony before train – seems we are all out for dinner – and he says it's not warm . . . Really taking to coffee. I seem to have a second wind – after three nights on board Amtrak. We hit a truck prior to Jacksonville and the Police held up the train. Sent large suitcase on to Penn. NYC. Sadly it will be dark at Savannah on arrival. Card to Stephen Thorne.[10] A few cards – through the night.

Sunday, 19 December 1999
    A day off after a long spell. Coward's *Waiting in the Wings* immensely enjoyable – visited Rosemary Harris who was her ever good – met Lauren Bacall – impeccable stage performance, welcoming and just great – held my hand for at least ten seconds – how about that? Also met chatted with daughter and son. Rosemary suggested we should meet and have a snack. No review in *Sunday Times. Wings* reviewer same nonsense star split as *Amadeus.* No question Lauren Bacall most, most incredibly powerful stage actress.

1999 New Year's Eve 2000
    Walked down to E24 and telephoned dear Ida to find she sounded well. Back to apt W45 St – then around 10 p.m. cabbed out to Brooklyn to Carrol St. Saw 2000 in with a very young crowd on the roof – a spectacular fireworks display. Danny, young Jewish actor, and Colleen, ran me back to Lower E9 at 1st. Had coffee with Danny – cabbed back home. Two police cars at Whitby, plus saw dear Rose, the Residents President. I guess the day, eve, cost me $50. Bed about 4:30 a.m. A sense of settling in to this ghastly but small haven of an apartment – and city. NYC

---

10   'If you should arrive in New York City,' it reads in part, 'I will do my best, you know I will, to find a little window for you. Sadly I can't promise I will – you will have read how demanding the press are out here. I find Shaffer's writing [in *Amadeus*] from the sublime to the awkward and awful to speak. I thought the performance I saw at the Old Vic was tremendous. Whether we will get there is all unknown – there does seem to have been lots of new pages passed around and I definitely have not clocked in yet – that is certain. Perhaps the wig and walking stick will point the way – my Italian is coming out Vietcong, Welsh Baptist, but then only the mob will notice, I'm sure.'

March 8/9 2000
 Somehow strayed along Ninth Ave and had a meal 11:30 p.m. in a small Chinese restaurant – was taken by the family atmosphere – the small daughter, talking all the English – such a beautiful fascinating face.
 Today eschewed Ollie's on Times Square and returned to the little restaurant – where I found the daughter studying the Bible. I found a moment to ask her to read some to me – which she did – 'very good but a little quick', I told her. She asked me if I was a teacher. I said no, I was an actor. It later occurred to me that her speed or lack was fine and I was in a sense wrong – only when words are being presented to an audience to create an effect is pace in need of concern.

Sunday 19/20 March
 Snow marred St Patrick's parade – though one young group provided much applause by topless show. Noel, over in London, married Kate. Patrick had his hernia op and Joseph rang to say he was fine. [...] Francis Delduca, who had already seen *Amadeus*, met and took me to dinner down near W11 St. Meanwhile Ida has become 80 years of age – and I must mark it somehow. Also send [...] two letters or contacts to ignored friends Maria José and Pamela Mozza – all in need of attention. Walked 11th – W46. Good. Finished David Hare: *Acting Up*. Excellent read.

Thursday, 30 March (191 performances)
 Yesterday before the matinee, after a fearful night of unrest – unwisely but most glad – met Michael, Finty, and Mrs Dame Williams-Dench at Pig and Whistle E55/6. Michael looked great – very late – a few drinks and off to matinee. Felt not good, booked Sorra the Estonian for next day. He confirms again that all is not lost. Cheer up. Relax.
 [...] Four to go before London possibility for 'leave'. What can I do about [*'X-Ray'*]? Mostly, yes that's the word. I am marked totally. I feel invariably quite 'perdu'.

Sunday, April 2/3
 Two hours across the Atlantic on BA114 on leave and decided to cross over, for in much need of a change – to say the least. Economy terribly cramped these days – and night flights – everyone desires to sleep. D[avid] Suchet [*who played Salieri*] climbed up the stairs specially to wish one a pleasant leave. Last evening at Broder party taken at Cafe Nicholes W52. – a Maime folk gathering impressive. Jake [Broder] as Mozart at matinee was bit wild animal – touching, grabbing, holding.
 I partially felt an unusual EASE of performance – perhaps more easily in the first act. But on reflection – a physical differential! Stop. This is supposed to be a BREAK. Let's just loll.

❑ JULIET'S TABLE

He's just been on a date with Gillian Diamond and because he can't sleep, he's come round for a chat. The cheek of it! He's got women all over the place, all of them eating out of his hand. I'm probably the worst offender. I should tell him where he gets off, but I know I never will, because he has been so kind to me.

He tells me that on Monday night he took Britt Ekland out to dinner. 'She could boss me around, you know, and I'd probably obey her.'

'You? Obey?' It's a cue to talk about marriage and I tease him mercilessly. He recalls John Gielgud saying to him, 'You never married?' 'Never,' Rigby replied. To which Sir John said, 'Nor I, thank God. Who would want to bring children into the world today?'

We laugh. He stays the night and doesn't emerge until gone eleven. I'm pleased because I've been able to work. He makes tea and brings a mug over to my desk singing, 'Happy Mother's Day to you, Happy Mother's Day to you, Happy Mother's Day, dear Juliet, from Llewellyn and me.' (Llewellyn is the cat.)

Over a late breakfast we discover the lovely word 'fecundate'; it's one of things we like to do – thumb through the dictionary looking for interesting words.

*

Troilus and Cressida and *Saved* (2001)

Peter Hall cast Rigby as Agamemnon in *Troilus and Cressida*, which was paired with Edward Bond's *Saved* for one of his US seasons. Jack Atkinson, our much loved mutual friend, and I decided to pay a surprise visit to New York to see the play.

We arrived in New York on 3 May 2001, and having enjoyed a matinee of *Follies* on the 5th, walked along to the American Place Theater to book tickets for the play. A matinee of *Troilus* was about to finish, so we hung around the stage door. I hid behind Rigby as he signed autographs. In a funny voice I asked, 'Can I have your autograph, Mr Rigby?' Without looking back he said, 'Wait your turn.' When he finally faced me, he was shocked, but obviously pleased. The three of us walked to Bryant Park for a cup of tea and a chat. Bryant Park is probably the most civilized public space I've been to, where people play chess uninterrupted, and talk, argue, discuss, and have fun. It was a favourite haven for Rigby when he was living in New York.

Our hostess, Rosalie Lemontree, joined us for the matinee I'd booked. It was performed in a sand pit. I found it an unsatisfactory play and a muddled production. Rigby, who shocked me by speaking in a convincing American accent, seemed more relaxed in a Shakespeare part than I'd ever seen him before (an opinion that Peter Hall shared, when I later spoke to him). I thought Rigby's performance was as powerful and grounded as always.

'*Troilus* got a bad review in the *New York Times*,' I had written in my diary on 1 May, 'but Rigby comes out of it well. He's got a punishing schedule.' Quite how punishing is made clear in a letter he wrote to Stephen Thorne at around this time:

✉ *[Terence Rigby]*

Dearest people [...] near the end of our eighth week of rehearsals and not at all looking forward to a full ninth, being already on previous six [...] believe that we are all [beginning] to feel quite pilloried by Sir Peter Hall

144

and his insatiable thirst to grind his fellows near to pulp in order to protect his personal reputation. I think it insufferable, and sense I shall never wish to work with him again – how nobody is buckled under it all is, for now, quite a wonder. He is an insensitive, selfish chap. Enough (absolutely insatiable). God how awful that one has to confront one's blessing. Does one really? I just hate wandering about in the physical condition of a zombie. I now believe he never ever knows what he wants, ever, and makes a positive creative virtue of it. Anyway, the port is with you. I've been invited to a gala where 'Sir' will feature, also Sir Ian Holm will recite W.S. this Monday – our day off of course. Bastards.

Following quite quickly, another letter which shows his frustration both with Sir Peter Hall and himself:

✉ [*Terence Rigby*]

St Patrick's Day 2001
   Having received from Sir Peter, Dame Judi, the crippling news of Norman Rodway's departure – I pause to say farewell, dear loveliest of men, with whom I had extremely recently in frivolous correspondence, regards *Troilus*. He was a rare outrageous man – and I shall miss him. Oh, I shall miss him. I have written to his lady via the SOA Theatre. Well – on with the motley. Tomorrow sees the last performance of *Saved* – a limited run of four or five weeks – and let me assure you that there were, are, good reviews both personal and overall – alongside the 'orrido' – again personal and overall. To fill my days, as it were, I have, since the first preview of the Bond, been rehearsing usually mostly 9:30 to 5:30 each day with Sir Peter + 2 assistant directors – using their rehearsal rooms at the same location. So it is as well that *Saved* is going, gone, dead parrot. The foothills of this most recent excessive mission having been reached – the ascent to Jove remains – in the round – at the same location. There will be a gnashing of teeth before bedtime. There really will. Any 'Aggard Hagamemnon will receive (if at all) sensationally cursory reviews, and that is certain – there is nowt like being prepared. Though dear friends always rush to reassure me that my fears of iambic tempo are excessive, as you do it naturally. I find in the end that they are either ill-trained twits like myself or sycophantic no-gooders. However, on the plus – I finally this evening got a scene in *Saved* right, after desperate, desperate struggles – NIL help from a sun-soaking Dominique Beach bum of a director. All down to doing some lip and diaphragm work – thank the Lord for Clifford Turner and the Cicely Berry Brigade. More on this area, but for now quite enough . . .
   The main acting area is a circular sandpit – that will be fun – dump the iambics – just try and stand up. Tony Church and myself are the two stray Brits. I'd dumped the Bronx that I started off with, and back to RADA-ish speaking. Spoke to Tony who is determined to stay in the Kansas area. Achilles is black, as is Diomedes (or rather Diomeedeees). Don't even

start on Greek names. I am class dunce in spades . . . I've recently had 15-years-sans-the-sauce anniversary. Well at least I have been spared to flounder. The older US chaps are a pretty entertaining likeable bunch and 'Wait until you see the Duke of Buckingham' tales go down a treat.

[Sir Peter] refuses to come and review our performances and leaves us to a fascist stage manager – on a day-to-day onslaught. However, I'm sure any missive this writer submits on this matter would rebound upon his own rebellious head – so I may cower quietly on the fourth floor.

In retrospect, I wonder whether Rigby felt so disgruntled by the way the play was directed that he just relaxed into the verse and spoke it with great confidence. It's interesting that he abandoned his Bronx accent and reverted to standard English in *Troilus*, though the *New York Times* was less than kind to Rigby's interpretation of Harry in *Saved*: 'Mr Rigby's delivery is so monotonous – and his low-rent English accent so broadly affected – that his lines are largely indecipherable.'

In August 2001, Rigby was back in London. We must have had one of our confessional sessions in Randolph Street, which resulted in a postcard dated the 13th:

✉ [*Terence Rigby*]

Dearest, about my favourite card – the Post Office (Manhattan) I mean: Sunday was most gratefully received. What a pity I find it necessary to blurt things out to you. Bearable I do hope but do regret. 'Yes I am a mess.' Good poetic ring to that. So you think we've 10/15 or so to go. Would Ladyship mind if we say, round it up to 20. Ta ever so. 'I shall wave my stick and spit' another poetic lurch. I hope that all pro. stuff is continuous triumph AND that your sojourn to Welsh Wales will prove a glorious, glorious rest and FUN too. Have you made much headway with the scandalising version of my Biography? I've certainly started on yours.

Ever affection, Lord Marylebone X

It was strange to read this postcard again. It describes the nature of some of our evenings together – the speculation about death, his insecurities, and mine. Ironic that he should joke about our respective biographies. Odd . . .

Another postcard, undated, but I believe dating from September 2001, is a Vermeer street scene with the caption . . . 'Marylebone-on-Sea':

✉ [*Terence Rigby*]

Wed.

Look, old girl – dashed bad luck you couldn't make the trip. Glad(ys) of course is not behaving – keeps sticking her dress up her knickers and dipping her toes in the tide. Not on – what! Sneaked off for a quiet donkey ride, much to Bertie's annoyance – very much reminds one of the old pig-sticking times in Delhi. Quite miss old Vicky now and then. Glad's off again – chasing the life guard. Ah well. Boxing Day perhaps. Chin, chin.

    Bugsy

Dearest. about my favourite card - the Post Office Mean

Gratefully received. What a pity
I find it necessary to blurt things out to you. Believable
I do hope - but do regret. "Yes I am a mess." Good
poetic ring to that. So you think were 10/15 also to go-
would Ladyship mind if we say, round it up to 20.
To ever so. I shall weave my stick another spit
another poetic lunch. I hope that all pro-
stuff is continuous triumph AND that
your sojourn to Welsh Wales will
prove a glorious glorious rest and
FUN too. Have you made much headway
with the scandalising version of my Biograph?
I've certainly started on yours.

Your affectation
Lord Mandible one X

Lady Camden

28 Randolph Street

Camden

London NW1

ZIP+4

ix Postcard

148

The Last True Believer and
Smelling a Rat (2002)

R igby played the title character, a British diplomat, in *The Last True Believer*, Robert William Sherwood's post-Cold War play, in its Seattle Repertory Theatre premiere.

✎ *[Diary]*

January 2002

Arrived in city [Seattle] January '02 from London. Rehearsals commenced January 11th. Went on monorail, my first ever, and glided about in the shops downtown. Fell in with an actress person, but didn't pursue the matter. Robert W. Sherwood was around all the time, it seems – and first several days were spent 'at the table' – a practice which is more well known here than the UK. It seemed to go on forever – without producing much – but there was a lot of rewriting or shaping going on – by RWS back at 200 Roy St. I had a free apartment – most practical. During some of the rehearsals I got emotion-shy and giggled a lot – I do not approve of being stared at before I'm settled – which I believe promotes this awkward situation. I say it myself – I worked very hard – writing my role out and used up three whole pads from Bartells Drug Store. Though Kevin [*the part played by Coby Goss*] and RWS and myself found a suitable haven in the Mecca Cafe-bar dive near Queen Anne.

This whole period – even today – was peppered with visits to the podiatrist – though generally I've worked less. Except in last three weeks when I started to climb Queen Anne Hill – a severe test – I never got to stop – 'puffed' less than three times. Now I've been told by Doc Meehan that four times a week is to be my quota – to build against high blood pressure. He also put me back on 20-mg Beta Blockers. I continued to strut and fret with sc. 1.4, though I enjoyed it – though early performances were perhaps gabbled – the sheer embellishment of much of my text was of major concern – and the rat-tat-tat-tat sequence with Coby. However, what I did achieve was a certain showing-off in the character. He was one of those supremely confident Foreign Office/ Varsity-bred men – utterly drenched in confidence – I also (in sc. 2.2: the important scene – as Leonard always put it) began to learn how to speak into the heart and faces of those in the auditorium – to always bore into them [and] – something of a miracle in personal acting terms – lost my fear of soliloquy. For now – hopefully for ever. I had written to Sir Peter Hall – and received a warm letter – talking about his new Greek venture at the NT in London.

❏ JULIET'S TABLE

Daughter Catherine rings from the Barbican. She's an associate director for Theatre de Complicite and is currently working with the National Theatre of Japan who are touring with *The Elephant Vanishes*. They've been in London for a week or so and apparently they want to see a typical British home.

'Will you make an after-show supper, Mum? We'll bring beer and wine. You don't have to make a fuss . . .' As if a bowl of crisps would do. Ideas, please. I ring various friends for inspiration and finally settle for a Japanese/Mediterranean fusion dish (recommended by Ned Chaillet), a large piece of topside, a pisaladière and various salads – all very typically English. Then I ring Rigby to help host the evening. Tim McMullan comes too, and so begins perhaps the most extraordinary occasion ever held around the table, upstairs in the sitting room, and out in the tiny garden. Have I mentioned that the house is next to the viaduct that carries the North London Line, and that every twenty minutes or so, when a train passes by, you have to raise your voice to a shout if you're outside and the house itself shakes?

About twenty Japanese and British actors, technicians, and Catherine arrive, with two interpreters. They all seem to carry cameras and take pictures of everything in sight – the table, the shutters, open and closed, the outside of the oven, the food coming out of it, my vintage clothes, and Llewellyn the cat. Rigby is entranced. After a quick catch-up with Tim McMullan (a fellow actor in *Richard III* and *Wind in the Willows*), he chats up the leading lady, with the help of an interpreter, and leads them both out into the garden.

When they suddenly leave en masse like so many Cinderellas, Rigby does the washing-up and tells me this has been a night to remember. 'Charming people. Charming.'

*

Seeing Rigby perform on Broadway, walking in Bryant Park, and having a meal in the New York Joe Allen's, allowed me to picture him more easily from afar. The Green Card was making its mark on his life in more ways than one. I believe he still had high hopes of making it big in Hollywood and in the meantime immersing himself in provincial productions, working with different directors, and perhaps, after some odd experiences, re-evaluating his opinion of Sir Peter Hall.

After *Troilus and Cressida*, I had a clearer idea of how he was able to take more risks. He was far away from the prying eyes of the media and press in the UK; he was being cast in unlikely roles for Rigby. He probably relished this.

What follows is another journal, not just of Mike Leigh's *Smelling a Rat*, but the traumas and amusement of being cast in a Julia Roberts film and his continuing exploration of the people and the streets of New York. I also sense that he is beginning to see the importance of chronicling material for his memoirs.

✎ *[Diary]*

Spring 2002

Before I returned to London – prior to Seattle – while down in Union Square – I sought out – at his earlier request – Nick Hytner – who was rehearsing at NY Ballet place near 20 West St – we had a coffee – gateaux lunch – and he was tremendously friendly – rehearsing *Sweet Smell of Success* – at that time prior to opening Chicago – which brings me to regret the Sh'ite Hawk reviews he has just got in *NY Times* – I hope it survives – it's a really expensive show. The same 'critic' had butchered us in *Amadeus* – disgracefully cutting up the sensationally good David Suchet. A show which I had had a poor time in – due to not being very good and the fierce domestic problems [...] – and being in total lack of sympathy with the lady S[tage] M[anager] – authority gone rotten. Bruce [Purchase] had tipped me about [her]. And indeed she was a pleasant good sort with strings of very impressive credits [...]. There was only one serious moment when I thought she was interfering with my interpretation – and I said so – publicly in front of Leonard [Foglia] – She was probably right – but I was momentarily 'saddened' – since I cared so much – was very committed to the piece. It did finally help me to understand the Finale a bit more – eventually – very eventually. Such embellishments. I'm lolling about with my boxes – not yet quite able to get away – and due out of my apartment in two days.

I start the new off Broadway Mike Leigh play April 8th. Have spoken to Jimmy Coate in LA about NY film but looks as though my Californian trip has yet again been put on hold. I do have some stern reservations about having accepted it. Nil style money. Thank the Lord for the *Tinker, Tailor* rerun of a Christmas ago. Seems to have built a lasting Reserve – for now. Have been taking much pleasure from the re-born Molière *Don Juan* show in the main house – the genius man Stephen Wadsworth at the helm – a lovely talented company. One chap actor saw my original Broadway *No Man's Land* – '76. I caught myself as our spy character now and then – speaking like Sir Ralph, my dearest pal friend – How much he and lovely Sir John – gave me – not forgetting my ever ever sponsor, Sir Peter. Julia, my niece, was in to see [*Last True Believer*] and seemed to be most thrilled.

She's an actress herself but I've not been able to see her – now lives in Vancouver – teaching, but presently involved in a Masque play up there as well. I found her truly lovely and affectionate and was glad she came. Had tea today with Helen Javid – my niece Joanna's friend here – with her lovely baby girl. Finally spoken again with John Dunhill – who's lost his mother's dog – and sounds a little grey – but at least he's discovered – with much help from Phyllis – a long lost daughter from his past. I like being in touch with him – he talks a lot – about all sorts, and his ardent pipe dream is returning to UK – after probably 25 plus years in Montreal. We all go back to the Kismet Club with John – and of course Dublin and The Open Air *Twelfth Night* with dear Kelly Fitzpatrick (USA) – a sad loss when it happened – and now.

I must pack that box – but before I do – I'm going to pop out for a midnight glimpse up at Mecca. I had an earlier unscheduled kip. Julia should by now have flown in to Birmingham to visit the family. Phyllis [MacMahon], who has been working hard on my behalf, to let my Devonshire Street flat – may, it seems, be on the point of success – for a three-month stint [...]

Post-script. NYC. I took Seattle–NYC Amtrak via Chicago. About 3 1/2 days – snowbound Montana – White Fish – which was quite goose pimply [...] Tiring smoking situation on The Three Rivers last leg into Penn Station. Went to stay at Seafarers – Union Square.

8 April 2002

First rehearsal *Smelling a Rat*, Samuel Beckett Theatre. Following my optimistic impression of my performance in *Last True Believer* in Seattle – Day One here at Christopher Street was a tiring, warm, crowded atmosphere and I wondered quite how it would come out – I have an immediate problem with the set layout even before we rise from the table, to block it.

I called Sorra a couple of days ago – not around – and fixed to visit Dr Gold on Wednesday. Accountant here Thursday – that's not at all clear UK< USA – and then there is what quite to do regards 166 Harley St. I did convey a message but again did agree to visit there after three months – which is up. Am trying to read, reread Act One before tomorrow's rehearsal. No. 11 is trying – 'the living factor' is not conclusive to work or rest – or the local sounds. Met Dan [Mason] after work and strolled in Washington Square – He's bright – talkative, pleasant – helpful – a pal. Joseph has been very unwell – and though I've written to him – lack current day to day news. Was able to sit in sun down on nearby Riverside East and wonder quite where the Twin Towers had stood.

Thursday, 18 April '02. NYC

Only today about Day 10 did we get into Act Two, meaning lot of time wasted – though I took a day off yesterday with a streamer of a cold. The work seems to be coming along OK. Scott Elliott [director] seems OK – in some ways very approachable. The rehearsal room is the pits – with echoes to boot – awful. A mini heatwave just now – can't wait for June 30th, our end date. This farce is 'new' to me – maybe I'll learn a bit – I cannot stand the way the table staff laugh all the time at work in progress – I'd prefer they just shut up. It's a cultural difference for me. Caro S. decided to withdraw after a week – quite a mystery – And initially horrific news of Henry Goodman being fired after 30 shows in *The Producers*. Penny Wesson was quoted as having phoned him after the matinee from London. PW was front-of-house manager at Goldsmith St (with Ted) during [John] Neville, [Frank] Dunlop, [Peter] Ustinov triumvirate in Nottingham. Saw Frank in NY about 18 months ago – wonderfully jolly man – goes back – back.

At open-air coffee house – NYCS venue – reflected over coffee – not advisable – varying highs, lows thoughts. Not very immediately productive one. Israel, Palestine in thick of it – Colin Powell floating the Middle East. This play in rehearsal. Mrs Muscular in Devonshire St block. Phyllis doing a good job – feel a modest nuisance – Freddie back from India for a while. Being made aware of desperate human poverty – it's tough, really tough for some – many I observe around E13/14 [...]. Here I am – much lack of control – with a bloody cell phone that I can barely work – and being buffeted around – without foresight or plan. Though I have thrown my hat in for *Copenhagen* [by Michael Frayn] at Seattle – I quite doubt that that will come up trumps – Why does it all seem tough to me? Can I believe that to be a good option – always? I am nevertheless sure that life has blessed me – so many times. I wonder how oppo Kevin oops Coby [Goss] is faring in Chicago. And how I shall move regards the Paddington Club! The women – young all here – are simply staggeringly pretty – with so many crazily beautiful moves. Discovered only this evening that Irene – Ukrainian of Dunkin Donuts E14 – is married with a six-year-old son – now in Ukraine. Seem to have known her for a year or so – very 'en passant' friendship.

Tuesday, 23 April. Shakespeare's Day. 2002
An unkempt start of day. 8:30 a.m. [...] Do more for oneself as opposed to work. Take care of oneself. About a month in now to my cell phone – and still having big problems. Each time you see the light in the trees – the forest moves – it's not all that amusing. Devonshire St seems okayish for 3, 4, 5 months – but the domestic strife is aggravating. Conditions in rehearsal room still [*indecipherable*] – New York *Daily News* were in today snapping [...] Feel chesty, and not easy to feel – well – in control.

8 May 2002
First preview of *Smelling a Rat* by Mike Leigh at Nouveau Samuel Beckett Theatre W42. Last two weeks at our dreadful rehearsal room at 154 Christopher – usual unproductive scenario. Can hardly say I look forward to our new venue even: it's also a strange 'shape', character-wise. B[rián F.] O'Byrne took a snap at me – well deserved perhaps – regrettably I had no response – that scene defeats me as yet – and I've no answers. I went to Michelle [Williams]'s loft for an hour or two. Delightful company. There's been some chit-chat in the *Daily News* I discover [around 28 April] and the odd photo does seem to have come out well – despite my misgivings at the time. Mike Leigh is now with us. He is very direct. Some last-minute

changes to the reading of the prison section caused me some problems –
after I thought I had it sorted. A lot of curious upstaging which seems to
be Scott E[lliott]'s style – maybe for this play. Importantly – I did phone
the club in Paddington [...] the Club is an important worrying matter. The
first preview had some very good moments – but. Michelle is clearly a very
special person – to me.

Wednesday, 15 May 2002
    Not at all feeling any lasting, firm comfort with this *Smelling A Rat* – no
matter how many times we do it – and we haven't even opened yet. Quietly
cursing my colleagues and director and author – and myself – the terse
scene evades me – it seems – completely. Extraordinary day – 3–4 hours –
spent at Actors Credit bank [...]
    Oh dear: Michelle – oh dear: Valerie.
    Second returned letter from CAH in Oklahoma.

12 June 2002
    Took a tumble on stage – toys – and spent 6–7 hours in St Vincent's
– hairline fracture of right wrist. The Saturday shows cancelled – no
understudies. Soft-bandaged up. Iago– Desdemona saga – very potent in
my head. Fidelma – J. Rayner – Dan Mason – all called to check on my
wounds. My three gentle gossipmongers. Trying to field off Lady Shaw.
'Cast' now off. Somewhat soreish but thankfully it's a stark reminder. Cigs
up NY $7:50.

Wednesday, 12 June 2002
    So much – actually – seems to have taken place since I last wrote here.
The tiresome rehearsals at 154 Christopher St – haven't been called and
waited so long ever, it seems, – often bumping into Jeffrey Horowitz –
TFNA [Theatre for a New Audience] boss. Very difficult to determine if he
will ever forgive me. He's achieved a lot. Stratford, etc. *Cymbeline*, which
Patrick went across to see. To my surprise: company of *Rat* feted by B[en]
Brantley *NY Times* review – He is the BIG ONE. *NY Post* OK, *Variety* good
– for me. Much talk of 1 Sept. extend – eventually got sized down to 14
July due to Michelle Williams, E[ddie] K[aye] Thomas commitments. Just
as well since our Irish colleagues took humbridge [*sic*] and lashed out – Life
has been most tricky perf.-wise since then – it's a small D[ressing]/R[oom].
This Michelle link crushes me – though I'm a clown of high order. RFK
Room is becoming after 2 months fairly claustrophobic – so many events.
    Back at Devonshire Street, Mrs Muscular has broken out and the Indian
students are off June 15th, this Saturday – Others may take on until Dec –
wanting 12 months though. The largest non pro problem is my Presidency
– I've written to remarkable Ray Gibbs – a somewhat high flown text –
thank goodness I can recognize this – though have to dispatch it. Thinking
off cuff when I can guarantee the AGM and 8 Boards. I probably should
consider my position. It would be a sadness but I know deep down that my
influence and energy for the task is low. I also know that if I am to have
– somewhat Oatmeal – an American career with a small 'c', I must free

myself from serious UK influences except family matters. The loss of Patsy Facchino made me think a deal along such sad lines. The idea of 34 or so performances here is reasonably discomforting – if not more. It's very hot, muggy.

Coming downstairs one morning, I saw the familiar pale-blue colour of an airmail letter on my mat. It's always such a pleasure to receive a letter from Rigby, so I make coffee first and sit down at the table to devour it.

✉ [*Terence Rigby*]

16 June 2002

Dearest Lady C[amden],

Had a silly trip on stage – it's littered with toys – tiny wrist fractures – was ghastly painful had to cancel two shows – no understudies. But back for Sunday matinee doing it all left-handed – tricky . . . Jane sent a note to tell me that you were in the Middlesex – but all superseded as we had had our chat days ago. Perhaps I should not be writing at this stage but wanted to say hello again soon – despite the spider scrawl. I hope you are settling well. Don't forget the Prof and the madman Simon Winchester would while away many slow hours for you. Depending on satisfactorily trying to mike up properly, I have decided from July 1st to let my flat for six months to a boy and girl both in their final years – which, showed on paper, means an amount of stability from them [*He talks about what he should do if he comes back to London*] . . . plus of course the occasional two-night weekend break in London with a very charming girl – I knew her a very long time ago – from Llansteffan as I recall. She used to like having the odd chap from time to time – and I believe she went into writing or something arty-crafty – anyway I'll give the public library a ring and see if I can track her down – you never know – she might have had a second wind. Life's like that, milady. I'm not terribly optimistic of much here – flop with agent, I'm afraid. Again had done so much for myself – had a lot of luck and what have I achieved? . . .

It's Shakespeare's birthday and I forgot – how bizarre can that be? Joseph was very down, but is now mended – hopefully with strength to spare. As for myself, I can never quite make up my mind whether I am less than 100% over – or have become a New York hypochondriac. I thought one night, 'To hell with it!', flashed my British Mastercard down at The Metropolitan Opera House and saw *Rigoletto* in Italian – the music of which I find quite heavenly. It's the only tape I carry in my bag. I do hope you persuaded someone – one of your chosen chaps – to come along and sweep the yard in preparation for your Summer recitals – and that my lupins are moving into form.

A few weeks later another missive, after learning that I'd recovered from a malignant melanoma.

155

✉ *[Terence Rigby]*

6th July 2002

Dearest Juliet, née Lady Ace. Ace high news – thank the powers that be. Not easy to express my highest delight as will be yours and all those that care for you – congratulations on seeing it through – truly. So let's turn to the latest Marylebone escapades without more ado, milady. I have it necessary to cross over to Brooklyn. Literally one street from the Brooklyn Academy of music, where we did *Richard III* back in 1992/3. An English pal has gone to Welsh Wales with his wife and child and has made a very pleasant deal that in the circumstances I could not refuse, though one Spike, a most neurotic cat, is all part of the deal. Good thing is, I can shove off when I like, as there is a back-up team of ladies happy to take up duties, at the drop of a doll's dillie (!) – this – so I have a little garden – one very huge tree – a fish pond, three goldies, and it's on two floors – and it's difficult to move about – never have I beheld so much semi-organized clutter – it's like a spilled-over library. I live in the spaces and of course I only smoke in the garden. Turning to Spike, he's a handful – meow meow all the time – often refuses food – and only seems at home when I am roaming around starkers naked – well I suppose he thinks I am John, since we all look the same starkers. But it's taken into the fourth day to get some sort acknowledgement of any sort – it's good training for Camden Town and you choose when and if they come around. Yesterday – my day off was horrendous 105° humidity and I was taking my wardrobe from Union Square – it was also Independence Day. I woke up this morning to a distinct purring and to my shock horror – it wasn't Spike – it was another cat – where you could imagine – couldn't corner it, to ban it, it took two hours – until it became clear that it belonged to upstairs – this place is so cluttered – five or six cats could actually hide around the place – I think there is a secret entrance. However, the domestic crisis passed. All this has not assisted my occasional panic moods – a vaguely new thing. In the midst of matinees, Saturday night is now. I hope you will not overdo the celebrations, but gently does it – for now. I'm certain I have your Welsh Wales number in one of my small diaries – so I can always keep in touch if you're out of London. I must say that though my wrist is technically better – soft cast removed – after writing and during the act of writing it does develop sharp nasty muscle pains. Hopefully it won't go wrong. Meanwhile I hope Daniel and wife are reunited – keep yourself well and truly well, milady – again such wonderful news – I will endeavour to telephone and get true update of your intentions. For now, congrats again – keep your powder dry, Laddie – all nonsense – the deepest affection.

TR de Marylebone.

✎ [Diary]

10–11 July 2002
Banner headline. *Daily News*. ROD STEIGER DEAD. He made 125
films. During '66/'67 he was at a party given in honour of Harold Pinter and
the cast of *The Homecoming* at Sutton Place – given by Milton Goldman
and Arnold Weissberger. As I left he was in front of a taxi queue but the
driver wouldn't take him – so he walked instead. The taxi seemed oblivious
when I mentioned it. That was the year of *In the Heat of the Night*. Today
I was moved on his death and was caused to reflect. My wrist hurts –
aftermath of my stage fall. Benjamin Dimmit and his nephew were at the
show, had tiresome if amiable drinks at West Bank, where our Last Night
party is to be held. Earlier had sent my Constitution letter to Stephen Foster
– for the Board Meeting. The show, personally, was a shade comfortable but
again the voice was a bit below par. We have to do two on the final day 14th
due to having Independence Day off –'boiling shower'. Slowly getting hang
of Spike the cat down at 130 Fort Green Place near BAM.
  Mike Leigh, in an interview with Matt Wolf (NYC), said that having
spent time with the company decided that 'everyone's got it'. He also said,
'Apart from the fact that Scott's a good director, he's also good at casting.'

10 August 2002. Post-Beckett Theatre
Been down in leafy Brooklyn now well over a month thanks to John
Rainer, Margie Chloe being in Porth Madog. Been amusing myself doing
some gardening and dealing with antics of cat Spike and the gentle gold
fishes. Am working on trying to relax down – a gentler spell of August
weather presently helping. Find myself constantly dropping into Plaza St
43rd at 9th Ave to see Martin, Mel, Geo., Arnie, Harry, Richard, Millie –
'what a bunch' – a small haven collectively. Also Bernie, who's intent on
employing me in his variety show. In recent weeks quite a few auditions
seem to have gone down the pan. *Fair Lady* (Austin, Texas). *Chairs* at
Guthrie, Minneapolis. A new Irish musical (Finney/ Gambon film) *Man of
No Importance*. Much better vibes from *Mona Lisa Smile* film which I did a
video test for Castings at Union Square. Ten days later had 'strong interest'
call – yesterday – after I'd decided against leaving town for shoreline Mary
Lou's place – swift request to meet Mike Newell – director (who goes back:
Mayor's Charity, Henry Livings' [1977] BBC TV film – Frank Windsor,
Thora Hird, Roy Kinnear, Ray Smith.) Very jolly and affection chat with
MN [Mike Newell]. Met 'Julia' Roberts – slim – easy – jokey – and
Producer. MN in NYC for one day – him now off to Los Angeles. These
meets took place 3 p.m. E23 St HBO Studios.
  Also discussed the Mike Hodges film chances – 30 Sept and 23 Sept
are respective start dates. Julia Roberts joked that I'd got the part because
I'd washed my hair. Overall I'm feeling lazy but it's been a racy couple of
days – left to reflect on my non-visits to see Marylou and Wally Gilman –
at Old Saybrook   which is where Katharine Hepburn lives. Met my dear
Puerto Rican family by chance for a meal – Debbie David a bit temporarily

lost – waiting to get to Pennsylvania and new home. Desiree and Tonston – [Tatiana?] now at E13 in residence. They saw dear Ida in an old TV film. We said we would lunch and get Patsy's Mass cards. It does not seem likely – to me – that either film will come through – and am still 'sad' that *Copenhagen* at Seattle fell away – am still glancing at the text – And thinking of an England trip – The flat, the Club, and such. Off airplanes right now. The Pakistani builders are drilling again – it's Saturday morning. 'They' promise no Sunday work. Must search around for some 'Fish Food'. Hope the weather doesn't start to burn up. Dear Liz Gill has died in St Mary's – and Phyllis [MacMahon], her 'next of kin', has gone to do Yeats with big Jim Ellis in Sligo. La Brasilia is in residence at 41, WC2.

2 September 2002. Seafarers House

During my move from Brooklyn – appalled that despite sent off a good-sized box to long-suffering Patrick (in this respect) – the weight of my trappings is now DOUBLE my normal target and next days will try to weed it down. Brooklyn was a good love-hate time – chief culprit the evil hot NYC summer and the gnat bites from gardening efforts – and the demands of the cat – the fish were as good as gold. Last few days have seen the welcome rains and more personal activity. Trip to Barbara Caruso – to the US Open and a bonus meet with Alan Mills the Wimbledon Referee and charming lady wife Jill. [...]

During recent 10 days – quite pole-axed to hear that the Julia Roberts film were not taking me on board – so very, very near but not near enough – a stern blow. Unlike Cleopatra whom according to WS age could not whither [*sic*], age seems the sticking point. Also lost the big UK Mike Hodges film to Ken Stott – a delicious performer but truly he is not me. Perhaps I will have a chance in time to see for myself. Then there was the poor time which took in St Vincent's and antibiotics though with a clear X-ray – but bronchial troubles.

The flat – the Club – the business – NY despite being reasonably solvent – the above are seemingly ever present surrounding tensions. There was also a visit – fleeting to see Wallis at Old Saybrook in Connecticut. Rather a spread-out manicured place though W has a truly enchanting place. She continues highly nervous and has a strong liking for me. I spoke to her this evening and wrote yesterday. It needs to be resolved that as far as NY goes, my agent is and does make me feel quite ill – he must be replaced – but that's not easy. A possible meeting regards the DC Festival Shakespeare and the call from Mr Horowitz are presently the only two live events in my calendar. I've initially booked in here for three days.

I interrupt this diary to include an amusing letter from Rigby. It demonstrates the kind of daily adventures he had in his wanderings around New York.

✉ [*Terence Rigby*]

28th September 2002
    Dear Lady Ace. The dark clouded morning heralded a welcome change
and clearly, the prospect was rain. It was already 11:00 a.m. as I work and
after a leisurely cup of tea or two – a required intake of tobacco – a shave,
shower – I headed off to the book shop, Barnes and Noble near Lincoln
Centre. The Met area. [To get] a book script – however I was headed
off at the Met as there was an Arts and Crafts fair. Very beautiful, very
pricey. So after spying a pretty woman, selling her jewellery, coffee – and
stalking another lovely beauty who was with her partner or guardians –
and in earnest conversation with a Norwegian painter immigrant – I got to
my destination. But there was no copy – not anywhere there, and it seems
in other branches. The rain had now dug in and despite cap and brolly, I
was starting to get wet. No pals in town in that area. I ducked into an Irish
bar and struggled through their version of liver and bacon and rang Alan
Drury to pick his brain (though I hastily add that I am always hoping and
pleased whenever he's working). He has by the way started to become
productive as a writer once more.
    After all that I decided to proceed down to 43rd St on 9th Avenue
and got even more wet. And of course, the meeting place of many I've
got to know was empty, and the array of tables and chairs, under cover,
had disappeared. It's a pretty well lit area, that, [so] by now dark, but
determined to rest down and somehow – I got a cup of tea and settled on
a wet bench though I got some freebie papers to sit on and was thinking,
this is a bit of all right after all – when I knocked my tea into my crotch
and it was all over the place. I was disgracefully soaked in every which
way, socks and all, on my way down to 43rd and this bench – a large
estate car had beeped me at about 47th St. and it was, most ironically my
Brooklyn actor pal and his daughter who had two letters for me and were
on their way to drop them at my new place. But an enormous coincidence
to see me. One of the letters was yours – the other from Mrs Roddy Hall.
I proceeded on to my bench – and following the first cup of tea upset, got
another – and settled again in the dying light and drizzle to read. Spots of
rain were dripping on to the text as I read. I left Brooklyn two weeks ago
and was in The Seafarers place a week – and now in midtown Manhattan,
but had to quit here a week from today. A fairly civilized studio.
    Your letter was dated August 29th so a lot has occurred during the
interim. I suppose it's a fact that after losing the Julia Roberts picture,
finally – I was prepared to consider regrouping with a trip back. But the
most curious thing happened [...] two whole weeks after saying I hadn't
got the part – they officially enquired again as if I was still available – and
that was one week ago. But, again now, more silence. Hence it really has
been – almost still is, something of a shaker. Tomorrow I meet a former
employer here, the *Troilus/Saved* man, who has a season in New York in
January 2003 to cast – and also this bit of nonsense in Philadelphia to be
dealt with this Thursday – an interview for an early Stoppard.

Last night, Saturday, I hurried back from the Connecticut town seaside home of an old girlfriend – the one who turned up at the matinee. I'm sure I mentioned her – on that occasion – having decided that she was holding such a strong burning candle for me, that staying around was neither sensible at this moment, nor indeed at another time. She is so nervous and vulnerable and simply seems, appears, to wish some action. Whether she wittingly realizes this or not, it's neither here nor there, perhaps, but I tell you anyway that I was a total gent and blew up the spare mattress for my overnight – though she was considerably winded when I told her I was going back the next day. However I did manage to talk to her to a calm departure. The one thing we did was visit the cottage on the seafront where Eugene O'Neill spent all his summers and which location is used – the house itself – for *Long Day's Journey* and *Our Wilderness*. The town is called New London – which is a short drive from Old Saybrook. The lady is a spinster who lives in her own house in a very crusty area – well it's all pretty crusty. I did visit there before but only spent 5 hours there – it's two hours each way, [a] real trip. Phyllis MacMahon is in the film [*The*] *Magdalene* [*Sisters*] – [it was] was shown in Venice and she took herself there under her own steam and stole all the newspaper interviews when the paparazzi realized she had actually been a NUN in one of those places – even photo in the *Evening Standard*. Well done, Phyllis. So don't destroy those old clips.

Much later today I reported to Jeffrey Horowitz, who oversaw the *Troilus/Saved* season – to be told that the new play by Richard Nelson [...] will be headed by Corin Redgrave, which made me mad. Another Brit without a card being squeezed past the Equity ruling and in fact taking a part I or many other actors could play – it does madden me. It's all personal power politics.

I also spoke today to my young married friend Patricia in Rio de Janeiro who would like me to go out for a holiday – she was one of those golly nice, really jolly nice girls who used to help clean the flat up – then she moved back and married a Scot in oil – I had a letter from Mike Hodges who of late considered me for a nice role in a new film – but he is giving it to Ken Stott. It was civil of him to write and he says 'we will [work] again together' but since it's over 30 years since we did, it may have to be something posthumous – which of course with digital is now possible. Later I saw at the Russian caff, my young friend who now wants me to help them prepare a scene from *Day in the Death of Joe Egg* – from the Sonnets to Peter Nichols.

Continued Later. Continuing mayhem regards the *Mona Lisa Smile* (the Julia Roberts film). Told last Wednesday that an offer would be made to me for the role – meanwhile would I be prepared to attend the first read-through today the 23rd? Yes, I said, I would, but when last Friday arrived – still no offer, no contract. Calls to London, Los Angeles SAG [Screen Actors Guild] (now a member), the best advice since I have no faith in the New York man. Sifted through it all and decided to go in and do it – but feared it might be a hidden-agenda audition, especially as they had rewritten my two scenes with her. Cut a long story – did the read-through and they today had a monetary offer – which is curiously out of tune with what I think it should be. So between costume fittings and such and continuing to negotiate a salary. But I shall not do anything explosive to lose the part. It's a very nice cameo which lurks through the film – a professor of Art History at Wellesley College – famous Ladies College MA – circa '50s – Meanwhile I'm expecting a film script from the London end – something to do with a bowls club, oddly. I truly must endeavour to get this away as it is becoming a long saga and I did appreciate your last encouraging affectionate note. Perhaps, perhaps, I could then top it up by calling you and bringing you up to date rather than waiting 4 to 5 days for delivery – I will try. Goodnight sweet princess!

And now it's ages later and I'm in a hotel on 71st Street, oddly enough same street as Barbara Caruso – and the film saga rose up again and I now have an offer to do this part and go to Boston to commence work on October 2nd. So that's the now at least. Well what a lot of puffing and panting this letter has been. But now I will truly get it off to you, hoping that you are in the pink and full steam ahead on your projects.

For now, ever sweet affection, Lord Marylebone.

I love this letter and continue to read it over and over again. It seems to sum up everything that is Terence Rigby. The calamities that beset him in the rain. The meetings in cafes. The doubts and insecurities over parts. His delight in Phyllis MacMahon's success; his terror that a girlfriend was getting too enamoured. His scene setting of O'Neill's stamping ground. How he so often happened to find himself in someone's street, as if it were by accident. His appreciation of Mike Hodges's sensitivity; his anger at Corin Redgrave and the Green Card business; his love of humanity; and how people from every walk of life were touched by him and he by them. That was his talent. That was the joy of him.

Rigby loved the fact that New York was more of a 24-hour city than London. There were more loners – like himself – who enjoyed their own company but still liked to get together with friends and acquaintances, at certain cafes, hotels, parks at particular times in the day and at night. Then they would disappear back into the fog of the city. He also continued to enjoy his tennis.

 [*Diary*]

Friday, 6 October 2002. Seafarers
Due to check out tomorrow. A glum day, but at least last evening took Barbara Caruso out to The Open at Flushing. Had to introduce the JP Morgan card to get ourselves entry. [...] It was pleasing indeed that Sampras

disposed of Roddick to enter semis – poss. Agassi match up for final – if Pete can overcome Hewitt – greater chance than Henman – (as for Ruds and his dopy comments . . . !) I feel tired and not able to give – to give.

Sunday, 27 October 2002. London via Lichfield

The various continuing shuffles from a short sublet at W54, to Seafarer, to Riverside ad infinitum, and the to and fro on the *Mona Lisa* project – reflect on the curious quality of life with one pleasant solace of having spent, by chance, time with Barbara C[aruso] who is standing up more than courageously against her difficulties [...] Decision to fly to London came willy nilly at 5 a.m. – woke dressed showered no shave checked out car to Newark – reinstalled cancelled ticket – and took the buffeting iron bird in a fell swoop. Leaving Rio and San Francisco to be visited and revisited. Maria José now calmer and Patricia in still gloriously happy form. At least there 5K$ waiting to boost the reserve on my return – also two further weeks on *Mona Lisa Smile.* [...]

The Bathroom Saga rerun, with Roy in to estimate as usual [...]. Saw my Dearest Helen at the Home in Florence Road – a desperate virtually unspeakable sadness to behold this great woman so faded – Life's ghastly relentless 'course' and dear Pat Mike Mackay who left us this morning nearby. The great mocking individual who showered our youths with pleasure sheer and constant. Found a pronounced disquiet regards the Birmingham accent which prevails – a mysterious dangerous ugliness. [...] It was good to see and dine with Brucie Purchase and Lord Vincent of NZ at the old Greek place. Look forward to Brucie 'Swan Song' at SOA [Stratford-upon-Avon] '03.

❑ JULIET'S TABLE

I don't like it when my friends go away. I feel bereft. Fortunately, Rigby writes letters and cards all the time. He's even said to me that he communicates better by letter than in person. I suggest that he should never come to visit me again and just write to me, but he says, 'I don't mean you.' However, I'm always impatient to open one of his airmail letters and I think he knows this, because he sticks them down with strong glue and sellotape to frustrate me and make me curse.

*

✉ [*Terence Rigby*]

7 January 2003

There are still a few quid to come in from the film. Though, ladyship, I'm not that rich, there's always a little reserve for kebabs and a couple of dainty fishcakes for whenever I next roll up at Randolph Plaza. Continue to see Struan Rodger a time or two. His lady Sheila was over – now he's missing her. Their *Medea* seems to be an unpopular smash hit – which often happens to really good drama on Broadway. Haven't seen it yet – heavy prices. I haven't done the San Francisco trip to see Maria José. Not quite sure what she really wants anyway. She won't discuss the matter on the phone, and I'm not sure I could cope. I mean, a heavy sub could be made available, I suppose – but that seems too simple a matter to be the one in view. I'm probably being a cynical bastard and failing to be a good friend . . . Any floating beaux, my lady? Or is it gentle footsie under the table with Chanson C. [David Cregan]. I am a naughty fellow making such comments. For now – dear Juliet – take care – keep well and wish me a little courage. Wonderful memories of West Hampstead remain. [11]

Oops-a-daisy and love, Marylebone de Manhattan

⊠ [*Terence Rigby*]

First day of Lent [*9 March*] 2003
I did manage to salvage the audition for the Lauren Bacall film – and was put on tape yesterday and await results. I picked up your Christmas letter again, to me, about Herbert Lom and your new-found society stance as a cocktail hostess. I am in a New York library writing this – with all the students of New York – it's extremely civilized.

⊠ [*Terence Rigby*]

14 May 2003. New York
I've been back one week – it seemed longer. The work of recent days, weeks and months doing that silly sausage of a show – then the iron bird flight, and back on to the set the following day – all served to disorientate. Now it's all over bar perhaps a bit of looping. Though Mike Newell has inferred a rough-cut preview [of *Mona Lisa Smile*] may happen almost immediately. He's also promised that he and I will have coffee together, he's here post-production for about a month. The final committee scene was shot at a seminary college attached to Columbia University up on 120th Street. Incredible to realize that I've been involved with the piece for since October 2nd last year – just over 7 months. Hopefully there will be something of me in the final product. But there is no knowing. This is, after all, the dreaded Hollywood scenario.

[...] Having prepared my New York agents for a possible disruption of association and gathered the interest of another, I have become somewhat uncertain. (Shades of Charlesworth shenanigans here, I feel.) But I need to do a little sorting. Had at least 2 extraordinary letters this week. One from the Lebanon-based Irish religioso (nun) and the other from Fraulein

---

11   This refers to the period I shared a flat there, with five other girls, in the Sixties.

163

Katrin, now of Florida, now married to another woman. She wrote to me after an absence of 12 years, saying she felt guilty for having seduced me during a period those years back, when I offered her a few months' sanctuary. Do you recall that phase of my life? It was no more than a fumble that went wrong, milady. Fact is I desired her quite badly, but know that she was even then of a different religious bent. As for the religioso – she is just totally incorrigible and needs to be put in touch with the bishop confessor. If one believes that there is that sort of thing.

[...] The centre of my day here seems to be my walks – and then I find myself first wandering hither and thither . . . cup of tea at a caff on 8th Avenue . . . a further stroll to West 42, Duane Radio to pick up cheap cigarettes, and lastly into the Russian caff to have my final evening cup with Sonia, Sofia, and Michaelovich. Then back to N45. Only the middle of the evening I had soup, the best in town at the Edison Hotel on W 46th Street. All these locations are in the middle of the theatre district. Yes, it's the silly season of Tony nominations. Vanessa's *Long Day's Journey Into Night*, also *Day in the Death of Joe Egg* and lots more. I finished *Lawrence of Arabia* by Robert Payne and have started to really read *Decline and Fall* the Evelyn Waugh first novel. It's extremely laugh-making and sometimes terse. For my sins remembered, I'm studying a draft of the tennis club new constitution. Fact, was on the phone to them earlier today. All that is as bad as [girlfriend] Radiographer [aka X-Ray]. Can't let it out of my head – though of course, with her, there is no contact at all. I can't let this note go without a reread as it's beginning to spread – and may need a sort of summing up to clarify a little.

P.S. No. I'm determined that it all speaks for itself so leave it as it is. Au revoir.

Special affection, Marylebone.

The Caretaker (2003)

Later in May 2003, Stephen Thorne received a letter from Rigby which, I think, marks the beginning of his serious falling-out with Peter Hall, which lasted for several years. It didn't stop them working together, but it seemed like a grumbling appendix.

He outlined a phone call he'd had:

'Hello, Terry. It's Peter. Peter Hall . . .'

'One might be forgiven for thinking excitable things,' he wrote to Stephen. 'However, he then went on simply to tell me that he was *not* inviting me to be in his production of *As You Like It* in the States. A month ago he was screaming for Green Card actors. Now he's bringing all these herberts over. How he's going to get them in, is beyond me. And that's one of the perks I was looking forward to, etc., etc. Ah well. I must quell expletives.'

He flew back to London and was offered the part of Davies in a new production of *The Caretaker* by Lindsay Posner at the Bristol Old Vic. Although very well received, Rigby found the whole experience of that production deeply traumatic. He felt he wasn't ready at the opening, and that would have distressed him beyond belief.

In a rare diary entry for 2003, he writes:

✎ *[Diary]*

A lot of things happened in the last eight weeks. All to do with *The Caretaker* – I found the rehearsal period tediously, nervously tricky due to reschedule – all the stupid table reading – but with a lot of help from Ben Delfont (our ASM) – and a couple of blow-ups in the rehearsal room. Although I tempered down to the director – he cannot be let off the hook – it could have been a personal disaster – in some respects I sense it was – But the relief of three good national reviews eased the depression. I felt nervous all the time and shaky with the text. There is talk of West End – I had laryngitis and had to visit a Wimpole Street doctor [...] Overall it was a blessed production. Lucky it was not a disaster. Harold P. was on great form at our Preview – a welcome reunion. He lent us his poems.

My digs turned out favourably [...] Saw little of Bristol. Have booked back to NYC Oct 7th. Not to transfer will be a serious disappointment, but it would be more fret and stress. Harold Pinter promised to let myself and Vincent D[owling] do *No Man's Land* in Chester MA. P[eter] H[all] seems to have taken option on Arts which could affect us. HP War Poems hit the spot.

A letter from Harold Pinter dated 6 October 2003:

✉ [*Harold*]

Dear Terry,
So pleased to get your letter.
You were an absolutely terrific Davies and for a change the reviews recognized that. Let's hope it will go on.
Wonderful to see you again – on – and off – stage.
Love
Harold

I have pieced together various bits of information on the delayed previews of *The Caretaker*. It was apparently announced that the previews were cancelled because Rigby had laryngitis – which his diary confirms he did. But the truth is also that he wasn't 100 per cent confident of his lines. This was so unlike him – the man who was always near perfect in preview and performance – but I was not aware of this at the time. It didn't affect his eventual triumph in the show, but he seems to have been distressed by the front-of-house explanation for the cancellation. He obviously contacted Equity on the matter and Christopher Ryde tackled the problem on Rigby's behalf.

✉ [*Sarah Smith*]

17.10. 2003
Dear Chris,
In response to your letter dated 9 October 2003, having now had a chance to talk to staff, I am writing to clarify the points you raised.
The previews were cancelled because Terence Rigby was not able to learn his lines in time. When we took this decision clear guidelines were given to box office and front-of-house staff and those patrons who had booked were contacted and told that one of the cast was ill. We felt it was a more sensitive reason for cancelling the performances. In fact we believe he had laryngitis for most of the time he was here because in the last week of the run we had to cancel two further performances at the request of his doctor. Simon Kunz [*who played Aston*] was not ill and I am really surprised that a member of staff told your colleague he was.
Finally the reason why all the images used to promote the productions this season have nothing to do with the cast is because generally the

production of brochures, posters, etc. is completed far in advance of casting.

I hope this clarifies any misunderstanding.

Yours sincerely,

Sarah Smith

(Executive Director)

❏ JULIET'S TABLE

'I sometimes wish that I had responsibility for a wife and children.'

I nearly drop a pan of potatoes.

'Say that again,' I say.

'You heard me. I've probably left it too late.'

'It's never too late. Mind you, by the time you've chewed it over for the next five years, and eventually get round to it, any child of yours would be ten and you'd be a hundred and five.'

He doesn't like that, and huffs and puffs, ready to have a go at me. At this point I put a dish of chicken stew in front of him, which changes his mood somewhat. I feel a bit shamefaced and backtrack, telling him he'd be a jolly good husband and father if he put his mind to it.

It occurs to me when he's eating that he's changed the way he dresses. The blazers, shirts, ties, and flannels have disappeared; so have the Crombie and the decent mac. He's wearing combat trousers with strange-looking pockets and buttons and zips. On top he's sporting one of a collection of T-shirts or rugby shirts and a gilet sort of garment that a fisherman might wear, with slots for knives and hooks and suchlike. On his head he wears a floppy denim hat decorated with a pink denim flower. He's read my thoughts because he holds out his hand.

'I bought this ring in a fair I went to, near Broadway. Jolly nice Danish woman.'   It's a feminine-looking dress ring with a blue stone. I nod my approval, but there's not a lot to say about it. I know he'll come back to the subject of marriage and children. I tell myself to say nothing.

'What's the point of it all?'

As ever, this negative slant to the conversation covers a deep-seated worry about his health. He's smoking heavily again, forgetting the triple bypass and the breathlessness. Occasionally he coughs up blood. I must not lecture or show any concern or disapproval, I say to myself. Be nonchalant. That's the thing to do. But he presses even further.

'I just wish I had responsibility for somebody.'

'What about your colleagues – especially when you're working on a play?'

167

'Well, yes. I feel concern for my colleagues . . .'

'And your friends?'

'I don't give a fuck for my friends.'

'Cheers!' I feel angry for all of us who regard ourselves as his friends, and I'm glad when he goes home early.

The next time he appears on the doorstep he says, 'You were going to tell me to fuck off, weren't you?'

*

ix. Kodak snap 1: Rigby at Juliet's table

Reading through my conversation with Douglas, I found a reference to the influence America was having on Rigby. He'd taken his lady friend to see the last *Godot* and they went round afterwards. As a Brummie herself, she really hit it off with Rigby. He was wearing his beige combat pants, a fishing jacket, and a hat which had a fur trim and a flower on it. 'And she said something about it,' recalls Douglas.

> And looking back, I remember Terence and the way he used to dress. I
> think this whole business of America, and doing plays that seemed to have
> no point in doing them, in places that had no point to them . . . and this
> whole change in costume . . . He changed from Sir Ralph Richardson into
> Oscar Wilde. But something I admired was that he was still wanting to

168

develop as an actor. Actually, it was real acting . . . The point of wanting
to do something again – was to play it. And it didn't matter if it wasn't
the Old Vic or the National or some student place in Ohio – you were an
actor playing a part . . . from what I could gather, for very little money.
And this costume change . . . Terry was Terry, and you didn't say, 'What's
this outlandish change?' But I get the feeling there was some attempt at
reinvention. But we never discussed it.

It was something to consider; a possible tying-up of loose ends. It seems
that Rigby was going through a period of uncertainty about his health
and his career at this time, as well as his dress sense. He was certainly
depressed. He regularly came back to London, principally to see his doctor.

This unfinished letter from Christmas 2003 was one he never sent, and
which was found among his papers. And we don't even know the would-be
recipient . . .

✉ [*Terence Rigby*]

It's a few minutes after 6 a.m. on Christmas morning – I've been sleeping
for perhaps 10/11 hours, having felt tired last evening, following a tramp
around during the run-up to Christmas. I don't know if I am below
par or just collapsing under jet-lag matters though indeed I've been on
English soil for several days. I came to see the witch doctors – one has
somewhat begrudgingly given me an OK – the other – I await reaction
to some tests – often the case that one has to wait, even though one pays
out 'good money'. But nevertheless – I do seem to be possessed of a
general D. I think I picked up that expression via an American – perhaps
it's short for 'Downwardly immobile'! Certainly I seem to be kicking
against mobility. My family has gathered in Bristol and I have declined
to join them – I am not – if ever, inclined to large gatherings of the clan
– especially when there are no trains running – to get out of town when
the conversation gets 'rough'. I am known to drop a few bricks where
Famille is concerned – though overall I have reasonable affection for
them all on an individual level. However they seem to basically think of
me as a loner – either caused by my job or a general waywardness. Nearer
London I have 3 different opportunities to friends' get togethers which at
this moment of writing I have no impulse to attend. En passant I wonder
how you will spend the Day. Do you make an effort to join in or do you
sit back and start a new novel – i.e. writing one or reading one. Michael
Redgrave's autobiography may come into play for me – my hardly ever
used TV has done a splutter, so old films are out – interestingly enough
only one channel worked anyway. Never was up on technology. I wonder
how that Beagle is doing on Mars? It was about to splash down a few
hours ago. I just fiddled with the TV and it came on for long enough to
tell me that so far Beagle has not reported in – but that all is not lost. At
about this point the TV went splutter again and a long green line extends
across the screen. Conversely – is that the correct word? – (I looked it

up in the Webster and am still unsure) – your message about *Mona Lisa Smile* did get through – though I will have to rerun it in order to soak up what it is saying – What I'm hearing is that I am in the film – and that there are credits, etc. – well, thank you for the message. I also learn – again without knowing about it – that there was a sneak showing at the Warner Cinema in Leicester Square plus a Q & A with director and one of the starlets (Maggie Gyllenhaal) – and when they talked about the British input I was talked about in very good terms. That I believe was Dec 12th. The director did tell me a month ago that he expected erased scenes to be included in the DVD – All that can really be said about this whole awkward scenario is that I, one way or another, spent eleven months on and off, in and out, of the making of this movie – and in the way of things must try and somehow feel a degree of satisfaction that I am 'in' it at all, and that it was my first USA movie and must adopt the attitude of 'Well – who knows?' – Let that be that.

Daughter Catherine and I went to the BAFTA showing of *The Mona Lisa Smile* at the Warner cinema. The little we saw of Rigby made us smile – he looked so avuncular, so pleasantly ruthless. It was a great disappointment to him that his scenes were cut to shreds – though perhaps it didn't ultimately matter that much, since the film was badly received.

The Birthday Party (2004)

Back in the States, Rigby was given the opportunity to play Petey in Pinter's *The Birthday Party* at the American Repertory Theater (ART) – the play that had bombed when it opened in the Lyric Hammersmith back in 1958, but which eventually, of course, came to be regarded as a masterpiece.

Towards the end of his life, Rigby set down his reflections on how he had approached the part, in a letter to his friend James Stephens, who was due to play the same role. 'I was doing it at Princeton,' James later explained. 'He played Petey in Boston, so he was giving me advice':

✉ [*Terence Rigby*]

Forgive the temerity of teaching grandma to suck eggs, but having played Petey during recent seasons, and from study and experience gained, I offer you this – allied to what little I know of your range of work.

I am convinced that Pinter wrote and intended Petey to be ineffective in a most amusing way. He does his deckchairs – plays a bit of ordinary chess (his only form of intellectual stirring) – and some with Meg's oddness in a good-natured way. But his Bible is the *Mirror* newspaper and allows himself a modest irritation as regards Meg's silly flirting with Stanley. Whenever that comes to the fore – he goes off to the deckchairs. I don't believe he is ever aggressive – maybe he once did his fair share, but that's all in the past.

Later, in Act 3, he slowly becomes aware of a certain oddity – with regards to the activity of Goldberg/McCann – and essentially would wish to defend the house in his own way – and is concerned that Meg should not be upset. However, in the final analysis – he is sadly conscious that he is mentally/physically no longer possessed of the ability to restrain or offer assertive resistance to the situation – and has let it go, and of course deliberately allows Meg to believe that Stanley is still upstairs in bed when he has in fact been led off by strangers.

Yourself – myself – both of us having a natural strength of presence – find such a role not easy to effect, but I think what I did and almost certainly you must do is to find a docility without losing anything. Perhaps a pair of spectacles, particularly for all the newspaper reading. Whether you can see it another way I do not know, and in the end it's up to you. Happily I got a decent notice or two – whereas the whole was shot down.

I think this letter demonstrates how Rigby approached most of the parts he played. It shows his understanding of the other characters, and how he should – or could – react to them. He looks into a possible back-history for Petey, and how time has rubbed off the edges, but that the essence of the character is still there.

Although Rigby was now concentrating more on theatre, both in Britain and in America, he still worked pretty consistently in film and television. He'd already appeared in *Funny Bones* (1995), where he played Lee Evans's agent, the 2000 crime film *Essex Boys*, and as Mr Caldicot in *Mrs Caldicot's Cabbage War* (2002). I quite often heard his lines for various parts in television. When he came across a tricky line, he never once changed it or added an 'Eh' or an 'Ah' to make it easier to say. He would work his socks off to make the line 'sayable'. He talked about words 'bumping up against each other instead of flowing naturally', and how difficult it was for an actor to speak the lines when that happened.

While he was working on *The Birthday Party* in Cambridge MA, he was also involved with the film *Colour Me Kubrick*, starring John Malkovich. He sent this postcard when he was filming on the Isle of Man on 17 February 2004:

✉ *[Terence Rigby]*

Lady Juliet dearest,
    As you see, still here – finding John Malkovich an extremely amicable talented artist. Perhaps I am understandably a shade tired – 3 days more on this – then Dublin, Boston-bound to recommence rehearsals for 'Birthday Party' to open Mar 6–27 only. Then what. I hope, Ladyship, all continues well for you – for yours. This is a very picturesque beautiful island – beaches, dales, hills, coves, and mountainous regions. We have had some hot sun over several days. The Cambridge MA rehearsals have been odd – the lady director is very off the wall and Harold would not approve – Well I don't think so. Nonetheless, Much love, God Bless – to all,
    Sir Rigby

I still have this feeling that Rigby regarded himself a guardian of Pinter's work and would report back anything that he thought was sacrilege.

From a letter dated 14 March 2004, it's obvious that Rigby disapproved of some wilful disregard of Pinter's genius and must have let him know about it.

✉ [*Harold Pinter*]

Dear Terry,
   Thanks for keeping in touch. I appreciate it.
   I don't know what the hell they think they're doing by repeating those lines. They never mentioned it to me.
   Anyway how is it going? I hope you're happier with Petey.
   Mind how you go and keep me posted.
   Yours, Harold

I'd already received a postcard from Rigby during rehearsals of *The Birthday Party*, but a letter then arrived which I read and reread several times. There's a touch of paranoia to it that still makes me laugh out loud.

✉ [*Terence Rigby*]

Dear Juliet,
   This has to be quick to catch the post. Thank you for your welcome note and one which I picked up on a brief 24-hour trip to my New York box room. You seem to be on an OK course, good to charge the batteries and proceed regardless. Easily said, yes. Just now, for Lordship – quagmires are afoot. I hope your pub evenings with Lady Morgan do not extend to letting slip confidences – I know ladies when a gin or two have slipped down – caution goes to the wind. I know you will rap my fingers, but I am a fearfully, if stupidly secretive cove – as you must know. Some instinctive defence mechanism. Not having any fun with 'Birthday' – apart from a crass production – we preview later this evening – I cannot get – this old man – I can't settle at all on his rhythms – mental, speech or otherwise and feel quite quite amateur – I mean it. The fags are doing me up – chestal problems, which do not help.
   Harold would hate this presentation – he's already denied changes, but they skip between the loopholes in making such differences legal – I suppose. I'm sorry you won't get any particular joy from this scrappy note – that I am just anxious to say hello, now you are keeping well. This technical period has been a pall – rushing here, there, trying to remember to eat – buy food for fridge – all too much for this ageing thesp. Oh well, let's be hopeful. Brave and all that. God! Well could just get Saturday 1:00 p.m. post. The 'Colour Me Kubrick' film wrapped yesterday or today and I'm sorry to miss the party which is in London tomorrow. Jim Davidson sent me an enormous beautiful bouquet of flowers. Got to go.
   Love, Sir Riggers T.

Waiting for Godot and *The Importance of Being Earnest* (2005–6)

There were several to-and-fro visits to the States during this period of Rigby's life, as well as the constant feeling that he was never quite in the right place at the right time, and his turbulent friendship with Sir Peter Hall now escalated into an almost paranoid state over the casting of *As You Like It* – Hall's first production of the play. Rigby's agent Peter Charlesworth found it difficult to understand all the ins and outs of his misgivings, but it certainly involved his Green Card and what he regarded as the by-passing by others of its privileges. There had been vague discussions about Rigby doing several small- and medium-sized roles in the production, and there had been hints that at some time in the near future they would remount *Waiting for Godot*. In a fax, sent on 2 October 2004, it's clear that Rigby was still finding it difficult to steer a middle ground between friendship and professional dealings.

✉ [*Terence Rigby*]

Dear Peter,

I do not wish to write this letter. I write it out of duty and because at this stage of only a little more than 5 weeks before AYLI rehearsals begin, for safety.

I am overwhelmed with difficulties regards doing this play. I cannot 'interest' myself in it despite that we have proceeded this far. It must be said that I am also surrounded with truly personal problems which are not unconnected.

At this time I feel a shade down and out – and I hate to say that, but it is true. I do not believe that I retain the emotional and physical requirements necessary for the safe conduct of the task.

There are several additional matters which I have not been able to grasp. The Green Card, which I have. Why is this important to you – who else has one? – Why is one actor, myself, so necessary as regards the whole?

Why has your producer been permitted to illustrate such lack of artistic appreciation in standing firm on his salary offer to me; of $650 less than my Ahmanson Theatre norm? Such a factor is grossly debilitating and has remained so in recent weeks. It has made me feel a very second class citizen indeed, and is painful and incorrect.

As regards 'Godot' – there is obviously no point in making any further comments, in the circumstances, – than those I have already made known.

Lastly, Peter, I must simply ask you to think through what I have written here and be good enough to respond. Warm regards ever.

Terry / Terence / Rigby

Rigby arrived back in London to attend the read-through of *As You Like It*. When he walked into the rehearsal room, Rigby was astonished to find that he wasn't expected; indeed, that he wasn't in the play at all. Sir Peter, apparently, was equally surprised. It's true to say that Rigby wasn't that thrilled to be cast in small roles (such as Oliver Martext in this one), and more than likely had gone through his usual deliberations –doubtless thinking that Sir Peter would take all this on board. When he obviously hadn't made allowances, Rigby walked out in high dudgeon.

Peter Charlesworth commented that Rigby handled Peter Hall at arm's length after that. Fortunately for Rigby, though, Sir Peter let it go. But it's no small wonder that he told Struan Rodgers that Rigby was 'barking'. 'It really upset him,' Charlesworth told me. 'It was his own fault, to be honest, but he didn't appreciate me saying that either. He turned up disregarding the fact that he hadn't had a call, or there hadn't been any arrangement with me for him to do it, and Peter Hall looked at him saying "What are *you* doing here?" . . . He seemed to have retreated very quickly'.

It's probably just as well, because Sir Peter was gracious enough to employ Rigby many more times after that, putting aside all the tantrums

❑ JULIET'S TABLE

'Your bravery knows no bounds,' I tell him after he's settled down with a mug of tea. He looks puzzled.

'The rat. I've never seen you look so pale.'

Llewellyn the cat had caught a rat by the railway line and brought it back as a present. Although Sloth (my journalist friend Richard) regards Llewellyn as heroic, his timing couldn't have been worse. There was absolutely no call for delivering a rat when I was entertaining my brother, his wife, in-laws and children to tea – and Rigby, of course, who had turned up, as usual, out of the blue. I screamed; my brother grabbed a broom and chased it out into the road. Dear God.

'I still feel embarrassed . . .'

'Barricade the cat-flap!'

I've already done that, and Sloth has volunteered to deal with any similar offerings, provided they're moribund.

'I've been to Denville Hall a couple of times, to see Robert Stephens. He's recuperating from a liver transplant.' (I'm tempted to say, patronizingly, that it could have been Rigby lying there in pain, in the actors' care home, if he hadn't given up the drink, but I resist the temptation.) He chuckles. 'I can't go there without a bottle of Scotch. He gets upset if I don't.'

I tut-tut disapprovingly, like a maiden aunt.

'He wants me to take him to Paris for a little jaunt.'

'I suppose you told him about the widow.'

From time to time, Rigby takes himself off to Paris for a few days. There's a widow and an artist who's in the process of painting a portrait of him. He's rather secretive about the widow, but she's definitely on the list.

'I might have done. I try to entertain him as best I can. He's my pal.'

It's around this time that Kenneth Haigh is in hospital after choking in a restaurant. Rigby is a regular visitor there as well, despite the fact that Ken doesn't speak much any more.

This is one of many occasions when I remember that, along with his talent, he is probably the most compassionate person I know. There's nothing to say about it except to have the kettle on and the tea caddy full of tea bags. And if he starts going on about X-Ray, who has disappeared off the scene for a while, I will listen intently.

*

I should have gone to Bath to see Sir Peter Hall's production of *Waiting for Godot* in the summer of 2005, but I didn't and I felt ashamed. After playing Pozzo for Michael Rudman at the National in 1987, Rigby was now reprising the role he'd first developed with Hall in the 1990s. He'd obviously swallowed his pride, and Sir Peter wasn't holding any grudges against this curmudgeonly 'ageing thesp'. The reviews were very positive, and there was talk of bringing the production into London, but there were problems with the Beckett estate, so it became clear that the West End transfer would have to wait. Shortly after this, Rigby accepted Sir Peter's invitation to play Canon Chasuble in an American tour of *The Importance of Being Earnest*.

At the beginning of rehearsals for this production, I received the following, rather grumpy, letter from Rigby, dated 20 December 2005. He refers to my daughter Catherine, who had studied drama at Manchester University and then, having worked with Simon McBurney of Complicite, went off to train for two years with the legendary Jacques Lecoq in Paris. Rigby's apparent disdain for her training – despite her extensive experience as both director and actor – is part and parcel of his general distrust of academia, of the intellectual brigade, from Peter Barkworth's improvisations at RADA, via those 'public school chappies' at the BBC, to the earnest theorizing surrounding some of his later New York productions. (And as I said, it's a grumpy letter.)

✉ [*Terence Rigby*]

Dear Lady C.,
    Yes, well you certainly took your time in replying – titting for tat I suppose. So no house sale – pity – difficult to convince people that one actually does not hear the trains at all, in time. Yes, not sure at all about Miriam Margolyes – seems friendly enough, but though a good actress – a tiresome one – one who always seeks CCC [*i.e. prime-centre-stage*] when not an integral part of the action. Whatever. I have my own problems – like being above the title with Countess [Lynn] Redgrave [*as Lady Bracknell*], who is OK – but really I am not more than a pivotal cameo, can't understand it. Bloody idiots. Got to go for medicine tomorrow at 8 a.m. Christ. On antibiotics for a stinking cold. Subway on strike today – New York a bit ghost-like – rehearsals cancelled as we are down in Brooklyn. I'm sure your alternative party will be a success, just like the cocktail dos. But you'll have to get in the washer-upper, as I will not be around [...]
    I'm afraid I do not remember [Peter] Donaldson – he must have been one of the several dogsbodies in *Henry V* – not that I was much more. I remember Malcolm McDowell was also a dogsbody in those times (regrettably short) – Have to get on. Fondest thoughts for Christmas and New Year.
    Sir T.

Rigby's letters from this time supply a much better diary of an actor's life, and of the production, than anything his old *Birmingham Post* friend could have hoped to receive, thirty years earlier.

✉ [*Terence Rigby*]

14 January 2006
    [...] We have a stagger through tomorrow p.m. – then our first dress rehearsal, odd guests allowed. I wish I could report myself to be more with it – I am not – the big stumbling – and one does need to be right on the button – It's not a grossly large part. I should mind my own business, but there is a good deal around me that is not right. I shall hesitate here

to dwell at length on all the aspects that concern me. I simply hope Sir Peter will pull it through – as only he can do – in the circumstances – i.e. circumstances as I see them – I recall his late work on *Godot* which just made all the difference in the end and ensured its potential success. It was of course very much a success. I'm sure you will read between the lines.

I'm staying at the fairly sumptuous Biltmore Hotel [*in Los Angeles*] – I did a month here during *Amadeus* and the surrounding district is slowly coming back to me. The hotel goes back perhaps even to the 1920s and used to be where the original Oscars were held – though then it was known by a different name. It's a desperate god-awful fact – but the lady friend of former days – who suddenly found me again (from Old Saybrook) is now in a hospice and cannot have too long to go. I visited her in the New Haven hospital twice but now things have moved pretty quickly. The rotten thing is that she has nobody – but an estranged sister – I keep in touch now by phone and letters which are hard to write. It's all a shade odd, in that we really did not truly get on – but such were her circumstances that I felt I simply had to become involved. I feel sure you will understand.

[...] Press Night is 25th January. I intend to stay at the Biltmore only until 21st but it is subject to change – it's very expensive. Alfred Molina dropped by the theatre today – he's doing *Cherry Orchard* at the third theatre in this complex. Ours, the Ahmanson Forum, is a 2,000-seater, and we are required to have microphone embellishment – that even I must say – I have been up the back, at the top, and it really is OK – a great relief. [...] Were you not all due today to have a send-off for Ned Chaillet? I think I am right, and I hope it wasn't too tearful and went well – I am sure he will have lots of London reunions with you gels in the future. [...] And now I must repair – rest – revise – and try and put more effort into what I'm supposed to be here doing. Excuse the shortness. Take care – good luck.

Marylebone. Terence R.

✉ [*Terence Rigby*]

25 January 2006

Arriving back from First Night, which all seem to think went very well – I had a lightning fluff, but had them laughing again immediately, thankfully.

I found this Grand Hotel in darkness at 1:00 a.m. – and guests were met and are given a pencil-like fluorescent candle which serves as the only power available – until, so they said, 1:30 a.m. – if that can be believed. It's a great pity as I don't feel like flopping into bed – hence I am writing this candlelit letter. Thank you for your card which did arrive today the 25th.

The long drawn-out rehearsal process made us feel the play – had become very dry – but we have been blessed with superb and large houses, which has made the play lift off – quite magnificently – and sent the Bath producer and Sir Peter and Lady Hall back to London in, I assume, high spirits.

God how I hate late First Night parties. I hate parties. It is enough to get through the show without having to mill about and try entertaining guests – of one's own – when really all I want to do is flop out. I think it has all to do with them drinking – and me, you know – not. However – it's over – and we can't complain about our reception – whatever the press says – it is without doubt going – has gone – well. The grind of repetition naturally lies before us.

Earlier before the show, I rang up my Old Saybrook friend – who is lying in, waiting to expire, in the hospice just outside New Haven in Connecticut. She was tremendously breathless and finding it so difficult to talk. I am more or less assuming that we have spoken our last words. Somehow the word 'balm' came into our conversation and I slowly quoted her some of *Macbeth* which deals with sleep. 'Sleep that knits up the ravelled sleeve of care – the death of each day's life, sore labour's bath – balm of hurt minds' – it all sounds so melodramatic, but it was cruelly real – and I know she appreciated it.[12]

Well it's almost 1:30 a.m. and I still write by candlelight. Ah, now as I write at exactly 1:30 a.m., Eureka! the lights have gone on again. I have been lodged here at the most random hotels that the rate is about double our hotel allowance, so financially it is not very sensible, and I am seeking around for a better deal though I am sure to miss the luxurious space of the rooms.

---

12 Rigby remembered 'Wally', and her death, in a later diary entry in February 2008: 'I had met Wally all those years ago when she was staying, along with seven or even eight other girls, in a large flat in Moscow Road, W2. Leased by Lynn Furlong, one of the original "Z-Cars" girls – who made the programme's call-up sign "BD to Zed Victor One" almost a national catchphrase. Lynn was quite keen that Wally and myself get along and indeed we tried hard – but this very sweet American lady was a shade meek, and I was by this time learning to drink. We were next to meet thirty years later when she turned up at a matinee performance of Mike Leigh's play "Smelling a Rat" at the Samuel Beckett Theatre on W42nd Street (a theatre which I am pleased to say, we opened). Not having met for all that time, it was a classic encounter, but we fell in surprisingly quickly and our next eighteen months I visited her up at Old Saybrook which was Katharine Hepburn country. I dare say that our friendship could have developed even then, but it had turned out that despite the distance we had put between each other, Wally had placed me on a pedestal, having accumulated lots and lots of cuttings of me over the years – she even had the original copy of my film script from "The Homecoming" film [...]. I just could not accept this kind of attention which she poured over me. I also remember how difficult, how very very difficult, she found it to tell me finally that she was a Jewess and that she had some years earlier had a bout of breast cancer. Not long passed before that awful condition rose up again. But in thinking back over this time, I believe it was the fact that she thought me so very very "special", that I could not cope with. I had gone off to Chester in MA to do [David Hare's] "Skylight" with Francesca [...] and for some reason had asked her not to come and see it – perhaps part of me was afraid I would finally disappoint – only to discover months later, that she had made the very awkward journey and caught my performance.

Another devilish thing of course are the extras – laundry, room service, all truly savage prices. But certainly, I am being paid OK – though only getting a few more dollars than my last Los Angeles trip – *Amadeus* in the year 2000 – and I have my New York flat to pay as well [...]

Where we work – the music centre – embraces three theatres – two for drama – the other, the Dorothy Chandler, is an opera house. The second smaller drama house is the Mark Taper – and Alfred Molina and Annette Bening are about to open their *Cherry Orchard*. Fred was in the other night, we have done nine previews, and was agreeably complimentary. I am managing to get on well with Miriam [Margolyes] – but only, I think, because I have made an effort – and last night I invented a lovely piece of business for her – so she is cock-a-hoop – she has crowds of fans – quite a lot of whom are invariably of her persuasion [...]

It was on this production of *The Importance of Being Earnest* that Rigby met James Stephens, an English actor who had lived in New York for many years, and who was to become a close friend. I remember meeting him once when Rigby brought him to Randolph Street. 'I was giving my Laine [the butler in Wilde's play],' James told me when we met after Rigby's death.

It was a Peter Hall production. We took a liking to one another from the start. We were both Midlands born and had a liking for pork pies and pickled walnuts. I noticed that while everyone sat together, Terence would be off in a corner somewhere. His idea of Chasuble was certainly not anyone else's idea of Chasuble . . . because Miriam Margolyes was playing opposite him, and she was in tears. He said, 'She's got this idea that Chasuble is in love with Prism . . . and he's not! He's not in love with Prism.' So I asked him, 'So what do *you* think he feels?' And he said, 'I

---

12   . . . I thought it was a breathtaking gesture, though I never did quiz her as to exactly what her appraisal was. In doing this play I had in fact put myself "on the spot", which I really was not used to. I had a sneaking suspicion that I was good but somehow preferred to determine that assessment myself. Only two others that know me at all saw my performance – though David Hare did send a best wishes fax. But [...] the writing was slowly on the wall, and Wally was deteriorating I was back in London and she was not answering the phone [... She] had been unable to cope and had been taken to New Hampshire hospital. Later I was back in New York and able to visit her, to take various essential things that she was in need of – a dressing gown and soaps and such (amazing that the medics had not dealt with this) and there was serious talk of a hospice [...]. Meanwhile rehearsals for "Amadeus" with David Suchet and Michael Sheen commenced in Chelsea, London, were now continuing, and finally we made our way to Los Angeles where we would open and play for two months – and that is when the phone calls [...] began. Wally had always had a love of the classics and whilst it sometimes amazes me, I found myself trying to create solace for her by reciting gently to her the sleep scene from the Scottish play. After a few days Penny let me know that Wally had died.

keep that to myself, James. So I have no idea what kind of relationship Chasuble had with Prism . . . He's just a man.' Peter Hall didn't interfere. I like Miriam, but she can be brusque . . .

I told James that, from what I could understand, Rigby felt that she just wasn't an ensemble player.
'Absolutely right,' he replied. 'She's a natural comedienne. He would say, "Miriam, you cannot jiggle." She *would* jiggle, and get a laugh from the audience. He didn't put a stop to it.'
'Terry and I did not get on at all in the show,' Miriam Margolyes herself told me. 'I think I got on his nerves, but I would like to pay tribute to him as an actor':

He had complete integrity, a mischievous sense of humour and keen observation. He hated bullshit, he loved acting, he was a true artist. But he would not accept that there was a romantic connection between Canon Chasuble and Miss Prism. He was wrong; I am right: but I honour his memory. He was much-loved in our profession.

The atmosphere cannot have been helped, however, by Rigby's failing health. 'During that show,' James told me, 'I suspected he wasn't very well at all':

We were in California. And he was very solitary. And I was driving home in the car once and he said, 'I get dizzy on stage.' He did go and see someone. I think he had a CT brain scan and the fact they didn't pick up that he had a brain tumour at that point . . . You could see that he wasn't well, and a bit wobbly on stage.

I told him I thought it was the cigarettes – he was already spitting up blood, and had had tests and scans over here. They thought it might be TB.

We got on well. He'd smell my wine . . . He told me he'd been a bottle-of-vodka-a-day man. He said, 'After the show, my pal [David Sinclair] and I would drink all night, then we'd go home and put a joint of lamb in the oven on a low heat and go to bed. Get up, go for drink, come back and have Sunday lunch.' But he [told me he had] stopped smoking and then started again in a film with John Gielgud. I asked him if he drove. And he said, 'Yes. I drove a Jaguar'.
'He had someone lying underneath doing the pedals!' I told him. 'You kept in touch, though. He introduced you to Charlesworth.'
'I came over and I saw you,' James remembered. 'He met me off the train. So we became friends and he would come to dinner with us in New York. Walk in the park. You could see he wasn't well, though. I thought it was his heart.'

Rigby wrote again towards the end of February 2006, soon after we spoke on the phone. We had both been somewhat through the wars, medically: 'For myself, I am slowly whittling down the pros and cons of my problems. Today I have two appointments in the same building in Beverly Hills and today, I'm glad to say, I am spared the bus: a young US lady [Diane Landers] has offered to drive and wait and bring me back. (I call her Kissy-Kissy – but that is a long joke in need of clarification).' And there followed an eight-sided screed, on hotel notepaper, dated 19–23 March, that is the nearest thing to a stream-of-consciousness that I ever received from him – and a vivid account of the punishing slog of the road.

✉ [*Terence Rigby*]

Dear Camden,

Well, I woke up in Arizona following a disgusting flight in from NYC – where I'd spent 2 days – we don't open here until today Thursday, on account of getting the sets here – by road. 5-hour flight in a smallish jet – hot, stuffy, crowded – the worst. All round the hotel the roads are being rebuilt so it's somewhat of a building site – there's a swim pool and people talk of 125° heat but just now it's a moderate 60–70 – just as well – I'm not a lover of heat. We will be in and out of here by Monday – the stay is peppered with matinees to make up the weekly take. Means we don't have much chance at all to investigate the place. I know the Canyon is not far but I think it's impossible to get there.

Regards 'the break' – which is from 27 March–16/17 April, when we open at Brooklyn – I'm dependent on my passport being renewed in time – I sent it to Washington but only last week. [...] Regards my medics scenario the basic problem has not receded – it's just become something I go through each performance. Very puzzling – I've 'almost' stopped worrying about it. [*At this point, apart from heart and chest problems, Rigby was suffering from a very painful hernia.*]

We start today with a matinee – providing the set has arrived in time to be put up. I had more good reviews in New Haven – but we move about so much – I'm not even bothered to go searching for them. Seems after conferring with a very pleasant cast that the only way of doing the Canyon would be to stay another day or days here.

I'm still getting updates of the *Godot* revival situation – late August in Bath, 4 weeks' tour then there is an option on 14 weeks in the West End, Ambassadors or Duchess – But it's still not concrete – and therefore I am not happy about it all. The old story. Miriam gone off to have a tooth fixed – she continues unhelpful in a vaguely charming way – she is simply not my style.

Sorry this is all ME. I hope you are OK – did call you without success.

Sorry, all for now, Marylebone x [...]

Well not quite all. A good opening Matinee – house – got a bit wrong but no chaos. Spoke with Phyllis [MacMahon]– she's off this w/e to do

75th birthday special for James Ellis in Belfast. Fact is, Jim's not been well – but it's going ahead. Today it's like the very best day of Summer that you might expect in England – but some folk here think it's a shade chilly. Now at least it's evening and more Marylebone-suited. I'll just burble on if you don't mind. Apart from all that, I really do not want to do this show any more – it's an awful thing to admit – but my interest is now nil. Of course one goes on and does it – to the best one can – but I'm irritable and although my colleagues wax on about the wonderful houses, etc. – it is meaning so little to me. I suppose there is only so much you can get out of a part – and I feel in the circumstances that I have wrung it through – and indeed though it can hardly be perfect – I can't get any more out of it. Also this duplicity I engage in with MM, for whom I have no regard – only complaints – what more can I say? Perhaps I am just simply short of company – an odd thing for me to say, admit – well, I can only point out my own shortcoming in that area as being the reason for that. 'You made your bed, bloody well sleep in it.' I will endeavour to concentrate more. It's odd but all these cities we visit – the theatre is always Down Town – and such places are just full of yawning great buildings – empty streets, – little sense of community – and for us, for me, just bloody hard work from which I am getting no feed back. I've been enjoying *Pride and Prejudice* – quite different from the film – now I've finished that unfortunately. Don't allow your thoughts to be cast down with my own – no doubt I will survive it all one way or another. Meanwhile I do very much hope that the 'sun is shining' for you – your aspirations – you know exactly what I mean, I hope. Truly what will occur in the next few days I do not know – so I hope I'll make the right decision – at least I'm not technically short of cash flow – so that is a help. It's just after 7 p.m. now – I'm by an empty pool at the hotel – Time to slog off back to the evening perf. – actually there is some sort of reception after tonight's show. Don't be too angry, irritated by my mood. It could all be solved if I was at your place now, with some fishcakes and a decent bit of cheese [...]   Affection – again.

   Marylebone x

Meanwhile I was getting to know our mutual friends Jane Morgan and Peter Acre – though back in the early days, if we all happened to be together, Rigby would bluntly ignore me: he wanted to keep us all in our separate boxes.

   On 27 June 2006 I moved out of my house in Camden Town. Since my new flat in Fitzrovia couldn't be occupied by me until two weeks later, I asked Rigby – now back in England thanks to Sir Peter – if he would take me in as a lodger. He wasn't best pleased. I paid proper rent and kept the fridge stocked up with basics. I was determined not to get in the way, so I spent as much time as possible out and about, or in my room. I told him I'd either be reading, or listening to Radio 4. He told me he couldn't stand hearing a radio through the walls. When I showed him how my digital handset plugged into my ears, he shut up. His disgruntlement was all show, of course. He'd bought steak, potatoes, and leeks for our first supper in. And he would either come and sit in my room or demand I join him in the kitchen.

On Saturday morning, Jane Morgan arrived, as usual. I was invited to join them in the Prince Regent. At around two o'clock I said I would have to go to John Lewis; Rigby announced he'd have to go there as well. We got a cab because I had an ankle injury and was limping. Rigby said we should meet on the top floor of the shop in an hour's time. I bought a bucket, mop, and various odds and ends for cleaning up my new flat. I then got the lift to the top floor and walked like a broken Roman centurion with my spear-like mop in my right hand, my bucket in the other. I saw people smiling at my halting gait and felt rather hurt by their lack of compassion. Then I turned to see Rigby walking in step behind me – mirroring every move, including the limp – with a long curtain track in his right hand. Two Roman centurions . . .

But it was clear that he had a lot on his mind. Sir Peter Hall wanted him to play Pozzo again in the remounted production of his *Waiting for Godot*, which would again begin in Bath, and then transfer to the West End as planned. He was pleased – very pleased – until he discovered that there were at least three 'dark' weeks when he would not be paid. There followed angry phone calls with his agent, Peter Charlesworth, who later gave me his version.

> He was never really emotional about anything, except when he was angry. It was hell with him, because he'd got it into his head that they were trying to cheat him, and nothing I could say would show that this was quite normal and that he was actually going to be doing very well out of it. He wouldn't have it and he sent me halfway barmy with it. Peter Hall was frothing at the mouth and I was going between him and Terry. I don't know how I straightened it out in the end, but I did.

It was the first time I'd seen the process of Rigby coming to a decision about something. I knew about the pacing up and down, and the mind changing, and the chain-smoking, but this was relentless. He hardly slept. He outlined his grievances over and over again; he didn't want my input, but he needed me there to take some of the flak. I was – possibly – marginally better than talking to a brick wall.

Towards the end of my stay he decided to refuse the part, and seemed to be at peace with himself. We had a lot of fun together. And on the day I moved into my new and empty flat he helped me. He lent me a camp bed, a chair, and bits and pieces of crockery and cutlery, as all of my stuff was still in store. Over the next few days he was a constant visitor. He washed down walls ready for painting and fixed my ill-fitting letter box. This was typical Rigby behaviour. He could be a pain in the arse, but when someone needed help, he was there.

A couple of weeks later, he told me he had accepted the part of Pozzo for the London run of *Waiting for Godot*.

Once again, I should have made the journey to Bath, but – once again – I didn't. I was buried in chaos, with two workmen, and a whole houseful of furniture and other rubbish, crammed into my small new flat. Rigby volunteered to store ten boxes in his flat for three months. I was grateful, but for some reason he was concerned that I wouldn't keep my end of the bargain. Just before the offer's deadline, I found myself having to pay someone to collect the boxes and store them elsewhere – for one more month. I discovered that that behaviour often occurred – that he would offer practical help and then regret it. Emotional help and support was another matter: he gave that in bucketfuls.

I eventually saw the latest *Godot* at the Ambassadors Theatre in the West End. Having seen Hall's previous production at the Piccadilly Theatre in the late Nineties, I was astounded by the production as a whole and by the acting. I felt for the first time that I was beginning to understand what the play was about. Rigby was in great pain during much of it. He found dropping to his knees unbearable and had to wear knee-pads. Nevertheless, he somehow garnered all of his energy to give a masterful performance as Pozzo – a character whose breadth of development throughout the play, in such a short space of time, would extend and exhaust even the healthiest of actors. 'In certain parts,' he told Douglas McFerran, 'I'd be holding my bollocks in my hand to get through a big speech.' This was because of his painful hernia, which dragged on – with Rigby continually turning down medical appointments on the grounds that 'I might have to go to the States'. He never did.

He wrote to Noel Murray during the run promising tickets, and added: 'Harold came in the other night and came back – said nice things – His 'Tapes' [*Krapp's Last Tape*, performed by Pinter himself] has now finished – I sense he was pleased it was over and done with. He uses a cane but is in stout fettle. Doing this play is a nightmare.'

The night Jane Morgan and I went to see *Godot*, Rigby had left two tickets at the Box Office for a couple of agents from Los Angeles. They didn't show up and he was extremely put out. In retrospect, I wish I hadn't gone round to see him. It was suggested that he take us out for a meal. He responded by escorting us to his favourite little place near Leicester Square. It turned out to be a greasy spoon with pretensions. In other words, they had wine: a cheap, warm, white wine, and one wine glass. I got mine in a tumbler. Having cooked endless meals for him, we thought his behaviour curmudgeonly. I left him rather abruptly at a bus stop off Trafalgar Square. Half an hour later, he rang wondering why I hadn't waited for him – he would have come back with me. I told him I was not best pleased to be treated so badly, but that if he hadn't rung, he wouldn't be any the wiser. It was the only time I expressed my displeasure so vehemently. It obviously made him think, because he did tell me I was easy to wind up and very gullible. I replied that true friends wouldn't take advantage of that fact.

I later learned that in the run-up to Peter Hall's *Godot*, Rigby often found himself in rehearsal rooms in Clapham. During and after work, he would sometimes visit Father Michael, who lived in the Abbey House of St Michael's Church, occasionally joining the brothers for lunch in the refectory. When Father Michael was officiating in the church, Rigby would wander in and make his presence felt – just by his stature and stillness. It seems he never really participated and may not have taken communion, but the visits were significant.

Father Michael told me that one day, Rigby got on to his knees and said, 'Bless me.' I envisioned this happening at the chancel steps, but when I was shown round the church, and then the house, he pointed at the doormat and said, 'That's where he asked for the blessing. We'd had lunch and he was about to leave.'

A feeling of great understanding washed over me now. Rigby, being the contrary man that he was, somehow couldn't have asked for a blessing in the church. He'd been wrestling with the notion that he wanted a blessing all during lunch – and only managed to ask for one at the point of departure.

❏ JULIET'S TABLE

So the table has been moved around the living room several times. In truth, it's far too big for my new flat, but today I think I've found the perfect location, under the window. I like to read Rigby's letters here and relive, laugh again, or be sad at some of the things he writes. Last year he sat in his usual seat and actually told me about meeting a sweet old man in a cafe. He loves adventures and was clearly moved to write an essay about this encounter. It could only happen to Rigby.

*

I met an old guy – really nice old guy, sitting at a table drinking coffee – in a nearby street – opposite Macey's, LA. He told me the city was a cross between New York and Chicago, where he had been born. He used to sell newspapers some 60 years ago here in downtown LA and that a lot of his family had been in films. He had also many years ago been a promising singer. Frank Sinatra and others had all at various times offered to help him – but he thought they all talked hogwash – and he only appreciated people who talked straight – so he went his own way. He is aged 83 years – doesn't get a State Pension, only Social Security and he had been down here since 1939 at the time when President Roosevelt was in the White House – until he reached the age of 94. He said that the people just kept voting him back into office. I was very surprised as I did not know that. I explained that I was here for a while appearing in a show – and had once also appeared in an American film with the very famous lady Julia Roberts, the film star who recently had twins. We started talking about boxing – and I asked him if he remembered the famous fighter Tommy Farr for the World Championship, which went 15 rounds and the verdict in favour of Joe Louis was hotly disputed. He said he did. It seems that he had met Rocky Marciano, the great boxer – after he had retired from the ring – at Marciano's hotel – and that he was a really good man and had arranged for him to have a room in his hotel for $10 a night. He told me he was later on the way over to the West Side to have lunch and a few beers – and that he always stopped by, at the cafe where we were sitting for his morning coffee. As our conversation continued – he said I would probably be surprised to know that Billie Jean King, the tennis player, was his daughter – and that his mother, who had played minor league baseball with boys – had taught her tennis, in the early days. This tennis connection of course thrilled me very much. I hadn't noticed during our chat, that there was a newspaper on the table – and by chance there was a photo of Julia R. at the Golden Globe Awards, handing out one of the prizes. He didn't seem to connect the fact that I had recently worked with her but explained she wasn't named Julia Roberts at all, but that it was Loretta Young to whom he had once been married. When I expressed incredulity, he insisted that people in the business were always changing their names and taking on new character – and that he had not long ago asked her for help to become a film extra – but that she had ignored him through her secretaries. He confessed to having emphysema – but nevertheless as the talk went on, he continued to chain-smoke from a pack of Pall Mall, but assured me he could still get about OK. Talking further about Show Biz it turned out that his cousin – at one time named Schwartz, now Tony Curtis – who of course was now famous and rich – but that as his family had kind of disowned him – that Curtis never came by to sit and talk with him – or offer him any help. I said to him, would he really wish to become a film extra, at his age (83) – and he replied that he spent all day kind of not doing much and that it would help him fill in a few days a week from time to time. I was really warming to this pleasantly dressed old fellow and really enjoyed my new-found friendship, when he suddenly announced that yet another cousin of his, who had changed his name, was Orson Welles – but that he too had been absent from his life over many years. At this point – I felt that things were starting to get a little cloudy but nevertheless did not hurry away – I had become fascinated and confused. It seems his name is Albert – or Al – and also sometimes he told me he is known as 'Lefty'. I was feeling hungry anyway and decided to leave. He said he often sat there at the cafe – and I said I would drop by again. Just as I was leaving he said, 'Don't go away angry.' I didn't.

FIN

I can visualize Rigby, daydreaming his way through the endless streets of New York or LA, in his combat pants and floppy hat, feeling entirely at home and at one with himself.

2007: The last of the best

I couldn't remember much about 2007 and my encounters, one way or another, with Rigby. Fortunately, I found my diary for that year and was surprised to find 44 entries about him and 24 meetings – and that was despite his Autumn residence in New York. My mind was elsewhere: I was still settling into my flat in Fitzrovia (and had accordingly assumed a new Rigby title: 'Lady Fitzrovia'); my close friend Tony Holland was seriously ill, in and out of hospital, and then dying that November, which left us all reeling.

On 1 January, the day before his seventieth birthday, Rigby had rung me from New York. He had no particular plans for his birthday but supposed he might take himself off to the Met for an opera treat. The second call from him came from New Cavendish Street, which was round the corner, so we had a reunion. And that was a month later.

A more detailed entry on 14 February relates how he came round after a visit to his cardiologist. I think he played down the seriousness of his condition, but he needed a nap before going home. Later he rang to say he'd like to take me to the Palms of Goa restaurant in New Cavendish Street for a Valentine's dinner. He lectured me on being too sensitive.

Two days later he invited me to join him and Phyllis MacMahon to view a studio flat in Hallam Street, just a four-minute walk from my place. For at least three years, he'd been toying with the idea of selling his Devonshire Street flat and buying a pied-à-terre. This was the closest he'd got to it. Someone had made an offer on his flat, and this had been tentatively accepted by the vendors of the studio. The portered block was pretty grand, but the actual space was claustrophobic. I think we all forgot the fact that his New York space was a shoebox, but that it suited him well. Maybe he thought he could replicate it here – but at an astronomical price. In hindsight, it was probably a good thing that the whole procedure fell through. His health wasn't good. Apart from thickening arteries, a worrisome cough and bad feet, he was still suffering from a painful hernia, which had troubled him greatly through *Waiting for Godot*. On 7 March he rang to say he'd had his premeds ready for the hernia operation. It didn't happen: the surgeons were too concerned about his heart. He would have to have an angiogram before they would consider proceeding. It was only natural for his friends to be concerned, and if he didn't get in touch, we would make enquiries. But he hated that. He regarded it as an intrusion.

So in the intervening days, waiting for news, our conversation drifted, as ever, into theatre and acting. He'd listened to a Radio 3 production of *The Homecoming*, directed by Thea Sharrock, and thought it was dreadful. It didn't come up to the Rigby standard – despite the fact that Pinter himself featured in the cast.

By 22 March, when I hadn't had any news, I rang him – a rare occurrence – and he seemed quite terse. I regretted my call. He told me the angiogram had been postponed and then choked me off for gossiping about him to Jane Morgan. We had to play by his rules. We were not to worry without his say-so. I decided to think of him as being invincible. He'd come through a triple bypass, and for the moment was able to take a very deep breath and get on with life. Surely they would throw him on to a stretcher if there was something terribly serious wrong with him? They wouldn't be so nonchalant as to ignore his condition – surely?

❑ JULIET'S TABLE

It's eleven o'clock in the morning and I'm still in my dressing gown. The upstairs neighbours are nocturnal, and have thundered about on the creaking floors above until dawn. Some days I lie abed in an effort to catch up on sleep. Today is such a day and Rigby is here, having risen, uncharacteristically early.

'This is like the old days in Randolph Street,' I venture. 'You in your usual place with your yellow mug.'

He laughs, picking up on my thoughts.

'Do you remember me saying, early one morning, how nice it would be if we could carry on talking until we both fell asleep?'

I do remember it, very clearly. It's recorded in one of my diaries.

'And I said – "And when we wake up, one of us will say 'As I was saying . . .'!" Ah, those were days. And all that.'

He starts talking about *The Homecoming* again and how the recent radio version hadn't worked for him.

'How about when you did Pozzo for John Tydeman? Did you enjoy that?'

'There were some good old mates in it. But I'm not sure. Tydeman was pretty robust in his praise.'

He's uneasy about the medium. All those 'Public School chappies'. We dissect Pinter and Beckett for a while before he begins on Oscar Wilde. *The Importance of Being Earnest* is still relatively fresh in his mind.

'There's going to be film of *A Woman of No Importance*. I'm up for it.'

'Which part?'

'Another cleric. Daubeny.'

'Type-casting. That's a shame.'

'This one's an archdeacon, though. Chasuble was only a canon.'

'You're well up on the Anglican hierarchy – being a Catholic.'

'Stephen Thorne's the man. Tells me what's what.'

'Still. Another film. That's good. Will Julia be in it?'

I can't resist bringing her up: 'My friend, Julia Roberts'.

'And Faye,' he says. 'Don't forget Faye.'

He's made a film with her – Faye Dunaway! – in Wales, called *Flick*.

I look at the time. 'I've got to have a shower and get dressed. I'm supposed to be in the Yorkshire Grey. If you hang on, I'll make us some sandwiches.'

We set off at around one o'clock and meet up with a jolly gathering at the pub, which includes Peter Donaldson, Nick Utechin, Mary Kalemkarian and Ned Chaillet. We revisit *Henry V* and its Sixties production for the RSC, where both Peter and Rigby played lowly parts. Eventually he saunters off to wander the streets and catch up with the other chums who inhabit his life.

*

One day in April 2007, when Rigby was withdrawing cash from a cashpoint in Manchester Square in Marylebone, he was attacked by two men. One of them grabbed him from behind and the other took his cash and made threats. The police were called and Rigby was taken to a police station and questioned about the incident. It seems unbelievable that anyone would regard Rigby as an easy target. Peter Charlesworth remembers it very well.

'He came steaming in here,' he told me, 'and said, "Can I come in?" He'd brought his token bag of cakes. He sat there for two hours, absolutely devastated and outraged. They must have been pretty brave buggers in broad daylight – to take him on.'

The next day he went to cheer on his brother-in-law Barry – his sister Catherine's husband – in the London Marathon, but was so stressed, he had a mild heart attack.

'He told me it was an angina turn,' Peter continued. 'He didn't look well when he came here and that was the day after. He stayed here for two hours drinking tea and eating cream cakes, and smoked fifty cigarettes.

God knows how he survived America without smoking.'

Rigby's sister Catherine thought he looked dreadful. He saw his consultant the next day.

❑ JULIET'S TABLE

I notice he's slowed down a lot. Coming up the last few stairs at Oxford Circus underground station, he is exhausted and has to lean on the railings. More and more I tell him to go straight home rather than walk me to my place in Hanson Street. His hernia operation is still on hold.

Today he wants me to go through his lines for an episode of *Doctors*, the daily BBC 1 soap. He's playing a 'lifer' who is en route to a more secure prison and stops off for an emergency examination by a police doctor: he's apparently had a heart attack in the prison van. I look at him and think 'type-casting'.

The last time he was round I'd admired his multicoloured striped socks. 'They've got a hole in the toe. You can have them.'

He still gives me his old shirts, some of them unworn. Today he hands me a bag of Liquorice Allsorts and a classy carrier which contains a pair of brand-new pink socks. They are extremely expensive and would look good on me if they were not size 12.

He tells me he's not speaking to one of the other tea ladies.

I take the warning on board. *My turn next*, I think. Then he tells me he's irritated by one of the others as well. I pull a face.

Looking more and more like the lifer he's studying, he tells me he's depressed and confused. And not feeling well. I know better than to quiz him. But it seems to me that he is just feeling unsettled again. Is he on the wrong side of the Atlantic? You can never tell. If he was in the States, he'd probably be thinking the same thing.

After he's gone I recall happier times when we laughed a lot more together. Something is very wrong, but he's not ready to tell me what it is. I determine to focus on the old Rigby, and recall walking down Baker Street in the early Nineties when he asked me if I could do birdsong. I had pulled on my lower lip continuously and let out a feeble twitter. Then he showed what he could do in the way of bird whistles. After a minute or two he stopped, very deliberately, took off his cap, laid it on the pavement and started busking.

I want those days back.

*

The 'Cup-of-Tea Ladies' broke the rules and contacted one another to give the latest news on Rigby's well-being. He was not himself and we were all worried. In typical fashion, I did not contact him, fearing a telling-off. But on the 25th of June, according to my diary, he turned up and bawled me out for not ringing him. He took me to the Palms of Goa in New Cavendish Street and told me he'd been offered a part in the West End, but had turned it down. He didn't want to talk about it, but this was something important he wanted to discuss with someone else – a man maybe? Whatever the reason, I was in the wrong compartment of his life for this disclosure.

One of the people he did talk to at the time was Douglas McFerran. 'I must tell you this, Juliet,' he told me.

> On that last evening we saw each other, he told me that he'd just been offered a part in the West End to take over, at very short notice . . . and he said to me, 'This is the part . . . Charlesworth told me: the actor who had the part has just been diagnosed with cancer . . .'
> So Rigby had said, 'What about the bloke who's riddled with cancer?'
> And Charlesworth said, 'Do you want the job or not?'
> And Terry said, 'That's the business we're working in . . . they don't give a shit about it. He's dying. The poor bastard's dying. He's dying. He's riddled with it.'
> I realized, much later, that he was as well.

Rigby continued to be irritable and irritated with his friends, but we all understood that he was very unwell and didn't want to be the centre of attention. I left a message to say I thought he was very good in *Doctors*. Rigby rang back to disagree and to tell me he didn't like giving out bulletins on his state of health. I said I could see him doing a banishment on me like the other ladies. He rang off and I knew I was seriously in his bad books.

He was threatening to go back to the States. He desperately wanted to be in a new production of *The Homecoming* on Broadway, starring Ian McShane.

Despite hanging up on me, Rigby showed up the next evening. At this time, my best friend's daughter, a television director/producer was staying with me for a few weeks while working on a show in London.

❑ JULIET'S TABLE

This is the second time that Rigby, who seems to be burping endlessly, has met Jo, my young lodger. On the first occasion, she had asked him what he did for a living. He was greatly amused by the display of ignorance on her part: 'What do you do, then?' she'd said in her lilting Welsh.

'It just goes to show,' I say, 'that I don't gossip about you all the time.'
He reluctantly agrees.

Now, when we're having supper, I tell him that Jo has taught me how to send texts on my mobile. Rigby and I both have the same antiquated model and neither of us is able to do more than listen to calls and voice-mails.

'Shall I show you how to text? It's quite easy.'

'Oh, go on then, if you must. I've only just managed to do emails.'

It's true. What's more, a one-line Rigby email takes him more than an hour to write, which he finds aggravating. A session in an internet cafe in the States costs over a dollar an hour.

He passes over his phone and I go to 'TEXTS'.

'Would you like me to see whether you've received any, first, before I teach you?'

He nods. I then discover that he has over 75 unread texts going back over five years. They are wide-ranging and I find it almost impossible to read them because they are so unintentionally funny.

He has missed countless extra rehearsals, costume fittings, appointment changes at doctor's surgeries, clinics and banks.

The list of women who have texted is endless and, of course, these are the ones that make me giggle – not because they're funny in themselves, but because Rigby's expression is deadpan. Expressionless.

When I try to teach him how to text, I know I'm going to fail miserably.

'Life goes on, doesn't it, without fucking texts, excuse my French.'

*

I reproduce below two pieces of information about Rigby's pursuit of Pinter, regarding his desire to be in *The Homecoming* on Broadway.

In a postcard to me he writes:

✉ [*Terence Rigby*]

I had lunch with Harold Pinter about a month ago – he was angry that the US management was requiring me to audition for a revival of 'The Homecoming' – for Uncle Sam – and would bloody well tell them so and to sort it out. Two days later, I heard from a New York pal that the role had been cast. I left a message to this effect on Harold's machine. Much later I called and got him and amazingly talked about everything except the business in hand – including that he was getting bloody old and Lady Antonia even older. Finally he said 'When are you going back to the States?' I told him and he said 'Well bloody good luck' and that was it. So no 'Homecoming' for me – but how very mysterious.

And one to Stephen Thorne:

✉ [*Terence Rigby*]

A part of his conversation at our lunch was interesting to say the least, if I can somehow transcribe it. It went thus.

'What's happening to all you chaps? I mean, look. I'm going to the first preview of my play *The Hothouse* at the National later this evening. Stephen Moore is playing the lead and a couple of days ago I went to a run-through, and frankly he didn't appear to know a line. It seems they've sent him up to Harley Street. I mean, I'm there in a few hours. I don't know what to expect.

'And another thing,' he continues. 'Bloody Peter Bowles, out on tour with a large role. After the first act drops, he goes in front of the curtain, addresses the audience with "I'm sorry about this, but I've got to go. I've forgotten to put the cat out." Goes off to his dressing room, climbs into his car and hasn't been heard of since. What's going on? I mean – that's not happening to you – or has it?'

I assured him that I was – (lying through my teeth) – that I was perfectly OK. But the fact is, I saw *The Hothouse* that night and, given a couple of hesitates, Stephen was terrific, and they had excellent reviews. It also had dear Henry Woolf in the show.

In August 2007, Rigby joined me and a couple of friends for an al fresco lunch in Fitzrovia. He was predictably late but explained that from time to time a gathering of old friends and colleagues would enjoy a liquid lunch in a pub in Notting Hill Gate. Apart from Rigby and others, there were his old *Softly, Softly* friends Frank Windsor and James Ellis – who said that, in the old days, Rigby and Sinclair would show up in Holland Park where everyone was always welcome. But in the pub, Rigby by now teetotal, of course, was the quiet one who came out with one-liners.

At the end of our lunch he described the whole mugging incident; how he had shat himself, and suffered the humiliation of sorting himself out in the police station, before being driven home. It must have had a profound effect on him to admit how scared he had been. But rather like the Zagreb incident, it took several months before Rigby was able to process the traumatic horror of it into a rehearsed tale to tell his friends.

Naturally, news of Rigby's mugging and heart problems reached his brother Joseph in Spain. 'Dear Terry (Hi, Kid!),' Joseph wrote to his brother on 5 June 2007, 'Hope you're well and feeling much better! I heard you don't want any more "effing" phone calls – understandable – but it was only out of concern – and we do want to hear from time to time . . . So we'll leave it that you'll keep in touch with Patrick . . .' The letter ends with more concern for Rigby – a typical Joe gesture: 'Dr. Conor Lynch is here in Spain this week – haven't met up with him yet, but I'll invite him over and no doubt have a discussion about you know who! Keep up the good work, Kid – hope you'll feel "on the mend"! as each week passes. Please let me know if I can be of any help – please keep in touch!'

One evening in late August, Enyd Williams, the Radio Drama producer, had joined me for dinner when Rigby showed up. I swear he knew when I was making a special effort in the kitchen department. For some reason, we started talking about Shakespeare's sonnets, and Enyd, who of course is into the spoken word, explained to Rigby how they should be approached. I could see Rigby's face setting into a fixed expression, at which point I gathered the dirty plates and retired to the kitchen.

Over the next two weeks he rang from Villandry in Great Portland Street to ask me to join him for a hot chocolate, and we'd spend a couple of happy hours watching the world go by. Then home for the inevitable tea and cheddar cheese. September the 13th was one such occasion where we covered every subject under the sun – except, crucially, that he was flying back to the States. Jane Morgan rang on the 17th to tell me as much.

He was forever changing his ticket, out of fear of the 'iron bird', or of making the wrong decision, but when he was able to garner up all his resolve and daring, he would go – then and there, without warning.

Back in the States, the fact that *The Homecoming* was going on without him still irked Rigby. In a letter to Noel he says:

✉ [*Terence Rigby*]

The projected production of 'The Homecoming' for which Harold P. had championed me for the part of Uncle Sam, the chauffeur – has gone all wrong. Vast skulduggery in abundance has deprived me of a Broadway return. So, it seems 'they' even have the temerity to discard the author's recommendations. Ian McShane will be playing Max – outstanding chap though he is – he's not Max. Anyway, good luck to them – I'll just have to accept that I was there in the golden years – and be satisfied.'

In November 2007, from the Golf Real Village near Marbella, Joseph Rigby wrote to try and persuade his brother to spend the forthcoming Christmas with nearly all of the Rigby clan at Sandford. Although suggesting various ways of avoiding the noise of young children, I'm sure he would not have been over-optimistic about his brother's putting in an appearance. He knew how much Rigby disliked Christmas.

Although he was so often away, for some reason I felt very close to Rigby during this time. When so many of my dearest friends were sick and dying, I was conscious that all my friends were deeply important to me. The following extracts from a letter to me, following a close friend's attempted suicide, show Rigby's compassion and concern. There was never anything forced in his kindness to friends.

✉ [*Terence Rigby*]

8th November '07

[...] more importantly, you will have got my short email regarding your awful shock. Apart from giving you my modest solace – naturally you sent me whirling along through your long and mostly unknown to me, friends – trying to place the dear unfortunate subject. I must only hope that whoever is involved, some calm has arrived, and normality is safely resumed. I would wish to say that such has never touched my life, but so many years ago, we did have a family tragedy, a wonderful cousin, he I'm afraid, died. RIP.

Essentially then, professionally nothing is happening – the only movement is the offer of *Antony and Cleopatra*, next February, a project which does not interest me. I put it on hold, but now they've come back and want to know before this coming Friday. The film I was chasing is still on financial hold and my contact with my New York agent is less than good. Of course I missed two if not three possibles for Broadway, due to being tied up in England earlier in the year, but although people have it that I am always working, it's 10 months now, and for me that's very unusual. Thankfully I do not lead too extravagant a life, though Devonshire Street bills do hit me hard and the reserve continues to be rocky. Thankfully I did get a percentage of my UK private medicine bills offset by my Screen Actors Guild insurance. Also my rent has gone up.

I continue to read perhaps a little too late into the early hours which affects my sleeping, so I rise later. I'm on a biography of Rudyard Kipling, which is fairly interesting – a lot of India and the States, where I've never been, nor will ever, I suspect, interests me – if only because my very dear grandma on Father's side, was born there, the daughter of a British soldier.

I tend to break my days up in two ways, by going for a modest lunch either at the Edison Hotel where the soup is hearty and where I meet a collection of actors around my age – and if wanted, answer their queries about the English theatre scene. Or, to meet my old pal Hughie (I may dine at their place tomorrow) at another cafe called the Cranberry on West 45th at 6th Avenue. They are a motley crew as they all go there from their AA meeting at the local church.

Sometimes it's just Hughie and me – sometimes it's a table of seven or eight, with an occasional lady. The stories are very good. After either of these venues, I might drop into Equity, which is on 45th at Times Square, and look at the notices about various upcoming showcases and auditions. Also boards with accommodation addresses all over the country. There's quite a large public room – only for actors, so at least there is somewhere for people to go to make contacts. There are auditions all the time, either there or at various centres around the city and they are called EPAs, which stands for Equity Principal Auditions. However, there is something curious about it all – which I found only by chance. I decided to go for one of these auditions and did a bit of Shakespeare – but when I told my agents they nearly went spare – it seems these auditions are for actors who have no representation and are usually run by some assistant to the assistant to the assistant of the director – and that the pukka auditions are only arranged through agents. I find this very odd. Anyway I shall continue to go when the mood takes me, as it does give you a bit of practice.

Rigby's belief that he couldn't speak Shakespeare persisted. For some reason he didn't trust his instinct in the way he always did with Pinter and Beckett. In his least confident moments he would still consult Stephen Thorne:

> I would ask him to read [Shakespeare], and I'm afraid, since I'm not a director, I would say, 'Actually I think it should sound like this,' and it was mostly to do with scansion and iambic pentameter – which he was very frightened of. Directors used to say 'Ignore whatever it is', but I would say '*No*, you can't ignore it. You must keep to the punctuation and the knowledge that it is written in a particular way.' It was like a seminar on Shakespeare. He would pursue the problem, and sometimes I had to say: 'Forget about *di-dum, di-dum, di-dum*, and just say this line – meaning "I'll go and do so-and-so" – and forget about what you've learned. Which is the basic thing. It's like riding a bicycle: you don't always think "I must keep my legs going round and round, and *that* happens . . ." It's the same as Shakespeare verse. If you do it enough, you will forget about all that. It will be instinctive.' I was just regurgitating other people's advice. I didn't think of myself as a teacher. I just tried to answer questions.

I discovered a rough draft of a reference Rigby was working on for a young Italian-American actor. It's another example of Rigby's kindness and concern for young talent. But more importantly, it shows how, in fact, Rigby was entirely confident in his own ability to speak Shakespearean verse.

☞ [*Terence Rigby*]

This part-time trainee actor, during the two years that I have known him, has made extremely commendable advances in his study of, and speaking of English, and is now at a point of breaking, in a formidable way, the difficult barrier of it being a second language.

He has excellent posture, moves well and has acceptably good gestures, without having had any formal training in this area. He would appear to have a talent in mimicry, and notes differences, clearly, in the speech patterns and sounds of not only different parts of the UK but also in

American and international peoples. His naturally light and, to a degree, nasal sound would be strengthened with tuition. He has an excellent memory – indeed a very speedy one, in learning texts – even in the more advanced and demanding words of Shakespeare. He is also now coming to understand the imagery which is used so frequently in the author's work. With him, I have studied *Richard III*, some Shakespearean sonnets, *A Day in the Life of Joe Egg*, some American poetry, and some extracts from Dostoevsky's work – *The Idiot* – and listened to his renderings from each of these subjects . . .

To continue with his letter to me, from around the same time:

✉ [*Terence Rigby*]

There's a bitter wind blowing up – I now find I need a vest and also a big woolly jumper – they do get a few hours of sunshine. Without warning I took myself off to see a preview of *Rock'n'Roll*, the Stoppard play which I ignored in London – and liked very much, bumping into Trevor Nunn, who was quite amusing, and Tom Stoppard, who was gracious – and Sinead Cusack who is quite special – I'd met her once or twice in the UK. As it happens, Harry Haun, a Press pal who writes for *Playbill*, had a spare ticket a few days later for the opening. So I went again, which included an invite to the party which was burstingly full. But I had my photo taken with a lady actress and was printed (posted?) on the web. 'What larks, Pip!'

I know one gets Charity Mail in England but here it's mammoth, I'd say I get about ten each week – I usually respond to people feeding ones and UNICEF, the rest mostly go in the bin. I won't detain this letter by trying to think of other things to say – so I wish you ever so well – and don't become a stranger. 'That' opens around 23 November. I wish all your family and friends well.

Affection.

Lord Marylebone

My friend Tony Holland died soon after this letter was written. A couple of acquaintances from London were in New York at the time and wanted details of his funeral. Rigby sent two weird emails that I misconstrued. Prompting the following letter:

✉ [*Terence Rigby*]

5th December 2007

Dear Juliet,

I think I may essentially give up the email business and stick to letters. My one-finger laboured style doesn't help me flow – thus creating a staccato style which lacks warmth – and I am of course always plagued by the time factor – so many minutes for so many dollars. However to turn to more important matters. Realizing that the loss of your professional pal has hit you very hard – I would like to hope that his service was, if ever they can be, a good and glorious tribute – to a man who was so very close to you in your earlier writing, and whose company was always special, in fact quite electric – and that a wide cross-section of his and your colleagues were able to be present. Though you will be down for a considerable time, I would like to think that you will not allow your loss to completely overwhelm you for too long – and that as soon as it's possible you will recover yourself and become the wonderful Lady Fitzrovia that you are. You have had a lot of trials during this last year to contend with – a lot of stress from various directions – you must not let this tragedy compound with others and quite bring you to your knees. Don't make yourself ill.

Though I referred to it somewhat indirectly in an email, I didn't thank you directly for your long letter – many thanks for that. Your BAFTA evening with Jill Balcon was clearly very special. Glad the film [*The Ballad of Jack and Rose*, written and directed by Rebecca Miller] was good, and great that Daniel Day-Lewis's mom was so well cared for by the studio. I will look around for the films you mentioned, though you are right that I am not much of a film buff – in fact I've seen more plays here in a couple of weeks than I would normally see in 10 years. I bet incidentally that you eventually had a great time with George [my grandson] and all his toys, all on your own as it were.

As at time of writing I have heard no news on my DC *Antony and Cleopatra* audition which I thought went quite well – I did 7 pages which I have learned – a couple of fluffs – before finding out they didn't expect me to have it by heart. Now I'm expecting to do an audition for *A Woman of No Importance* – but not the film I spoke of – but for Yale Theatre Productions. About the same time as the DC Shakespeare play. Goodness me, it is getting tough and cold here – having to dress up much more and choosing not to venture out except when essential – which makes, what with my place being so small – for a bit of claustrophobia. I believe my Green Card meetings are now completed, I'm just waiting for an official word on my extension . . .

I steeled myself to see the final run of *The Homecoming* – quite a curious evening seeing that play. It turned out less than good – essentially it's a non-adult production – they are all too young. However, in my head the play stood up, though I imagine I was making allowances all the time. Despite Harold's recent silent behaviour I sent him off an appraisal – since I know he will not be coming to New York. He has not acknowledged my note. You probably know that the stagehand strike is over and the lights are back on on Broadway. But the writers' strike is still in full flood. Glad the boyo's book [Ray Jenkins's biography of the pacifist Francis Cammaerts] has come out (pass on my congratulations please – and I will have you take on board my well meant advice – about looking after yourself. Take care. Good luck.

Always – as ever, Marylebone.

The Homecoming got brilliant reviews in New York. In a letter to Noel, Rigby reiterated his view that 'Ian McShane is too young – they are all too young – it makes for a non-adult presentation. How fitting you should mention Paul Rogers – what a power house he was in the role [of Max].'

2008: A long journey home

As Joe had written, Catherine had invited all the family for Christmas 2007, including Rigby, but no one ever expected him to show up. But on Christmas Eve, when all the children had been found beds, and the adults had consumed more than 'the safe driving limit' of wine, Rigby telephoned from Bristol Parkway. It was gone 11.30 p.m., and there weren't many people around. Catherine was delighted but said there was no one sober enough to pick him up. She recommended he get the next train to Temple Meads, and a taxi from there. As luck would have it, all further trains had been cancelled and a free taxi service was provided to ferry the remaining stragglers to Temple Meads. Rigby's driver reckoned he might as well take him all the way to Sandford. He'd booked into a local hotel, knowing it would be a tight squeeze at Catherine and Barry's house. He described the visit to Noel Murray in a belated Christmas card.

✉ [*Terence Rigby*]

Dear Each,
    Late but not entirely forgotten – Just back from food-stuffed 3 nights at Rigby Gathering, Sandford, near Weston-Super-Mare – sister Catherine, 14 adults, 4 babies – Sneaked off to local Hotel Ski Centre – quiet, odd, only 4 in the hotel. Duty done and not too bad though too much TV (not for me).

Catherine recalls that he stood over her when she was making the gravy and asked for some to be decanted before she added some wine.

Her husband Barry said that, as usual, Rigby was courteous, monosyllabic. No real conversation. He liked the fact that Rigby called him 'Bar'. It acknowledged an underlying affection, despite the difficulties in communication. Eleanor, their daughter, said she didn't really know her uncle. They'd only met about four times, but she didn't regard him as special. She had been brought up, she said, to regard everyone as equal and therefore he was just her uncle. It wasn't until she was at university that a boyfriend took her to an Art Cinema that was showing *Get Carter*. She nudged him in surprise, and said, 'That's my uncle.'

Rigby left the gathering on Christmas Day to record a greetings message on my phone. I was with my family for Christmas in Cambridge, and was sad to have missed him. As the New Year approached, he didn't get in touch, and I was miffed, but not surprised, that for some reason I was being excluded from his visiting list. I knew that his departure for Yale was imminent.

On 3 January 2008, Rigby attended the Marylebone Health Centre. He came away with a prescription with nine items listed: 'Bisoprolol. Amlodipine. Sotolol. Beclometosone. Clopidogriel. Imdur Durule. Atorvastatin. Aspirin and Nitrolingual.'

On Friday 4 January, Rigby wrote to Noel and Kate Murray:

✉ [*Terence Rigby*]

Plan is a Tuesday 5th off-again to merry old New York en route to Yale (New Haven) – about 2 hours train equidistant to Boston – rehearsals start Feb 14 – the show is due to collapse in a heap around April 10. I have feebly started my memoirs – Feeble is about the right word. [...] Here in my paper-strewn kitchen I am being kept company by my hard-working Bendix whooshing my smalls about – one never need be alone if you have a trusted Bendix. (There is a line or two in 'No Man's Land' which I'm afraid I paraphrase: 'Imagine waking up with only the furniture staring at you' – Not even a very good paraphrase.)

I took myself off to see the new London version of *Importance of Being Earnest*, only to discover how good I was as Rev. Chasuble. Penelope Keith just ordinaire as Lady B – not good enough – 'ordinaire'! Jack Worthing was reasonably first class – otherwise it was below par. Only matter of significance on the night was my pointing out to an usher that gentleman two rows in front of me looked unwell and in need of attention. Poor chap was eventually carried out dead as a door nail. RIP. Not a St John Ambulance bloke in sight – They seem to have vanished like many another thing.

Haven't had a peep out of 'Mrs Sinclair' this Christmas – usually I do hear through Roddy Hall (had a card from her) – Last knockings was Alexander ringing me in search of possible digs while I was away in the States – but I think my mooted prices put him off. Sinclair memory still gets well aired when pals meet – he still raises much, much laughter.

Oh dear the Bendix is screaming to have its water changed – there's always something – I must get on.

Tons of warmth and mirth.
TCR

On Saturday, 5 January 2008, he rang at last. I was cooking dinner for Ray Jenkins and me. I invited him to join us and (surprise, surprise) he did. I added some pork sausages to the venison ones in the casserole. Rigby seemed to be on good form, but he hadn't shaken off the worrisome cough that continued to plague him. I discovered later that his consultant was concerned that he might have contracted tuberculosis. Since his father had suffered from the same disease, he was naturally very worried. And I guess fearful that he might pass it on to his friends.

He didn't get in touch again until over a fortnight later, on 23 January, when he phoned and said he wanted my assistance. He'd written his presidential speech for the Tennis Club AGM, wanted to dictate it to me – by phone – and then email it to Jane Morgan's computer so that she could print it up and give it to him on his way to the club. He dictated the first part which I duly sent, and then a little later, he dictated the second part which I also sent. I gather he then got a cab to Jane's and picked up his speech. Unfortunately, Peter Acre (Jane's partner) had only printed the first part and Rigby didn't realize this until he arrived at the club. It later transpired that it was just as well, since the second part of the speech was somewhat controversial. He took his presidency very seriously and he was very concerned that there were too many plans afoot that didn't have unanimous approval.

On the same day he received a card from Mike Hodges:

✉ [*Mike Hodges*]

Dear Terence,

What a great letter – many thanks. You never seem to stop working, which is only right – You're a great actor. Did I tell you that Carol and I have become friends with [the painter] Anthony Palliser (via Charlotte Rampling) in Paris. What a wonderful portrait he did of you. I too, hope that we work together again soon – although I move slower than a snail between films. Best.

Mike (Hodges)

Several days later, I was put out that Rigby hadn't rung to thank me for my efforts on his behalf and assumed he'd gone to Yale.

Wrong again! He turned up out of the blue on Wednesday the 30th. He said he'd delayed his departure. He took me to the Palms of Goa in New Cavendish Street for a meal. He seemed to think it was my fault that the second part of his speech hadn't arrived on time. But my 'lodger' Jo showed up later and fixed my computer, so that I was able to demonstrate that the email was sent quite soon after he'd dictated the piece to me. When he'd gone, I realized he'd left behind his floppy hat with the pink flower.

❏ JULIET'S TABLE

Tonight is one of those times when I don't feel like cooking. It happens. As I rummage about in the freezer compartment, the door buzzer sounds. It's Rigby.

'I left my hat.'

'I know. It's there. I meant to ring you.'

I sense he wants to hang around. 'I'm having frozen fish and chips for my supper. D'you want some?'

Silly question. It's food, isn't it? He never says no. I pour out a trayful of frozen chips and two solid triangles of cod. Then I make his tea. Maybe it's because he has walked into a warm atmosphere from the outside cold, but the inevitable coughing bout takes much longer than usual to settle. No point in mentioning it.

When we finally settle down to eat, it's obvious he has something on his mind. I wait.

'You know I've decided to write my memoirs . . . I'm not getting anywhere.'

'Too much to say?'

He nods. 'Where do you start? I've started three times. Not good, mate.'

'Fay Weldon says she nearly always discards the first forty pages. It's the hardest bit, finding the starting point.' He looks at me for a long time – it's longer than a Pinter pause. Now what?

'Will you help me?'

Without a moment's hesitation, I say, 'Of course. I'll do my best.'

I should have hum'd and ha'd perhaps, but I didn't. Instead, I cool things a bit by telling him that I'll give some thought about how to set about the task. It'll be easier by letter. If I kick off now it'll sound like one of my student diatribes at Goldsmiths or Arvon.

'There's no pudding. I was going to have a bag of Liquorice Allsorts for a treat. Is that all right?'

'Lovely.'

'But you can't have the brown ones.'

There's a momentary twinkle in his eyes, but then he looks serious again. It's another 'topic'.

'I'm changing my will. I was going to leave all my possessions to my nephew. All my tennis memorabilia and that. Pictures and things. What do you think?'

'I don't know.' I think hard. It's none of my business what he does.

'Well, I suppose if I was one of your nieces or nephews, I'd like to have a keepsake. You were very pleased that Sir John remembered you. That little magnifying glass is a lovely thing to have. It was me that showed you it had a whistle on the end of it.'

'So you did.' He's thoughtful now, and I don't want to interrupt what's going on in that complicated brain of his. I go off to make more tea. As I stand over the singing kettle, I'm worried by the breathlessness and the persistent cough. And neither of us should be eating fish and chips.

He tells me he's going to New York next Tuesday. I tell him I'll believe it when it happens.

'You've missed the fish pie. You wrote to say you wanted to sample it. Tough.'

'I could come for Sunday lunch.'

And that's how we leave it. I'm amazed he wants to come again so soon. But as I stack the plates into the dishwasher, I have this feeling of dread. Memoirs? Will? The terrible coughing?

I don't want him to go away. Richard Johns went to Bologna and came back in a box.

On Saturday I bought all the most succulent pieces of fish I could lay my hands on and prepared a good fish stock with the bones and shells. On Sunday morning I made a strenuous effort to produce the best pie ever. It was almost as good as the one I made when my son brought me some linen-wrapped cod straight from the Arctic Circle.

Out of consideration, I had suggested that Rigby should come for 2.30 so as not to rush him.

He arrived quite late as he'd called in at the Bricklayers Arms for a drink and to meet up with old cronies, Paul Redfern and others. He said, very enthusiastically, that the pub was now serving dripping on hot toast for £1.50 and you got two slices. I resisted the urge to shout at him but I was not best pleased that he'd spoilt his appetite. Nevertheless he still managed a gargantuan portion and proclaimed it to be the best he'd ever eaten. I told him not to lie and he giggled.

This was the last meal we ever had together. An occasion of laughter, bickering, and quotes from *A Woman of No Importance*.

As he left he said, 'Don't become a stranger.'

*

Rigby left for New York on Tuesday, 5 February 2008. The following week he was sitting in a station cafe, waiting for a train to Yale, blank exercise book and pen to hand:

⮕ [*Terence Rigby*]

Yale. A Kind of Prologue. Book. Valentine's Day, 2008
    I am sitting at Grand Central – waiting for a train to New Haven (Yale) to depart. Readers who may have stayed the course, may know that on this my 71st year, en route to perform in 'Woman of No Importance' – although the Venerable Archdeacon Daubeny is a relatively small though amusing role – that things being as they are, that I am again treading over thin ice. April 12th is the End Date and I am sure that my final words on the event will prove of great interest – if only to me. My arrival at New Haven put me in a reflective mood since this is where I came to visit my 're-visited' friend Wally Gilman in the local hospital: Wally, who I had known thirty years earlier in England and who died in a local hospice about a year ago. My final phone calls to her from LA where I was doing 'Earnest' were naturally very poignant – She even had trouble just holding the phone up to her ear. (RIP.)

Barbara Caruso met up with Rigby before he went off to Yale. 'The phone rang,' she recalls:

It was a rainy night in New York. He was on 72nd Street and said 'I don't suppose the kettle's on?' It was about 11.30 at night. We talked and he said he was going to visit Old Saybrook the next day. She was in hospital and had asked him to buy some make-up for her. She was concerned about her appearance. I told Rigby there was an all-night drugstore on 72nd Street and I offered to go with him. He bought make-up – the whole kit and a mirror and all sorts. The last thing you would imagine Rigby doing. He was ill himself. He never gave this friend a name. She was known as Old Saybrook and lived quite close to Katharine Hepburn. She died not long after this.

It was around this time that I began to encourage Rigby to approach his memoirs in earnest. I suggested that he keep a notepad of twenty-six sections, divided alphabetically, and to enter the topics as and when they struck him – 'Beckett' and 'Buckstone', for example, or 'Parties' and 'Pinter' – and then write down his thoughts as they came. I thought that would be a less daunting method than to start from scratch. It is maybe because Rigby took up my advice that the material he managed to write, in his diary and elsewhere, supplies a disconnected sequence of set pieces.

    Rigby began rehearsals at Yale of *A Woman of No Importance*, and settled into the familiar routine of getting to know his fellow actors and probably every pretty waitress in the vicinity. It would be essential that he find out all the late opening bars and eateries. He wrote me a letter describing the whole scene.

✉ [*Terence Rigby*]

St Patrick's Day, 17th March '08

At Yale University rehearsing. I hope that I find you in at least reasonable, if not excellent health and spirits. That you may by now have finalized or be near to – the sale of 28 Randolph St [my basement flat] – but the writing is progressing with no real red flags from the authorities – but the prospect of a bit of extra reserves enables you to gallivant at will – and that your immediate family proceed well. No doubt you will have been muttering darkly about the lack of contact. Well, fact is my cup floweth pretty full now – a new play, a company of strangers both fairly decent sorts – new accommodation – a one-bed apartment quite near the rehearsal room and theatre, and weekly runs to the large supermarket to gather in food for the week – courtesy large van – will stop to recount, the party's small though colourful and I do get a lot of free time. It's very lazy making and my general disposition is mingled with inertia – I sometimes go and sit in on rehearsals even when not needed, to remind myself that I am in the play. Costumes arrived – oddly from CosProps UK – and moving into theatre is beginning too – technicals begin on 14 March. Looking around the cast, I'm tempted to think that some sort of leading roles are not inhabited by the right people – a certain necessary Englishness could well be absent and I do think it is a difficult piece of work. We have several senior students attached to us – two actors, one actress very talented – plus stage management, lighting, sound and costume design. Rehearsal schedule 2:30 p.m. to 11 p.m. – because the students have classes to attempt as well. To them of course, it is a most excellent and rewarding experience working with pros. The town is teeming with bright young things, male and female, and overall they respond to being greeted in the streets, following a quite substantial meet-and-greet gathering in the theatre earlier on. I guess it's not unlike the sort of atmosphere that one may experience in Cambridge or Oxford – we have access to the Yale library and also if you're up to it – the gymnasium. The students also have their own theatre, plus many spaces, and show our productions of many classics like hot cakes. Last week, 'Pericles', 'Godot' and more. By way of variation –without any specific theme, these last three weekends – well, part of Saturday and Sunday – I have trained into New York – the wonderful Grand Central Station – it's around one hour forty minutes, basically at a cost of £10 plus taxes – to deal with mail and get overnight sleep away from the workplace. In American terms such journeys are commonplace the place being so vast and large cities. Tomorrow I may take a car ride with one of the actors. But then you've done that sort of thing yourself.

I continue to read. Just about to finish book on Orson Welles – the [Simon] Callow book – dense but revealing. Quite what a guy Welles could have been if he hadn't been so off centre – he could have run for president. Utterly fascinating. I have made little – but some inroad with my own memoirs. Maybe I've got 8 to 10 foolscap in the bag – but my enthusiasm – motivation is low. The need to write them is evasive.

My agent Charlesworth called up about an episode in a Linda LaPlante – but par for the course he had my end date wrong.

Now a great deal later – sounds silly, I mislaid your correct address again. I hope it's 23 – 3 – it just does not sound right. We've had snow, wind, and lots, lots of rain – seems just like Birmingham. Not done much moving around – didn't go to New York city this weekend – and oddly celebrated St Patrick's day here on 9 March, something to do with Palm Sunday being usually in April. Apart from one short postcard in months – to Jane – Bruce is the only correspondence I've engaged with – it's been one of those periods. Technical rehearsals are tiresome and stretched as the various important issues are all discussed by third year students – and part of the policy is that the process is part of their training – so they aren't given time overall, I believe, in the policy process, also they are very charming people. I wish there was something more to say – there simply is not.

Warmest, Marylebone T.

Back in London, Jane Morgan and I broke all the rules again about not gossiping with each other and swapped reports on Rigby's well-being. The visit home at Christmas clearly demonstrated that he was not a well man and we became anxious for news.[13]

A Woman of No Importance duly opened, but Rigby had for some time complained about dizziness and shortness of breath before going on stage. I had suggested he avoid smoking for half an hour or so before his first entrance. On 3 April, Jane Morgan rang to say that Rigby had collapsed and was in hospital. He had a pain in his leg. The next day, Jane rang again to say that Rigby had cancer of the lung. I was devastated.

By the following Saturday, 5 April, a secondary cancer had been diagnosed: a brain tumour. I felt helpless, and then angry that he was so far away.

---

13   Following Rigby's death, I talked at length with his friends Barbara Caruso and James Stephens (who were both extremely important to Rigby in those last months of his life), and was therefore able to piece together information from both sides of the Atlantic. It still affects me very much to trace this journey towards his death. It is exemplary of Rigby's character – a man who embraced drama and conflict – that he found it almost impossible to make clear decisions, and would only allow certain people to know all of the truth, while apparently in complete denial to others. I, for example, had to pretend I didn't know that he was terminally ill, and still encourage him to keep on writing. I wanted him home so that I could cajole him into finishing his memoirs, taking dictation if necessary, but I didn't dare suggest it.

What happened is perhaps best described in Rigby's own words in a letter to Kate and Noel Murray from the following day:

✉ *[Terence Rigby]*

6 April 2008

We opened fine and last Saturday another actor offered me a lift to New York plus our lead actress Kate Forbes. After about 10 mins my left leg started to tighten up as if clamped – and then began to vibrate and lurch like a piston – I had to ask to stop – not easy on these Freeways.

I lurched out of the car and my leg was non-weight-bearing, and I fell, twisting on to my back on the grass and staring up at The Plough through some overhanging branches. My leg was still thumping away for many minutes – The Police medics were called and an ambulance took me into ER at St Raphael's Hospital, New Haven. After 7 hours they were going to release me – 'purely muscular' – but as we continued to chat – he changed his mind and sent me for a scan and due to that diagnosis they have held on to me. I regret to have to inform you that I am seriously ill in two parts of my body and that's it.

It's not been a lot of fun these last days – I've seen more doctors, nurses, specialists at various times of Round the Clock – than, well, I don't know what. I'm just saying activity round the clock and sleep is difficult to achieve.

At the show they have my understudy on – James Bundy, Artistic Director and Dean of Yale Drama has been in several times and being 'all help necessary'.

I decided to call Lynn Redgrave who lives in Danbury Connecticut, she has been through all that Breast stuff and is a strong open patron – she was terrific spending an hour or so on the phone talking me through as much as she could.

I also on Day 4 here, called brother Patrick – the only other person I have spoken to – apart from them you are the first to get this situation report. It's very difficult to know who to tell – not to upset the already upset cart if you follow me. I think if you speak to Pat you had better say I'm having a poor spell (no details). Do you see what I mean? It's tricky. I remain, with many decisions to make – Therapy is essential there is no option on that – Where? When? – New Haven, New York, London – Am I fit to fly? Can I by hook, crook, or madness get back to the show for the final week.

Dear Friends, take care –

Terry

'He actually rang me,' Peter Charlesworth told me, 'when they'd diagnosed that he had cancer of the lungs, and I was so amazed that he should ring me. He said to me, "What shall I do?" – and never in all those years had he ever said "What shall I do?" And the only thing I could say was "Terry, go

210

back on the stage, that's where you belong".'

Back in England, Patrick had meanwhile told his siblings the bad news, and had rung Jane Morgan, who was given permission to tell me. We all felt so helpless. Everyone wanted to rush over to America to be of some comfort and use to Rigby. But he would have blasted us out. Nevertheless, I was seriously tempted to get on a plane and pretend I was on a shopping trip. He wouldn't have bought that. Letters had to be newsy, unconcerned, funny – not easy in those ghastly circumstances. Sitting helplessly at home, I felt pissed off with him for being so far away, so unreachable.

Rigby's diary for this period is laconic:

✎ [*Diary*]

Friday, 11th April
Returned to show – collapsed towards end of Act III.
Medics – St Raphael – discharged 2:30 p.m.

13th April
Train to NYC with Anthony. No key.

Lynn Redgrave advised him to go to New York to the prestigious Sloan-Kettering Hospital, which specializes in the treatment of cancer. As with every other major quandary in his life, he would have pondered long and hard before making the decision to go to New York. A big consideration, I'm sure, was the fact he had a base in New York and a supportive group of friends who would all be concerned for him. He endured radio therapy before making the journey.

When he was strong enough, they operated to remove the brain tumour. There were moments of great anxiety when it seemed as if he wouldn't survive the trauma. I wrote in my diary: 'Please God let him be OK.' That was on 23 April. Two days later, he actually spoke to Patrick. But on the 28th, I heard that he was back in intensive care. He had a clot in his leg and pneumonia. Four days later, he had a clot in his lung. Clearly, Rigby was a man of great physical strength and determination. His cussedness paid off. By 11 May, he was having more therapy. On the 19th, he said he'd like to have a holiday in Spain.

He was back in his studio flat by 25 May. Jane had spoken to him and he'd said my letter had arrived safely. On the 29th I plucked up the courage to ring him. It was wonderful to hear his voice and have him tell me off as ever. I later found a lined exercise book which included his diary, begun on the same day. Considering that Rigby was suffering from a brain

211

tumour, his written thoughts are quite extraordinary. I cannot pretend to understand all of it, but here are some extracts – the jottings of a jobbing actor punctuated by poignant, unheralded swings into memoir, and private fears of the unknown.

✎ [*Diary*]

29 May '08. NYC.
A few days ago my Edison Pals presented me [with] a copy of the *Village Voice* review for the recent 2007 revival of 'The Homecoming' – an event which had held much interest – almost intrigue – for me during at least the last two years. The writer was Michael Feingold who since the mid Sixties has seemed synonymous with the Voice Drama output [...]

30 May '08
From where I sit under the awning [...] sipping tea – learning to drink and eat again – after the scorching of my oesophagus – a clear line advert appears to the right, and staring at me is 'Thurgood' starring Laurence Fishburne – directed by Leonard Foglia, who directed me in a new play 'The Last True Believer' in Seattle – by Robert E. Sherwood. Later we revived it as a rehearsed reading at – wait for it – yes – The Actors' Studio on W44 St. Arthur Penn and Leonard went for each other's throats. This West 45 St is deep in the Broadway area of theatres and there are memories and reflections of the past – what was – what might have been – indeed what very much was – just Robert W. Sherwood now married [...] quite a brilliant text man – just not yet carried it off – finds managements confusing. Saw Patrick Stewart across this very street yesterday in company – being feted for his Scottish Play – I'll catch up with him. Saw also Michael Feast about 6 weeks ago, who's playing Macduff – he finally made it to Broadway. He could have come over in 1976 as he was the fourth man in 'No Man's Land' (Foster) – sadly he had at that time other things in his eyes – Lady Covington for one. ('Don't Cry For Me Argentina' the first rendering). Somehow Sir Peter Hall glided him away from NYC. I was sad about that – we were very fond of each other and replacements are rarely satisfactory, and we opened at the Long Acre without him.

Questions for Dr Ryzri 5 June 2008
• What improvements have been evident since the brain op and the seven (14) sessions of Radiation treatment over 33 days. Am I able to travel – when? Is it easy to communicate my situation to UK hospitals to good effect? Expectancy!
• What would be the side effects from now on with Chemotherapy?
• Is the view of Dr Bronner likely to be of heavier effect?
• Discuss Insurance aspects!

8 June. NYC. (I'm guessing at the day)
Yesterday For some reason I woke from a snooze to turn on 'The Tonys'

– a really ineffective programme about the annual awards. Since way back in '66 when Alexander Cohen presented the first-ever TV awards from the Shubert Theatre – hosted by Kirk Douglas – it was naturally . . . a total non-starter . . . Endless little patch-up cuts – and to add proper insult the real drama plays reduced to solitary half-second blimps. 'The Homecoming' which I saw during its last rehearsal – the Sullivan '08 version – somehow was up for 3 awards as opposed to our original 5 of which we won 4. But the point was – it was perfictory [*sic:* perfunctory] – as were reference to 'SeaFarer' the [Conor] McPherson play and Stoppard's 'Rock 'n' Roll'. At the time of writing I do not know of any results.

Kit Plaschkes (Whitby) and daughter of Otto our film producer [of *The Homecoming*] says she was in charge of some sort of party – but declined me an invitation. After all it was only the *40th Year Anniversary of Winning* – bastards. It is really to be wondered at that Harold seems to have distanced himself from the presentation of his plays – for so it appears – seems. Kit Louise P. sent me the most amazing floral display I ever did behold. (Is that just a little Southern?)

8 June '08. NYC
Whether they were Shermans or even earlier ones, to die under the waves of Normandie in disarray – they were tanks loud large and as they hit the main part of the High Street – the kerbs of the pavements were tossed and scattered into the air and dumped on the roadside. The USA had arrived in force.

This I saw from the upstairs room of The Talbot Arms (pub) where Father and Mother had billeted us to – in Upton-on-Severn, Worcs – following the German Air Force bombings near Castle Bromwich – an RAF station which was receiving freshly made Spitfires [*sic*] on an almost hourly basis from an industrial factory called Fisher and Ludlow. There was no publicity as Churchill would not wish to inform the 'L[uftwaffe]' [...] Us boys played tennis there and football with Father Michael McGreevy et al – Christmas morning was I remember a gala morning.

10 June '08
The City is hot as hell – 96° – and I'm wearing the top of an old Burton suit – somehow I do soak it up well. My desk 'abundant' with several dozen letters of all descriptions – a quagmire of paper. Brother Patrick rang on behalf of Jane Morgan to pass on the passing of dear Bruce [Purchase]. Barbara Caruso had already been in Putney during that loss. BC is being so very attentive [...]. PET scan looms tomorrow, follow-up next week 19th June. Where from here, there – paper work, paper work. Packed some American Express into my back pocket for fear of being stranded for cash. These 'bills' invoices are ghastly, confusing – fearful. Some good news from SAG – and American Actors Fund to call this week.

About 11 June. NYC. Hospital
Up at 6 a.m. to fast before PET scan [...]. Slaughterous wait at First Ave. 67/68 with delightful Barbara in attendance – that ghastly liquid – and the

long torpedo hour – always longer than informed of. Sloan-Kettering. Next assess. 19th. then who knows. Had information chat [...] – now awaiting more info – regards overall picture. New York Hot. Sat in a children's playground 1st/67th. – waiting for the cross town Lincoln Centre M66.

12 June. NYC
   Zagreb. Director Dan Curtis ('Winds of War') was finally fairly pleased – the new leading British actor in the air – a swift trip to greet at the airoporto – a civilized deal, with Sir John G. rested and no doubt eager to start. Zagreb was itself again . . . except . . . a modest contretemps on the tarmac – a gesturing 'incoherent' artist – surely not being held on the plane – oh my – a passporte losta – Jesus Christ! What is it about these limey bastards? And [casting director] Rose Tobias thought her long morning's work was done, and 'Sir' Robert, as he was to become, failed to notice their concern.

16/17 June
   Lunch Hughie at the CoCo W45 – alone – quite often so – not a lot of talk. Then to Bryant Park and a closed off lawn. Six films showing including 'Arsenic and Old Lace' – shades of Station Road Erdington, St Thomas's Club. Dad – Ray Moran – Legs seem to carry me where I wish to go but do not strengthen to striding about pitch – I need to improve this. I have to do follow-up in a couple of days and must settle the burning questions – I'm not failing – tough – tough. That will not do.
   The WRITING of mine is decidedly lacking in BITE.

18 June
   Yes, fine, we get no younger – there are danger signs but Corporate Global USA seems to be saying 'There's a very good chance you are not well – you'd better be wise and get insurance' – and yes, folks – here it is. I have noticed this and it's worrying – depressing state of affairs. There just does seem to be a lot of 'all of it' about, just now [...]

19 June
   I was down at the Memorial today to see [Dr] Rizvi for his appraisal of most recent PET Scan. He seemed unusually civil – and I was vaguely interested and did ask some questions. Overall, all seemed not too terrible and he OK'd travel and the chemotherapy should, if at all (my choice) start around July 17th 08. He gave me some précis papers to show in the UK and we kind of left it at that – his bedside manner still very wanting, though fairly clearly I do not help.

25 June '08
   Un Deux Trois. W44 St. Naturallement. José did not exactly recognize me – the shaven look (bald head) avec beard grise – He launched into his evening meal – I eyed up a très charmant blonde bar lady and ordered pâté sur le table. Relaxed with that red drink I can never remember the name of. No, it's not Campari – that's to do with J.G. Devlin's pronunciation of the

outrage actor Kenneth Parry . . . Monsieur Le Boss was mostly in evidence – What does he? Pâté tasteless – does one mention it to le garçon? Clearly a waste. Had a civilized late brunch yesterday with Simone – Jill Turner – she forgot the tea bags and the cake. I forgot the DVD: 'The Smallest Picture Show On Earth'. The 'place' on 9th at 40th sells Irish breakfast – no longer impressive. Barbara saved my bacon having found my lost wallet – lost diary – serious echoes of 'Amadeus' when I dropped $1,100 in a restaurant and lived to tell the tale. Thank goodness for a man called Ravel and my 'Amadeus'-actor pal who had a mobile phone.

I had been amazed to receive a letter from him in this turbulent time. The writing was shaky, but that aside, it was a perfectly normal, chatty letter – did I expect to be reading the deranged thoughts of a man with only half a brain? – and I was gratified to see that he had taken my suggestion that he write a memoir to heart.

✉ [*Terence Rigby*]

30 May 2008
J: Receiving your card, letter, intelligence – thank you. Not up to speed at all, at all, with my scribbles – at all. Even Bruce was personal delivery via Lady Caruso and Virgin Air. Walking well. Times Square. Bryant Park. Calves tighter, but I make it. Poor digestion. Hoping to overcome that. Heart burnish. Bowl-of-chilli donation and fruit-cake donation from Simon Tanner (ex RADA) rather a lost cause. Trying some over-the-counter stuff later. Well, you got your '08 project with Jane [Morgan] in – good. Yes fish pie would go down well – hopefully. Glad you had a Chez Vous after your recording – jolly handy what with the [Yorkshire] Grey [pub] and all. So pleased you had Stephen Thorne. Did do a telly with Gwen Taylor once. She was the lead detective figure – rather giggly at times. Not seen her for years. Good news on Randolph [Street] at last. What a shower. I mean, to have Thorne around simply makes one's morning, noon and late evening. Surprised to find you still with lodger Jo. I know you love memory of her mum and such but hope she won't become a permanent fixture for you. Oddly, Harold Pinter wrote a couple of early essays on that subject. You could blog it [...].
Sister Catherine was here that 10 days – pretty jolly with her jolly lady friend. I see Miss Dunaway has been larking about in Cannes – not a dickie about our film 'Flick', which was to be a Welsh flagship cinematically – you might Google, that's the word, that as well. Dir. David Shiel, I think [*in fact it was David Howard*]. Gosh. 1:30 p.m. and still lounging in me knickers.
Ta-ta, Marylebone.
P.S. Yes, started book myself – but from now, as I've said – low on output – but good idea.

His New York friends visited him at the Sloan-Kettering on a regular basis. 'A friend rang,' James Stephens (Rigby's friend from the 2006 production of *Earnest*) told me later, 'and said that he was in Yale doing *A Woman of No Importance*':

And that he was unwell. That he was in hospital, and was off. Then he went on again. So I rang him and asked where he was, and he said Sloan-Kettering. I knew exactly what that was about. So I asked what he wanted . . . fruit and that. So I went down to see him. One didn't talk about health, but in SK it was obviously cancer. So I went to see him two or three times a week. And he said, 'I've got nothing to write on, James.' So I went off to find a pad.

The hospital is on the East Side. A strange area. No shops to speak of. I finally found a little shop and asked, 'Do you have writing paper?' The guy gave me a pad and I said, 'Haven't you got any without lines?' And he said no. So I took it back to Terry and he said loudly, 'It's got lines.' So I told him that was all they'd got.

'Oh.'

So . . . Then he had an operation on his brain and afterwards he was quite perky and I thought, he's going to be all right. But I thought there's an underlying thing he's not telling me . . . and I asked and he said, 'Fuck off.' He was all right for a while and they kept him in hospital. He was grumpy but seemed to be getting better. I went down there and had a cup of tea with him. I'd called Charlesworth and asked if he knew about [the situation], and he said he knew but he didn't have the number.

When I saw Terence again he said, 'James, I want a word with you.'

I said, 'I called my agent, Terence.'

'Yes, I know. But you gave him the number.' He gave me hell for that.

I thought he was going to survive. I really did. He came out of hospital. I collected him. Got a cab to his place – Did you ever go to his place? I tell you, Pinter would have been proud of him and how he lived. I walked in. It was Pinteresque. There was an iron bed, an old army bed with a thin mattress, and this wide. No comfortable chairs. A tiny writing desk. No kitchen – a hotplate and a saucepan – no kettle. 'I'll buy you an electric kettle.' He didn't want one. It was stark. A tiny bookcase. Nowhere to relax at all. Tiny little bathroom. He'd just bought himself an air conditioner.

I called him the following week. He sounded disoriented and I said, 'Where are you?' And he said, 'I'm sitting in a park,' and I said 'Where?' 'It's just down the street.' I think it was between nine and ten. He was sitting in direct sunlight wearing a heavy coat. He'd lost his pills. 'Well, they're not the sort of pills you can get from a pharmacy. You have to get them from the hospital and they're going to mail them.'

I asked him how long he'd been without them and he said about four days. He must have been in immense pain. So we wandered to the pharmacy. The pharmacist said, 'Why didn't you come?' I don't think he ever took them properly. And of course dehydration had set in. He only took them when he remembered. I then didn't see him for a couple of weeks because he was annoyed with me over the Charlesworth thing. He called and said he was back in hospital again. His sister had been over. I wasn't the only one who visited him.

There were plenty of women, of course. I went to see him and the first time he was odd, but then the second time he was raring to go . . . I thought he's fine, he just needs to medicate properly. We went up on to the roof patio. His sister came to fetch him back to London. He said, 'What's the point in going? The doctor's given me eighteen months. I was hoping for ten years.'

I said, 'Why don't you go back to London right now?' It was a question I asked him all the time. 'Why are you here? You've got a wonderful career in London.'

And he would reply, 'I don't want to be in London any more.'

This rather shocked me. 'He didn't have regard for his friends and family over here?' I asked James.

'I can't say that,' he replied. 'I would ask the same question. Finally he knew he should. To be honest, I was pissed off with him, because he didn't . . . But he comes back . . . and dies.'

'Immediately.'

'The sod.'

I'm almost weeping angry tears. 'He could have come back earlier and written the book himself.'

'He was very well looked after. And he was pain free. And when he went home [to his flat] a nurse would visit him. But he didn't medicate himself properly. And he wouldn't come back.'

'How did he spend his time during those weeks?'

'He would come to the Polish Cafe, near Broadway. Full of actors. Every day. Spent a lot of time there. And round the corner in another cafe.'

'Did you meet the Chinese family?'

'No. But I met Barbara Caruso. She was a constant visitor at the end. I think she might have been his advocate. There were things that had to be done . . . Or perhaps his sister. They had to spend a lot of time sorting his insurance.'

'I found a statement about his illness written by him.'

'I suspect . . . When he castigated me about Charlesworth, I said, "You're not going to lecture me as if I were a child, are you? Because if you are I'm out of here." So he shut up. I said, "How many times have I visited you in hospital? I've brought you pork pies!" – There's a shop called Myers of Keswick, it's like a little bit of England . . . pork pies and sausages . . . He said, "Could you get some pickled walnuts as well?" . . . !'

'He grumbled about Catherine filling his fridge with food he hated,' I told him. 'He was so graceless . . .'[14]

'My wife is a wonderful cook,' said James, 'so when he came to dinner he loved it. But he didn't cook for himself. He had two electric hotplates!'

'When was the last time you saw him?'

'The last time I saw him was the day before he was discharged. He was in extremely good health, I think.'

'The flight did for him.'

'Did you see him?'

'Yes.'

James smiled. 'I tell you what. When I saw him last, he was as bright as a button. On great form. I thought: he's going to make that eighteen months. He was perverse. Rigby borrowed my wife's Beckett . . . it was a first edition, never to be produced . . . She showed Rigby, who asked to borrow it. I asked him if he'd finished it. With a twinkle in his eye he said, "No".'

During one of these short periods when he was allowed home, he caught up with Michael Feast, who played Foster in the original production of *No Man's Land*:

> I was playing Macduff in the Rupert Goold/Patrick Stewart *Macbeth* and Terry came to see it – and surprised me, because I didn't know he was in New York, by coming round to the stage door. I was delighted to see him but could see he was very unwell. Being Terry, he played down the severity of his condition so I didn't really know how ill he was. We exchanged numbers and arranged to meet soon. I didn't hear from him and assumed he'd got a job somewhere, but then just before I left New York he came again to the stage door to apologize for not having been in touch. He told me he had to have some more treatment and he looked much less well than before. We said our goodbyes and had a hug but I still didn't realize quite how ill he was. The next thing I heard was that he had passed away.

I also spoke to Diane Landers, Rigby's friend from LA. She spent time with him when he tried his luck in that great city. He was seeing several doctors, she says, because he was constantly feeling dizzy, and had, what seemed to her, emphysema. He wore a holster monitor for 48 hours and was scanned and X-rayed. He was reluctant to go into detail about his condition, so Diane didn't press him. When she heard that he was in Sloan-Kettering, she made the journey to New York to visit him. He had just returned from a CAT scan and didn't recognize her.

---

14   '[My] Sister Catherine who was over for 10 days being golly jolly,' wrote Rigby to Stephen and Barbara Thorne in June 2008, 'and filling the fridge with things I did not fancy.'

'He seemed disorientated and in great pain,' she said. 'He was kindly to the nurses and staff, given the situation, though he did not seem to be holding back tremendous shouts of pain upon being shifted. It was his booming stage voice, no doubt. I'm sure his outbursts were not due to his upset with the staff, but rather his great pain from duress. Memorial Sloan-Kettering is, after all, the best in New York and top in the US.'

Rigby, who for years and years battled with his faith, continued to drop in at various churches and cathedrals on his travels. Sometimes they were merely tourist attractions for him, but at other times, he embraced the familiarity and comfort of Catholicism. In his wanderings in NYC that Summer of 2008, he picked up a novena (a devotional prayer), and tucked it into his diary:

> O Mother of Perpetual Help
>
> I honour your holy name,
>
> I praise you with my lips,
>
> I venerate you with my thoughts,
>
> I pray to you from my heart,
>
> I trust you in your powerful intercession,
>
> I call upon you in every need,
>
> In times of temptation, protect me,
>
> In times of suffering protect me.
>
> In times of affliction, strengthen me.
>
> In times of discouragement, renew me.
>
> In times of perplexity, guide me.
>
> In times of doubt, lead me.
>
> Whenever I call to you, hear me.
>
> Mother of Perpetual Help,
>
> Pray for me.

All the novenas that his mother included in her letters to him remained in the envelope. This one was clearly very important to him, and he kept it close.

Barbara Caruso was a constant companion during the short time he was at home, often visiting Bryant Park together – a favourite destination in New York (and where Rigby took me and Jack when we came to see him in *Troilus and Cressida*). She'd seen him not long after an operation to remove his brain tumour. It was the only time she'd seen him frightened, she said. He was sitting on a chair in his gown, and he jerked his head violently downwards so that she could see the scar and the stitches.

'He shouted, "For Christ's sake, I've just had my head opened!" It wasn't addressed to me. It was addressed to the heavens. That was the only time. It was heartfelt and it was a cry from the heart.'

'In his last days,' Barbara told me, 'he began to trust me more':

> He would talk about his last relationships a bit and how he had failed. And what a destructive force those drunken years had on his life. He recalled that when he heard Sir Ralph Richardson was in hospital and was going to die, he found himself outside the hospital but unable to go in because he was so drunk. 'I was disgusted with myself. The memory of it. I lost a lot of time.' But he made up for it. He began to reach out to people.

I asked Barbara if Rigby ever talked about the woman we jokingly referred to as 'X-Ray':

> We were sitting in Bryant Park, towards the end of his life. He wasn't eating but I got him a cup of tea. It was 9 p.m. and I wanted to go home to cook supper, but he started talking about life and love. I thought this was the moment to ask him if he'd ever been in love. He thought for a moment and answered, 'I guess,' or 'Maybe.' Then he mentioned her by name and what she did.
>
> 'She was probably the person I could have made it with, but she didn't understand that I had to go away to the States or wherever the work was. She didn't understand.'

But that was maybe the closest he got to making a life with someone.[15]

I finally tracked 'X-Ray' down in July 2011, and she kindly agreed to talk to me about her relationship with Rigby. I began by asking her how they first met. She explained that in the late 1980s, around the time Rigby was in *Crossroads*, they'd both been invited to dinner at Jane Morgan's, along with Rigby's director at RADA, Robert Peake. Then a few years later, when Rigby was in *Bajazet* at the Almeida, they had met again by accident. He invited her and Robert to see the show, and had supper together afterwards. Thereafter, they met when Rigby was playing Albert the Horse in the revival of *Wind in the Willows*. She had taken her nephew and niece to see

---

15 Diane Landers told me Rigby spoke of the same woman to her – a 'lady friend' who was a doctor in London, 'with whom, I believe, he had a romantic relationship. I think she meant an awful lot to him and he seemed to be troubled by the dissolve of the partnership. He was also close to a friend in Bilbao – I believe by the name of Maria. He often mentioned her.'

it, and Rigby was apparently most attentive to the children afterwards and took them to the cafe. Over several cups of tea over the months, they began to get to know one another really well.

JA   What did you make of Rigby as you got to know him?

X   He was a great story teller. A great story teller. And he was an interesting person to talk to. I really can't remember. It was such a long time ago . . .

JA   It was obvious over the years that you were deeply important to him. Were you aware of that and was he important to you?

X   Yes. But I suppose I felt that I wasn't always important to him. And because of his working pattern and my working pattern it wasn't always easy to meet. I work nine to five and have to be up very early. He was in the theatre so he was working late. It could be quite problematic. We might say Tuesday's a good day and I would put it in my diary, then it wouldn't be for him. It sounds silly and petty – but we got over that. Once I'd got used to the idea that it didn't really matter then it was fine. But it took a while. And yes, I did know I was important to him, but he would rarely say that in public. We did meet someone once and he said, 'My very special friend . . .' He was a great one for making you feel special to him without admitting to it.

JA   It was clear you were one of his cup-of-tea ladies, as Jane was, and Phyllis, and me. He talked about you; he said there were times when you both found it difficult to communicate. Did you think that?

X   Yes. There were those months when he had the bypass and he wasn't well, and times when he went off touring to Scotland and America and – seems funny now – but it was a time before email and texts. It all seems so silly now. Eventually he could email and write texts.

JA   I showed him how to text and we found texts going back five years or more!

X   He could do *faxes*. He was very good at looking after my god-daughter . . . He would have been thrilled to know that she had got into RADA. She would put his paintings on the wall.

JA   Ones he had painted himself? He used to use bits of old cardboard . . .

X   Shirt-stiffeners!

JA   I don't know how true this would be, but . . . I interviewed Barbara Caruso – an American friend he met at RADA. She spent a lot of time with him in his last months and he talked about you. He implied that you couldn't cope with his being away so much, particularly in America, and that perhaps you didn't understand what an actor's life was like. Is that true?

X   Do I understand what an actor's life is like? Yes, I do understand what an actor's life is like . . . in that nothing is certain . . . you never know when things are going to happen . . . and unless you're going to be in a set play you never know where you're going to be . . . and it was clearly different from my life, which is set.

JA   Do you think it could have worked on a permanent basis?

X   Yes . . . but then we hit a period of non-communication . . . that happens . . . it's dragging over old ground, but maybe we weren't communicating at that time.

JA   I think that's accurate. There were times when he seemed to walk away and then times when he thought you weren't interested. He was so complicated, wasn't he?

X   Yes. I think perhaps I'd got to a point where I'd tried long enough .

JA   I didn't know him as well as you, obviously, but I know he found it hard. He talked about you. I didn't know your name. He always used nicknames. You were 'Radiographer', and I would then refer to you as 'X-Ray'. Banter. Sometimes he'd think things were back on track and then at others he felt you'd backed off. Were you hurt or did you just say 'Oh, well . . .'?

X   I felt I'd given it all my energy.

JA   Do you think you could have lived together permanently?

X   My job is permanent, but we could have got round that.

JA   Do you think he was capable of real love?

X   Yes. I really think he loved all of us . . . and if you look at him as a character, he had a lot to give. He would do anything for anyone. He would stop what he was doing and help.

JA   That was his saving grace as far as I was concerned. But he could actually be vicious. Did you ever see that side of him?

X   No.

JA   I didn't think so. He did say sometimes that he wished he had someone to care for. A wife. Children. He couldn't manage it. How would you sum up your relationship with him?

X   He was very nice to be with. We had a lot of good times. We could walk along and not necessarily talk . . .

JA   What do you remember most about him?

X   Oh things like . . . I'd be coming out of work and he'd be there, waiting. The way he would answer the phone with 'Double-eight four nine' without explanation. Listening to stories . . . and just laughing.

JA   Did he listen? He would talk for two hours and I'd say, 'Would you like to hear what I've been up to?' And he'd say yes – but plough straight ahead

	without bothering.
X	Yes . . . But I prefer listening to talking.
JA	He was quite jealous of Robert, and when you went off to Paris and places on your own.
X	But I couldn't just take off. I could say I was going to Paris next week or something. We got to the point where I would go and if he came, he came. It took me a while to realize that that was how it had to be. He loved trains. And once we went to Paris and on the way back on the boat we had to go through Passport Control. I got through first and then he went after me and it took forever. Then we saw a mouse. But they said we couldn't possibly have seen a mouse, but we said we had. And on the way out at New Haven, we went through Customs, and they stopped him. I just stood looking. We hadn't got much luggage, but he was carrying a bag and because he'd been on television they stopped him. He got quite upset about it. When he went to America, I did plan to go once.
JA	Was that Florida? He wrote to say you were there and . . .
X	Yes. I was in Florida, and then I went to New York. I also went to Washington but I can't remember now what was on. But I had family in New York so I saw him a couple of times.
JA	I can't resist asking whether you ever stayed in Dieppe: I told him I'd never speak to him again if he took anyone else there!
X	We did have a *meal* in Dieppe – where he ordered a seafood platter and I had fish. When it arrived, the platter was filled with winkles and things, so I had to eat his food and he ate mine.
JA	So you were only passing through: that's a relief! It would have been impossible to do this work without speaking to you. There are so many pieces in the jigsaw that have to be fitted together . . .
X	There was a man at the funeral who walked up and down the aisle looking at us all. He would have loved the detail of it all. Whatever else was going on, there'd always be something else to look at.
JA	He was so proud of his hand washing. And when he finally bought a washing machine, I couldn't believe it.
X	He only did that when he rented out the flat when he went to America. He flooded the restaurant underneath several times.
JA	And he, in turn, was flooded from above. Did you meet many of his friends?
X	I knew Jane already. We used to walk through London looking for [David] Sinclair . . .
JA	You looked after him in the flat, didn't you, when he'd had his bypass?
X	Yes.

JA   I remember him telling me that I mustn't tell anyone about his bypass, but
      then I discovered he'd said that to a lot of people.

X   He didn't want to be looked after. I don't think he realized how bad he
      would feel after the operation.

JA   Did he get in touch with you when he knew he had got cancer?

X   No. I'd only got back a few days before. Jane told me. She'd only known a
      week.

JA   Jane knew before that. But she was sworn to secrecy. I don't know why. I
      think maybe he thought he would get over it and work again. I think it was
      right to respect his decision . . . He seemed to be slowing down a lot. And
      he was in a lot of physical pain – particularly in *Godot*. He used to wear
      knee-pads . . .

X   He used to complain about what directors would make him do. Wearing
      that armour in *Hamlet* . . .

JA   We all had our own roles . . .

X   I remember once, we were sitting outside, having dinner by candlelight.
      There was a slatted table and we didn't realize until afterwards that the
      candle wax had dripped through on to his shoes. He didn't notice until the
      next day . . . He never had a lighter for his cigarettes. He could never find
      a lighter or a match – I used to carry matches! He could never find them in
      his many pockets . . .

JA   Did you know him before he changed his dress style? He used to wear
      blazers and suits.

X   Yes . . . and polished his shoes. He used to polish mine as well.

JA   It was strange. I don't know whether America liberated him or not.

X   ... Braces. The hat with the flower. The hat he had when he played Albert. I
      used to borrow it when it was raining.

Rereading my conversation with X, I am amused to see how my curiosity
– and possibly my envy – creeps through the whole piece. It's probably the
only time in all of my interviews that I felt a pang of regret that I had not
experienced the level of gentleness and obvious adoration that was clearly
hers. But when she talked about carrying matches for him, it suddenly rang
a bell. There was a toothbrush in my bathroom, stored in its cardboard
tube, standing against a mirror. Even after months away, he expected to
find it there. Like the plaque on the table, he was marking territory. What
did he leave in his other haunts?

❑ JULIET'S TABLE

Rigby's papers are spread out on the table. His last diary entries range across his usual interests and preoccupations: theatre gossip and memories; old friends; tennis; an eye for a pretty girl; and the constantly draining 'paperwork' of his illness. His handwriting becomes increasingly shaky. Following his operation, these diary jottings, letters, and notes, were written on separate pieces of paper, clearly taking a huge effort. I find it hard to read these extracts, let alone reproduce them here. But the description he made of his illness to the authorities for insurance purposes is harrowing. He wouldn't talk to anyone in such bald terms, about his decline, the advancing cancer or imminent death. But his honesty and bravery shine through.

*

 [Diary]

27 June 2008
Shlepped to Screen Actors on Madison 275 – taxi – chest uncomfortable. Took first pain pill to see if it helps. Positively 'oozed' over receptionist – as was convinced I was going to cock up the 'paperwork' which seems progressively more intricate.

Getting up later, reading [Sheila] Hancock—[John] Thaw book [The Two of Us] – it's great – dazzling memories of RADA. Wondering if to write to SH. What a great bonus to 'hear' of Michael Blackham – 'the dark sheep' – doing a one-man show [The Tree of Life]. SH delivery in prose of truly dramatic events is simply, to me, devastating – the recalling of her first husband's duties as a sort of Bombardier – flat out on his belly punching out bombs and firing a 'machine gun' in defence at the same time. Can only call it – the STILLNESS of her delivery.

Temp around 80°. Hughie, Catherine have gone on hols for the Summer – up in Maine. Oddly back in the Sixties that's what Gary Merrill (husband of Bette Davis) used to do every Summer – we went kind of clubbing with him and Michael Craig. We did our Broadway 'Homecoming' before being bought out by Julie Andrews for 'Star'. I remember delivering the cable to Sardi's – he was with his brother (agent) taking a late lunch. Found myself on corner of Eighth advising a couple to dine at Sardi's – could hardly believe my own ears, saying 'I've been eating there for over 40 years.' [...] Amazing, en passant, how little has been heard of Wimbledon this year [...]

27 June 2008
Late – 10 p.m. I hopped on M16 [bus] which said 'Waterside' – Don't remember being down there since Jayne Goss was in Town [...] Her dad Reggie was a great noise at the now defunct Green Room Club [the actors'

225

club in London] – formerly the very Hon. Secretary, when the Hon. Secs were Hon. Secs. Short tale of he who was President being mildly told off by a newer member, having complained of the swearing in the Club. It being pointed out that the President was as guilty as the others – the authoritative riposte was: 'Yes, well I am the fucking President.' And on Jayne – suddenly a link exists it seems between [*actor*] Bunny May and Myrna Haigh which might merit a card. [16]

28 June. 6:30 p.m.
        Amy – the tennis player – appeared. At last, I thought, finally, I shall observe her Hitting Up [*but*] the courts were flooded – so that was it. It remains in abeyance and it being Wimbledon time as well. I 'met' Amy some several months ago, wandering in and out – towards or away from the local indoor-outdoor on W43rd. (Another time, another life, could have been a sort of paradise.)
        I slip away to 1976 when Sir Ralph took me 'to play tennis' at the Indoor Bubbles over at the East Side Tennis Club. Dad had just died and this was Ralph's way of saying something. He didn't feel well enough to play so we ducked out – for a modest lunch instead – and talked about things like 'Did you like your father?' A question I found very very difficult to answer. Father was a colossally complex man. Based on what very little one could recall of him – a would-be Conservative MP – an honourable man – a gentleman – an inordinately quiet, silent man – a cool vamper of the piano – highly evident at Christmas-times and friends' birthdays – there was certainly a book in him, plus he read endless piles of FBI Detective Stories and Cowboy novels. From somewhere, when it was officially known that I had thought of choosing an actor's life, a hardback copy of 'An Actor Prepares' by Stanislavski appeared out of nowhere.
        But Amy was still a mystery – a tennis mystery – to unfold. Earlier that week I heard from Jenny Hoad, former No. 1 Australian lady – who sweetly keeps in touch – and who I hope to visit in September 2008 for the Vet. Lew Hoad Tournament at Compa Mijas.

A few days later, Rigby wrote a letter from New York to his old friend Noel Murray, which, as well as including a few map-sketches of the area (with an arrow pointing from the Hudson river to 'London'), also attached a note from the caretaker of his apartment that reads: 'Just keeping in touch. Will call again':

---

16   When the actor Kenneth Haigh had a dreadful choking fit in a restaurant, from which he never fully recovered, Rigby visited him on a regular basis. On one visit he was reunited with Myrna Haigh, Ken's estranged wife, and the pair of them worked unceasingly to get Ken the appropriate treatment. It was yet another example of Rigby's extraordinary kindness. I often wondered if it was the only way that he could express his love for his friends. For all that he appeared careless of their feelings, he would usually come up trumps.

✉ [*Terence Rigby*]

1st July 2008
This is how, often, messages arrive. I think this from Jim – my pal. Speaks a kind of Spanish lingo, but not sure he's ever been to the mainland or kicked France up the rear end.

Today is a critical sort of day as if I decide to stay NYC the treatment should begin 17th July. So I'm cutting it fine on seeking advice in UK. I really need to go – tonight, tomorrow, day after for sure.

Just imagine if Shakespeare had written, not 'Tomorrow, tomorrow and tomorrow' – but 'Tonight, tomorrow, the day after creeps in this petty pace from day to day . . .'

Well, so much for the Shakespeare Irish Canon.

Not much to advance to you except it is pretty humid which is always uncomfortable. Sit around and chat on the benches on W43rd St at Ninth Ave until quite late at night.

Yes. At the 24 hour Westway Diner – I guess they've got to know me and naturally as a tip is the order of the day – service is civil. Had a very civil p.m. today sitting with Miss Caruso in Bryant Park – essentially a large triangle running along 42nd Street between 6th And 5th Ave.

We sat chewing various cuds – the area is peppered with gracious tall trees and all around is vegetation growth – and the games of Boules à la Française is played – and chess is played. It is unquestionably a haven in warm weather and is also interesting in rainy times.

I happen to be reading the John Thaw/Sheila Hancock book which is overall quite fascinating [...] I recall one occasion when the RADA charabanc had to be directed complete with cast en route to somewhere like Glyndebourne to pick up the bleary cast members who had over-sleepied. It was an O'Casey play 'Bedtime Story' with Caroline Mortimer – Johnnie Mortimer QC daughter. John must have been in the Priestley play we were doing – anyway we all got there with much merriment.

I wish I could be more explicit about my movements during the next 14 days but it really is very complex and I am truly confused with the situation [...]

If you sense sometimes that I am starting to scribble a bit more often – don't let it worry you to writing – it's not meant to energize you into action. Take it easy. Day at a time – relaxez vous.

✎ [*Diary*]

3 July 2008
Scoured press for news of Nadal–Murray match – nothing except Nadal had gone through – hopefully Murray will have his day. Unhappily, these pages are becoming meaningless pages, not the more authentic meaningful prose that was intended. Can't all be Chekhov at once. Did pop in to my beautiful church on W46 today – first for a while. [...] MUST get this UK trip together NOW. Does seem but a moment or two since I wrote to Tennis

[Andy] Murray inviting him to practise at will at our Club, possibly to the chagrin of a few, no doubt – at the time his mum (surely it was not he) sent me a very stilted 4x6, more like a get well card – Now he's World No. 10 at least and in with the big boys. [...] I do hope I shall make the September tournament.

12 July 2008

    Friday or so. Ever been in possession of a large diary and all the trimmings – and still don't know the date? Clearly the answer is yes. I was sitting under the arches – under the benches (on) – in fact very much like the setting of the opening long shot of 'Touch of Evil' – sur le point of shooting off a few proverbial to Lyme Regis –when Dan Frazer's face loomed into shot – he who was top cop in 'Kojak' and various other NY series of some years ago [...]

    10 p.m. Surrounded by 6/7 NYPDs taking late supper early breakfast – at the local diner – I've been off appetite again so I'm trying to lessen it up a bit – cool . . . .

On 26th July, Rigby was eating Complan. It was said he had become confused. By the 29th, he was back in hospital. They said he shouldn't be on his own and he was struggling with another bout of pneumonia. He drafted his will on 4 August, naming his nephew and godson John Rigby as principal legatee.

    I asked Barbara Caruso to tell me about the last time she went to visit Rigby in hospital.

It was the last time I saw him before he went home with Catherine and Barry, his brother-in-law. He wasn't in his room and I panicked, so I went to the lounge where he sometimes sat. And there he was.

    On our way back to his room, he took me past various rooms and waved at people. He took my arm in a gentlemanly way. We came to the room of an Italian woman who was dying. She said, 'Come in. Come in.' She was being attended to by several nurses. She was very ill. He went in and chatted to her for a moment than he motioned for me to join him. It was the last thing I wanted to do, to go and talk to someone else who was dying. Then she said to him, 'What's the matter? What's the problem?' And he said, 'Cancer. Lung cancer.' I think he was honest because there was no point in not being honest with this woman. She said, 'Nobody talks to me. Nobody stops by. They think I'm too ill. Stay.' She asked all kinds of personal questions and did he believe in God. And he said, 'Yes.' And she told him God would help. 'It's not the best but you should continue to pray.' He shook her hand and off we went. I was quiet but moved. He didn't say anything.

    We walked in silence to his room. He had lots of bits of paper around his room and said he was trying to make a will. I told him to leave it until he got back home. I said I must go. He took my hand and he said, 'You will not be forgotten for all you've done for me.' And I said I'd see him soon because I was coming over. And he smiled and kissed my hand. He wasn't frightened. I think he was supported by his faith and he was spiritual. The only time I saw him frightened was that first time I visited him.

On Friday, 8 August, Catherine and Barry brought Rigby home to England for the last time. It was an arduous journey, despite travelling first class. Catherine had always been afraid of turbulence: Rigby remembered this and held her hand to help her through it.

Back in Devonshire Street he went straight to bed while Catherine got in touch with his doctors and the Macmillan nurses. I knew I should give him time to rest but I was increasingly anxious to see him.

On Saturday Jane Morgan went to visit him with Phyllis MacMahon. She'd come up to London from her cottage in Kilve. She stayed with me for the night and described how very weak he was.

On the Sunday lunchtime of 10 August we both went to see him, but he was asleep. I met Catherine for the first time, and her friend Margaret. I asked if they needed more bed linen. They said they were running short, so I said I would leave them in peace and return later with some sheets.

I returned at around 5.30. He was being attended to by a nurse who was trying to sort out his medication. Patrick and Joseph had arrived, and we all talked about those last months. I explained my relationship with Rigby. Eventually I could bear it no longer and asked if I might talk to him. His eyes were closed, but I was determined he should know I was there.

'It's Juliet,' I said.

He opened his eyes and repeated my name, twice. I told him he looked like King Lear, with his bald head and big bushy beard. He laughed. I took his hand, kissed his cheek, and talked a little about how good it was to see him. Not wishing to tire him, I left him to sleep.

He died at around 10.30 p.m. that night.

I thanked God that I'd gone back with the sheets.

Funeral, wake, and celebration

When I go to a funeral, every other funeral I've been to comes into focus – therefore it is a day for reflection as much as a day for a public demonstration of grief. And we all grieve in different ways. I remember thinking that the service would be something to endure and that the wake would be the time to get drunk. So I decided to wear Sloth's Salamanca straw hat and Rigby's white shirt. All three of us would be connected – good old friends.

My daughter Catherine and I walked through Spanish Place to St James's Roman Catholic Church. We were early, but already lots of people were going in and the hearse was parked outside. Inevitably, the shivers went down my spine. He was definitely dead. Catherine Sparks (née Rigby) greeted us. She was wearing Rigby's favourite colour – purple – and looked lovely.

The church, which was eventually crowded with friends and family, was the grandest I'd been into for years. It shone with polished brass and gold, and there was a profusion of flowers. The service was conducted by Father Michael, who set the tone of the proceedings in the most apt and comforting welcome. The congregation settled into an expectant but secure involvement. There was no sentimentality. We learned about Rigby's background, his religious upbringing, his departure from Birmingham – and sometimes from his beliefs. Michael Billington, the *Guardian* theatre critic, spoke about his work and his talent, Jane Morgan described her friendship with him; and Father Michael's niece Geraldine sang magnificently, her voice echoing around the vaulted roof. Catherine spoke of her brother's last year and how he strove valiantly to finish his last play in America.

Then there was the Mass. Father Michael surprised us by saying that if we didn't want to take communion, we could cross our arms and show that we wanted a blessing instead. I watched everyone queue for what seemed like an eternity and suddenly I knew I wanted to be blessed. I've no idea why – maybe because I didn't want to be left out. I am glad I did that. Father Michael murmured a few words that I found comforting. Turning back from the altar I remember being stunned by the hundreds of blurred faces. They had all come to honour Rigby.

We stood as the coffin was carried down the nave. This wicked, lovely enigma of a man was going to be missed.

≡ I had a small walk-on part in the life of Terence Rigby, whose death, sadly, was announced yesterday.

Back in the 1990s Rigby, who had built up a seductive practice in British theatre and television, suddenly decided to relocate to New York. But his initial application for the Green Card required was turned down because he was too close to his referees: people like Peter Hall and John Gielgud. So, out of the blue, Rigby wrote to myself and Bernard Levin asking us to endorse his application. Whatever we said, must have done the trick, since Rigby spent his last decade happily commuting between the US and the UK where the work offers still came in.

Why did Rigby decide to go west? Meeting him five years ago, when he was rehearsing Pinter's Davies in *The Caretaker* for Bristol Old Vic, I deduced it had a lot to do with his background. Rigby came from the Birmingham suburb of Erdington where his dad ran a two-man firm, making hydraulic packing. I had a great-aunt who also came from Erdington and, from my childhood memories, it was a place you'd want to get out of. And you could see that a Birmingham boy, with a love for acting, would have entertained fantasies of the bright lights of Broadway.

In reality, Broadway is a bit more like a grotty Birmingham suburb than we care to admit. And Rigby was honest enough to confess that his early years in New York were a struggle. He lived for a while in the apartment of a partying Puerto Rican family with a fire station underneath and a night club next door. Eventually Rigby got his own tiny New York studio but, even when off-Broadway work came in, life was still tough: he told me he earned a meagre $286 a week playing in Mike Leigh's *Smelling a Rat*. But Rigby was sustained by occasional movie work, the loyalty of old mates such as Hall and Pinter, and by his own immigrant version of the American dream.

What Rigby's curious career conceals is that he had a vital quality as an actor: physical and emotional weight. It was this that enabled him to play the thuggish Briggs in Pinter's *No Man's Land*, Stalin in Robert Bolt's *State of Revolution*, and the bullying Pozzo in Peter Hall's most recent, and near-definitive *Waiting for Godot*. 'Weight' is a hard quality to define: Timothy West has it, as did the late Leo McKern. But what is fascinating about Rigby is that he possessed it from the start, which is why he was a natural for TV cops in series like *Z-Cars* and *Softly, Softly*, and why he was so brilliant as the boxer, Joey, in Pinter's *The Homecoming*.

I suspect that kind of weight is becoming increasingly rare for a simple reason: because of the abolition of mandatory student grants, fewer working or lower middle class actors can afford to go to drama school. What chance would a young Albert Finney, son of a Salford bookie, have today? Or indeed a young Rigby with his small businessman background? — Michael Billington, *The Guardian*, 11 August 2008

The wake, which was held at the Paddington Sports Club, had been happening for several hours. We'd found a table outside and sat quietly, watching Rigby's friends and family in the clubhouse as they exchanged memories and condolences.

It was late evening and the light was good. The couple playing tennis didn't seem to mind the throng of people on the lawn, some of them drifting in and out of the clubhouse. We drank good wine and nibbled Thai delicacies, served by young Thai waitresses in national costume. This was the inspired setting for Rigby's wake, and our little crowd remained in situ until closing time, when most people had politely left. But how could we leave when Julie Covington was singing softly in the darkness and Rigby was so obviously there?

ix. Kodak snap 2: Rigby at Juliet's table

❏ JULIET'S TABLE

When friends of Rigby come to my flat to be interviewed, I show them the brass plaque and tell them the story of this table. John Rigby shares his thoughts on his uncle and over a period of months brings piles of archive material for me to sift through.

There's a bottle of red wine on the shelf – set apart because it was given to me by Rigby the last time he came to see me. For some reason I couldn't bring myself to open it. But I feel the time has come to share it with friends who loved him as much as I did.

And that's how, one evening, I cook a celebratory meal, and Stephen Thorne and Jane Morgan join me. Stephen brings his precious hoard of letters and cards from Rigby, together with Rigby's account of David Sinclair's funeral. I've managed to find the cassette of Rigby's readings of a chapter from Job and the Shakespeare sonnets. This has been transferred to CD and I give one each to Jane and Stephen.

When they've gone I listen again to the readings, which actually end with my feeble attempt to read from Corinthians. But after that there's a little background chatter where Rigby talks about Dieppe and chuckles. He never let me forget about Dieppe.

*

On 24 October 2008, I joined Jane Morgan and Peter Acre on the train to Birmingham. We were going to Rigby's memorial Mass at Erdington Abbey church. It was raining in London, but cold and bright when we arrived at the church. The family was there to greet us. They were pleased we had made the journey. We sat near the front of this pretty church. It's light and airy and, like most Catholic churches these days, the altar is placed at the nave end of the chancel and the priests officiate facing the congregation. I was glad to see Father Michael McGreevy, who led the service in London. He was joined by another family friend who now works in Liverpool. Catherine spoke on behalf of the family, describing Rigby's life since the cancer diagnosis. She talked movingly about his stoicism and the belief that he would recover and work again. He got up from his hospital bed to join the cast for the last performance. Whenever Father Michael talked about this good man, I found myself thinking, 'This good, *wicked* man!' – meant, of course, with great affection.

At the reception in the church hall, I met many of Rigby's childhood friends. They came from near and far with their memories, cards and photographs. Many of the women, who had never left Erdington, said they had been girlfriends or had acted with him in plays put on by the Youth Club and by the local amateur drama society. Two men said that at school he was regarded as something of a rogue. One of them said he could never have imagined that Rigby would go into the theatre – let alone become a prestigious actor.

The family kindly showed me the house in Bratby Grove. I mentally measured up the rooms and tried to visualize how a family of seven, and all of their friends – sometimes a whole football team – could have fitted in. Trixie clearly performed miracles in the tiny kitchen, turning out dishes of stew and soup for the five thousand.

Rigby's relationship with his mother was complicated; somewhere in his papers by now piling up on my table I found a letter describing his absolute exasperation with her, and he was obviously racked with guilt at the way he treated her – the depth of which can be seen in the outpourings of his Zagreb experience. In later years, though, he talked very fondly about her, and though he threw away all the letters he received from friends, he kept every single one of his mother's. 'She was an amazing character,' Rigby's nephew John told me when I asked about her:

> To be honest, I haven't sat down and thought about her in any great length, since she died, when I was at university. But what I do remember is this enormous capacity for love, and wanting everyone to be cheery and happy and all right. She cared about everyone so much, and loved them so much. And even though you knew she was at various times going through really rough times . . . she was this amazingly stoic character and decided the best way was to just keep going. And when I think about my dad [Joe] and [Aunt] Catherine, and the way they are, it is so obvious that they are her kids. But Terry was different. That isn't to say that he didn't care about people. He obviously did care about an awful lot of people and an awful lot of people cared about him. He didn't go about it in the same way. A quieter way . . .
>
> Actually, perhaps Terry was more sentimental than me. To be honest, I don't really keep any letters. At all. Because I think, 'I know you love me' – 'I know that that happened' . . . It's gone. It's history. Maybe there was a bit of that in Terry, but I don't want to paint him as if he was completely lacking in sentiment or emotion. There was clearly strong emotion and sentiment. And keeping all of the letters that you receive from your mother is a very good example. I wonder why he felt he couldn't be more open. Is that the impression you got? That when he saw you, that he was holding things back, that he wasn't as open as he could be, really opening up and letting you know everything that was going on?

I replied by telling John about a conversation Rigby and I had had, in which he confessed to finding he could be much more open with people in letters than in 'reality', in face-to-face conversations.

'Oh well,' I said, 'why don't you just fuck off, then, and I'll just *write* to you?'

'Well, I don't *want* to write to *you*,' he said.

I was particularly moved by my conversations with John. We got to know each other quite well over a period of months because he shared so much material, including reviews and photographs, that he thought might be useful for the memoir you are now reading. The more we talked, the more I recognized elements of Uncle Terry creeping through, and I was stunned by the remarkable likeness between them when I saw photographs of Rigby as a young man, and the resemblance extended to his character.

And actually there are things that are similar . . . you are kind to call it 'gravitas'. As you get older . . . I think you start to realize that you can only really try and be happy when you accept that you are who you are. And I am quite a serious sort of guy. I have to face it. I think an awful lot. I am very committed to my work and work extremely hard. And there are times when I need my own company. I enjoy walking for long periods of time through the streets of London. I feel I have never cracked it on the woman front . . . . There are about half a dozen things I think I share with him, and I don't know why that is. Although we never really talked about these things . . . maybe that's why there was that (*connection*) . . .

There are these complexities about him, and difficulties about him, but what seems to come over, time and time again, is that though he was difficult and treated people badly, on what seems to be a regular basis, there was always something about him that would bring him back to them, or them to him. A lot of good things in his nature. That makes him interesting. He wasn't a saint – but he wasn't a terrible person! He was a really interesting mix of the two. And I suppose I think he had a really fascinating personality. You could burrow around forever and still only scratch the surface of Terry Rigby...

I found John's words hugely helpful in cracking some of the dilemmas I knew I would have to face when trying to paint a picture – this picture – of him in words. I knew I was going to have to try to assess who he really was. He was so compartmentalized in his life; he, more than anyone I have ever known, was a different person to practically everyone he met.

No matter what role he was playing, Rigby always looked like Rigby. There was no helping that. But he was perfect for television, in particular, because within seconds he was so obviously a second-hand car dealer, a police constable, Stalin, or Bomber Harris, that one somehow forgot who it was we were watching. He had an uncanny knack of inhabiting every character he played, and this was largely due to the careful research he did, and his acute observation. Moreover, he not only found the essence of a character, but the humour and the particular integrity of whoever he was playing. That's a rare gift. He tended to sneer at physical theatre, but employed so many of its tools instinctively.

He had very strong views on what acting meant to him. 'You have to come on stage knowing where you've come from,' he once told his young friend Angela Bull's father, 'and leave as if you're going somewhere. It should be new and fresh.'

When he worked on *Man, Beast, and Virtue* with William Gaskill at the Cottesloe, the warm-up exercises and improvisations didn't appeal to him. He seemed to prefer the traditional route of read-through, discussion, character study, and rehearsal. I recall that he would read the script over and over again, until he had found his place in it. Unlike some actors who underline their part and don't bother too much with scenes in which they don't appear, Rigby embraced the whole play and understood what his response to any given character should be. It meant that his performances were firmly rooted in truth and integrity. Those were the qualities that perhaps his greatest ever collaborator, Harold Pinter, admired in him, the terse force of his letter to Catherine speaking volumes:

✉ [*Harold Pinter*]

Dear Catherine Sparks,
    I was so shocked to hear that Terence had died. He was a dear friend of mine – since 1965 – and a terrific actor. He was wonderful in my plays. He meant a great deal to me. He was a man of such great honesty and absolute integrity.
    I send you my deepest condolences.
    Sincerely,
    Harold Pinter

If you asked Rigby what he thought the play was about, he would often say that he didn't know. He just obeyed his instinct. And he almost always got it right. He would have denied having anything in common with the experimental working strategies of Mike Alfreds and Shared Experience, but he instinctively employed the methodology.

    Perhaps his approach to character is best glimpsed in the practicalities of the letter he wrote to the actor James Stephens, quoted above, who had asked him for advice on playing Petey in *The Birthday Party*. Most of all, though, he is very certain of his 'natural strength of presence'. (No false modesty here!) Rigby might have shown his natural uncertainty and reticence in other areas of his life, but in acting, he was always on safe ground. It's interesting that on a scrap of paper on which he listed his 'favourite roles', it was Pozzo in *Waiting for Godot* and Acomat in *Bajazet* – not noticeably easy parts – that earned the bright-green ink of his self-approval.

But then I think of Stephen Thorne telling me how very uncertain Rigby was, when they first met in the early Seventies, of his ability to speak Shakespeare and other classical works. Despite his early success in *The Homecoming* and the popularity of PC Snow in *Softly, Softly*, he lacked self-confidence. But as his friendship with Stephen grew, he felt more able to ask for advice. 'It was around the time of *No Man's Land*,' he told me. 'He would ring up and ask my advice about things to do with the text, or if he was asked to do something out of the ordinary like a broadcast.'

I asked Stephen whether Rigby ever asked him to listen to him, to comment on his delivery or his reading.

No. He would ask me what I thought afterwards . . . if I'd heard it, or whatever, and comment then – which one had to be very careful about, because I always thought the best thing to do was to be positive and encouraging with Rigby. As I've said before, I sensed that he had a vulnerability and I didn't want to lose him as a friend. For some strange reason, he wasn't the sort of person you could say (and I have friends like that), 'No, that was quite dreadful, you know you could do far better than that. I think that what you were doing was rubbish.' He would ask advice or questions in such an almost naive and trusting way that you would have to answer it . . . And I didn't have the answers! But he would ring from America – and God knows what it cost him, because it wouldn't have been cheap – at any hour of the day, it didn't matter. I would read scenes with him, in Shakespeare, and I'd go and get my copy, and did this for auditions or whatever, and he'd say 'What does that mean?' and 'Is that how you say it?' And we would read through the scene . . . for hours on end.

Despite his brilliantly deadpan sense of humour, Rigby never mucked about in rehearsal or performance, and he would regularly express his anger at what he saw as the bad behaviour of other actors. He believed in the concept of the ensemble, and was very cross when his fellow actors overstepped the mark and exploited every laugh in a comedy at the expense of the other players. In a letter of condolence to his sister, James Bundy (the Artistic Director at Yale, who directed him in *A Woman of No Importance*) remembered him as 'a wonderful actor – utterly professional, imaginative and supportive of others, and his bravery in the face of illness was deeply admirable. All of us at Yale who worked with him felt privileged to be in his company . . . Terence reminded me how to live well as an artist, and he will be in my prayers.'

Rigby's generosity, both on stage and off, is remembered by both young and old. 'He was in my opinion a most uniquely gifted actor,' Michael Feast told me. 'He was also in my experience one of nature's gentlemen and someone who I will always remember with very fond affection.' Apart from being a protector to his fellow actors – like the pregnant cast-member he made me invite to Sunday lunch that time – he would also and always give them their moment, and give advice on business and getting laughs. Jim Davidson, who was in the 1995 film *Funny Bones* with Lee Evans, sent Rigby a bouquet of flowers to thank him for his help. Angie Bull, who came from Birmingham and had followed Rigby's progress since her teenage years, recalls how, when she announced she wanted to go into the theatre, he sat with her in her parents' house, reading through some scenes with her. He then advised her on audition pieces for Drama School. Thereafter, he often turned up at fringe venues to watch her perform. Afterwards, with pork pies and baps at the ready, he would give a critical appraisal of her performance.

I sought a professional opinion of his craft from his old friend Phyllis MacMahon:

> I thought he was a wonderful actor. His stillness and his voice – he had a beautiful voice. What impressed me was that although he'd worked very hard, there was a quality about him that made him a real person. You can have actors who are very, very good – and technically brilliant – and in the same sort of way, it almost takes away from the performance because you know what they're doing. But you'd come away from a performance by Terry and you'd know it was *technically* fine . . . He believed in the character, and that's what I loved about his acting.

Rigby held writers' words in high regard. He rarely changed a line or asked for changes. He would work hard to read the line as written. Occasionally he would cuss at the crassness of a line, or the fact that it was clumsy in construction. Some actors put an 'Um' or 'Eh' in front of a line, to make it easier to say. He wouldn't. He understood the rhythm, and would repeat it until he'd got it right.

Sometimes he'd arrive at my house with a sheaf of paper covered in his elegant longhand. This would be his part, written out over and over again. Apart from asking someone to hear his lines, this was his preferred method.

Rigby's Seattle diary includes some rare details of his approach to a part, and how he liked to interpret for himself rather than be told what he should be thinking. 'It would be nice to find out what acting is all about,' he writes in his Toronto diary. In later life, after spending more time in the States, he talked about learning to speak into the heart and faces of the audience. That period, which included *The Last True Believer* and *Skylight*, was important to him· he lost his fear of the soliloquy, and trying out new things, away from the London critics, became a liberating experience.

I don't think Rigby ever stopped studying and learning the craft of acting – RADA was only the beginning. Douglas McFerran reminded me that the kitchen table in his flat nearly always had a script propped up against a pile of books; it would often be a dusty, thumb-worn classic that he would discuss with great authority. His long walks in Regent's Park allowed him to practise his vocal range and perform the sonnets and soliloquies he loved so much. He never needed tricks to carry him through a performance; what you got was everything he had to offer on that night. He would often be deeply dissatisfied, and since he was his own fiercest critic, he would immediately set about improving his performance for the next night.

At the beginning of his career he felt that he didn't measure up to the 'public school chappies' he found himself acting with. He must have realized towards its end, or so I hope and trust, that he was up there with the very best of them.

❏ JULIET'S TABLE

So here it all is, spread out on the table.

I'm astonished that after returning so much material to the family, there's still barely enough room for my mug of coffee.

There's my file of letters from Rigby – a box full of the picture postcards he sent – a folder bulging with the photographs I took of him in my kitchen – a stack of interviews, typed out and highlighted – a tape recorder and neat piles of cassettes – all carefully labelled, and very precious. All my desk diaries are there as well, with Post-It notes stuck on to the dates that are relevant to Rigby's life.

This has been my work for so long.

I thumb through a bundle of notes I've made – reminders, questions, queries, new starts, false starts, things I must do. I take a deep breath and ponder for a moment on the enormity of the task thus far and, now that I'm nearly at the end, the terror I feel at the prospect of finishing it. But how can a life so full of contradictions and impossible choices ever be finished?

He would take days – weeks – *years* – pondering the right path to take; to make a decision, only to ignore it at the brink, and then jump in, feet first; and then battle against the current without a life jacket. In those early years the choice lay between becoming a priest, or a Wimbledon champion, or an actor – all bold choices showing his latent talents in so many different directions. He opted for the RAF for his National Service because he wanted to be a pilot; then grew into a man who was afraid of flying, who hated the 'iron bird'. When he could afford it, he crossed the Atlantic on the QE2, which he loved; but he still remembered the thrill of being invited into the cockpit of Concorde.

Such perversity.

At RADA, where he'd had to borrow money for the train journey to the audition, he must have felt relieved to be on his way. Only to be told by his tutors on arrival that he'd never lose his Brummie accent and therefore to go back where he came from. He survived that, but the stinging blow to his confidence left its mark. He told me in later life of the 'pronounced disquiet' he felt 'as regards the Birmingham accent' on a subsequent visit home. That happens to us all – I thought *my* father was posh until I'd been away from Llanelli for a year, coming home to find him ridiculously Welsh. Most of us embrace the difference – so why didn't Rigby? It suddenly strikes me that he tended to align himself with his father, who was from a middle-class background, rather than with his mother, who was Irish working class . . .

I look across the table and tut-tut in his direction.

He loved his posh girls and their genteel backgrounds – not that he was ever Lady Chatterley's Mellors. Far from it. He just stood a bit taller and became more gracious and indulgent in their company.

In an old newspaper article, Rigby tells us that at the age of sixteen he had been something of a loner, roaming the streets with a Woodbine behind his ear, not minding the rain. He knew all about pauses and silences long before he encountered Pinter – or so he claims. But reading all that again, I just wonder if it isn't all a bit pretentious and an excuse for the 'awkward bugger' he really always was. Although it sounds romantic to think of him breathing in the street life and the atmosphere of his surroundings, I discover that his nephew John does much the same thing now – without thinking anything much about it at all.

At the end of rehearsals and performances Rigby would rarely mix with the company: he would disappear, and find his own amusement. Was this a deliberate ploy to get out of rigorous debate and lively banter? Did he feel intellectually inferior to his colleagues, preferring to don a cloak of enigmatic speculation? His absence was certainly very firmly registered.

Looking now at the pile of interviews, his friends and colleagues constantly make reference to his silences, his need to sit on the periphery of discussion. He would emerge, sometimes, bolstered by drink in the early days, to sing an aria and weep at the beauty of it. But at the same time, he must have thanked his lucky stars to have made the acquaintance of his life long friend David Sinclair. And vice versa, for David needed Rigby, too, both as a social foil and as a financial prop. Rigby, sitting in the corner, brilliant study that he was, took in everything this 'public school chappie' had to offer. The true bedrock of their friendship was laid there, and they were eventually equals – known as 'the odd couple' and loved for it. Over the years, he found his niche, his place in the scheme of things. As his fame grew as an actor, he came to realize that that was probably enough to carry him through any situation. Good manners, reticence, and being a good listener are all important in the make-up of a guest list. Rigby, however, would always go one stage further. If he didn't feel comfortable, or disliked a member of the party, he would take up position at the kitchen sink and begin washing up. Then, when everyone had disappeared, he would feel he had earned one-to-one time. That's what he liked and often demanded.

'Bloody hell, Rigby,' I say, across the table to empty space. 'I was so lucky to be one of your friends. You made it very difficult, though, didn't you?'

Douglas McFerran, Phyllis MacMahon, among many others, pointed out that one always had to accept Rigby's friendship by Rigby's rules. OK. But those rules could change in whip-stitch.

'What was it you said? You got "as far as Warren Street and changed your mind"?'

So much contradiction in his assertion that he couldn't give a fuck for his friends. Silly man! He would have laid down his life for any one of us. He supported us all through the bad times with overwhelming love and consideration. And that's why when strangers say, 'How did you put up with the way he treated you?', the answer is simple. Because his kindness always outweighed the *un*kindness he was capable of.

I sift through the interviews and find the transcript of my inadequate telephone conversation with Peter Hall. Rigby had a turbulent relationship with Sir Peter throughout his career. Called him all names under the sun and wrote petulant letters. Then he would describe him as his mentor, the man who gave him so many opportunities for so many years. And for all that he endlessly grumbled, he would long for Sir Peter to arrive on a tour and pull the production back into shape. It is to Peter's credit that he largely ignored Rigby's contrariness and continued to place great value in his performances.

And who wouldn't? Terence Rigby the actor always gave his all. I've sat opposite him at this table long enough to know that no one ever worked harder than the chain-smoking, tea-drinking curmudgeon that he was.

'What's the play about?' I'd ask, and he would swear he didn't know.

He just knew what he was doing with the character.

'What a load of old bollocks,' I'd tell him, and he'd giggle at me.

It seemed to bother him that he was an instinctive actor – as though he'd be found out any minute now. But his instinct never let him down, because, in fact, subconsciously, he used every means possible to arrive at a character – as well as his innate understanding of the part. In typical manner, he said he hated improvisation and theatre games; couldn't see the point of physical theatre or sessions round the table dissecting the play. But he deployed all of those tactics, even to the extent of using (without realizing) many trendy experimental exercises . . . except that in Rigby's case it would be done while wandering around London, or sitting at someone's kitchen table.

The biggest contradiction, of course, was his insistence that he didn't understand iambic pentameter. Nonsense. He'd played Macbeth to great acclaim, and spoken the sonnets in the carefree tones of a lover. And recommended a young American actor to a producer by praising his good understanding of the form. How would Rigby have known that, if he was the dumbo he professed to be?

He often described his Catholic upbringing as a curse, as an inhibiting factor in his development – all that guilt. And yet his wanderings would often end up in a church, though not necessarily a Roman Catholic one, and sometimes he would regularly seek out his dear childhood friend, Father Michael. He kept some of the novenas and still remembered the prayers and chants. Perhaps he was on his way back to the Catholic fold when his life was cut short. But who really knows?

In trying to make sense of Rigby, his friends and colleagues would often reach for images of concealment: 'He hid behind his answering machine'; or 'He hid behind the character he was playing'; or – in the early days – 'He hid his shyness behind booze'. But when alcohol stopped supplying that prop, the something-to-hide-behind, Rigby became a different man in many ways. He was getting older, and although longevity brings out one's reflective nature, he gradually began to realize what a boorish young man he had been. I believe he settled for being himself, and for living the life he felt comfortable with – just as John Rigby had said. The answering machine was a convenient way of avoiding people, not something to hide behind. If he wanted to talk to you, he'd interrupt his own message, say, 'Just a minute,' then go off, make a cup of tea, find his cigarettes, and settle down for a long chat.

'I think I communicate best in letters,' he told me, and he did open up in lengthy correspondence with friends and colleagues and, particularly, his family. He never wanted to quarrel with any of them, but as in all families, there were occasional frictions. He once wrote to Noel Murray saying that, while he loved all the members of his family individually, he was wary of family gatherings. Isn't that true of most of us?

He certainly did love his family. He kept most of the letters from his siblings, and his mother's letters were bundled up along with the novenas she regularly sent him.

And yes, again, he loved his friends – on his terms – and we grudgingly allowed that.

'We mustn't seek him out too regularly: he doesn't like routine –' Are you listening to me, Rigby? '– and somehow, we mustn't ignore him either, must we?'

It's bit like Little Bo-Peep: 'Leave him alone, and he'll come home, wagging his tail behind him . . .'

Why did his actor friends allow him to stand at the Stage Door and give them copious notes on their performance, when he himself was outraged if anyone attempted to tell him how a part should be played? I simply can't fathom how he couldn't see how unfair that was. But it's just another example of how much his friends loved him – that not only did they tolerate his criticism, but they appreciated and took on board what he had to say.

But of course there was no harsher critic of his own acting ability than Rigby himself. Only once – during the run of *Bajazet* – did I ever hear him say, 'Last night I gave the performance of my life.'

I start putting all the research material into a special 'Rigby' drawer. The battered table is very nearly ready to move to its new home in Highgate.

There, now.

So . . .

It's done. I have kept my promise to Rigby.

It's an unsatisfactory account – there's so much more to say. But this is mainly my view of a man who sat at my kitchen table and drank tea with me.

Looking back, it was much more important for me to be the same every time we met. That was expected. I could sometimes see the shyness – or reticence. At base, I believe he just wanted to be taken seriously.

I wrote earlier that I stopped short of reminding Rigby of the full details of our first meeting in 1964, and what happened when we got back to his lodgings.

So here goes.

He'd already told me he wasn't paying for a taxi to take me home, and I'd have to stay the night. His attic room had two single beds, and he indicated which one was mine. We undressed in the dark and when we'd settled down he began to open up a bit. At last we were having a proper conversation. That worked very well for me because, at that time, I shared his reticence. But it was odd, I thought, that this bluff, large, confident-looking young man should need darkness as a cover. The next time I stayed, the sheets were clean and starched and we recited poetry across the room to one another. Later, he invited me into his bed, where I seem to recall that we clung to one another companionably. There was more affection than any passion. I think that suited us both very much and boded well for the renewed friendship all those years later – which broke through so many boundaries and ventured in so many different directions.

But it strikes me now, that if I had this extraordinary relationship with Rigby, just imagine what he got up to on the days and nights he spent with all his other cup-of-tea ladies.

The mind boggles.

I look across the width of this table now, and see the brass plaque glinting through a sea of paper.

'RIGBY SHLEPT HERE.'

I smile at the place where he sat, and ask him to help me, please, to do him justice. Then I decide to talk to him, and promise I won't swear, or cuss him for not sticking around long enough to write his own damn book.

*

244

Acknowledgments

My first thanks must go to Rigby's sisters Catherine and Caroline, his brothers Joseph and Patrick, his nephew John, and his cousin Peter, for allowing me to write this personal memoir of their beloved relative. I am deeply grateful to them for their practical assistance. In addition, this book could not have been written without the generous time and patience of those many contributors who have so kindly shared with me their memories of Rigby's professional career and personal qualities, and allowed me to relay them here. Many thanks, then, to Angela Bull, Michael Billington, Barbara Caruso, Jocelyn Chan, Peter Charlesworth, David Cregan, Russell Davies, Peter Eyre, Michael Feast, Sir Michael Gambon, Bill Gaskill, Sir Peter Hall, Mike Hodges, Diane Landers, Simon Langton, Douglas McFerran, Father Michael McGreevy, Phyllis MacMahon, Ifan Meredith, Tim McMullan, Miriam Margolyes, Maria Miles, Noel Murray, Tony Palmer, Dorothea Phillips, the late Alan Plater, Judith Robinson, Struan Rodger, James Stephens, Stephen Thorne, Frances Wilson, Adele Winston, and 'X-Ray'. (Every effort has been made to contact any remaining copyright holders. The publishers will be glad to make good in any future editions any errors or omissions brought to their attention.) I must also record my warm debt to Ned Chaillet, Nick Hern, Nick de Somogyi, my brilliant editor, Anna Trussler, and Simon Trussler, for their variously invaluable help in steering my manuscript to publication. My son Daniel, my daughter Catherine, and my niece Maggie already know of my gratitude to them.

Juliet Ace, 2015

Author biography

Juliet Ace is a prolific drama writer for radio and television including *Eastenders* and *The Archers*. She trained and worked as an actor and teacher.

She started writing in 1976 and three years later won a Gulbenkian/ Arts' Council Award for New Writing.

Juliet Ace has contributed many original plays and dramatisations for BBC Radio 4.

Her screenplay for the Welsh film *Cameleon,* was nominated for a Welsh BAFTA, won a Golden Spire Award at 1998 San Francisco International Film Festival, was shown at Cannes and invited to the Edinburgh Film Festival.

Juliet Ace lives in London.

Other works by Juliet Ace:

Radio – script: *The L-shaped Room* (2004 serial) by Lynne Reid Banks. Dramatised in 10 episodes.

Radio – *Blind* (2002) directed by Gilly Adams, BBC Afternoon Play starring Mali Harris and Jennifer Hill.

Radio – script: *Young Victoria* 10 part serial (2001) based on the letters and diaries of the young Queen Victoria, starring Imogen Stubbs.

Radio – scripts: *Her Infinite Variety* (1999) 5 short modern plays for Shakespeare's women. A *Woman's Hour* serial produced by Ned Chaillet.

Radio – script: *The Captain's Wife* (1998) starring Patricia Hodge. One of Juliet's successful sequences of semi-autobiographical radio dramas.

Film – script: *Cameleon* (1997) a 90 minute drama set in the Second World War, starring Aneurin Hughes and Daniel Evans.

Radio – script: *Zinar's Tower* – (1995) Radio 4 Monday play, directed by Shaun MacLoughlin, starring Zia Moyheddin and Karzan Krekar.

Television – script: *Out of Order* (1984) 150 min BBC drama starring Sarah Badel.

Stage and radio – script: *Speak No Evil* 1980, first performed on stage in Bristol and then for radio, directed by Enyd Williams.

Acting for television - *The Fox* (1973) BBC 60 minute drama.

Radio – *Lobby Talk* (1990) Radio 4 play, directed by Shaun MacLoughlin, starring Andrew Sachs.

View more information about the author and Terence Rigby, online at:

en.wikipedia.org/wiki/Juliet_Ace

www.terencerigby.info/index.html

www.thestage.co.uk/people/obituaries/2008/08/terence-rigby/

sounds.bl.uk/related-content/TRANSCRIPTS/024T-C1142X000104-0001A0.pdf

"The Lady Camden"

TcR
Dec '89

x. Green felt-tip drawing by Rigby of 'The Lady Camden'

248

Lightning Source UK Ltd.
Milton Keynes UK
UKOW 00102141805 16

274448UK00001B/6/P